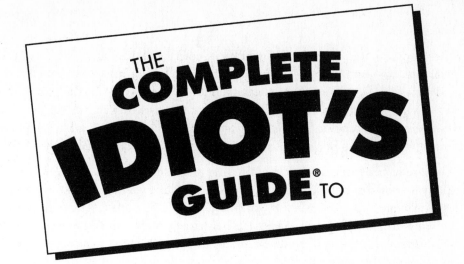

Playing the Fiddle

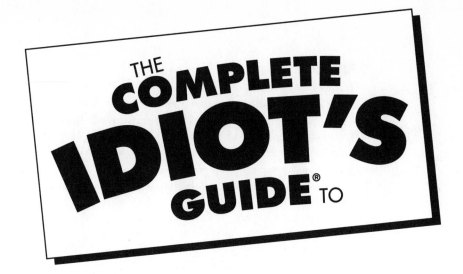

THE **COMPLETE IDIOT'S GUIDE®** TO

Playing the Fiddle

by Ellery Klein

ALPHA

A member of Penguin Group (USA) Inc.

ALPHA BOOKS

Published by the Penguin Group

Penguin Group (USA) Inc., 375 Hudson Street, New York, New York 10014, USA

Penguin Group (Canada), 90 Eglinton Avenue East, Suite 700, Toronto, Ontario M4P 2Y3, Canada (a division of Pearson Penguin Canada Inc.)

Penguin Books Ltd., 80 Strand, London WC2R 0RL, England

Penguin Ireland, 25 St. Stephen's Green, Dublin 2, Ireland (a division of Penguin Books Ltd.)

Penguin Group (Australia), 250 Camberwell Road, Camberwell, Victoria 3124, Australia (a division of Pearson Australia Group Pty. Ltd.)

Penguin Books India Pvt. Ltd., 11 Community Centre, Panchsheel Park, New Delhi—110 017, India

Penguin Group (NZ), 67 Apollo Drive, Rosedale, North Shore, Auckland 1311, New Zealand (a division of Pearson New Zealand Ltd.)

Penguin Books (South Africa) (Pty.) Ltd., 24 Sturdee Avenue, Rosebank, Johannesburg 2196, South Africa

Penguin Books Ltd., Registered Offices: 80 Strand, London WC2R 0RL, England

Copyright © 2008 by Ellery Klein

International Standard Book Number: 978-1-59257-768-2
Library of Congress Catalog Card Number: 2008924713

10   09   08   8   7   6   5   4   3   2   1

Interpretation of the printing code: The rightmost number of the first series of numbers is the year of the book's printing; the rightmost number of the second series of numbers is the number of the book's printing. For example, a printing code of 08-1 shows that the first printing occurred in 2008.

Printed in the United States of America

Publisher: *Marie Butler-Knight*
Editorial Director: *Mike Sanders*
Senior Managing Editor: *Billy Fields*
Senior Acquisitions Editor: *Paul Dinas*
Development Editor: *Ginny Bess Munroe*
Senior Production Editor: *Janette Lynn*
Copy Editor: *Amy Borelli*

Cartoonist: *Richard King*
Book Designer: *Trina Wurst*
Cover Designer: *Becky Harmon*
Indexer: *Tonya Heard*
Layout: *Brian Massey*
Proofreader: *John Etchison*

Dedicated to my parents, Jim and Nonnie Klein, whose encouragement and support has been invaluable to me and my fiddling.

Contents at a Glance

Contents

Introduction

Like many people, I started playing the violin in school. My first teacher, Mrs. Walker, came into my second-grade classroom with her daughter, who played us a tune: "Turkey in the Straw." That common American fiddle tune must have planted a seed in my mind. I spent years in orchestra and string quartets, and learning concertos in private lessons. But I knew by senior year of high school that I wasn't cut out to be a classical player. All those auditions, technical exercises, and formal events just weren't for me.

So I decided to check out fiddle music—and I was hooked. All of a sudden, I was spending hours practicing without even thinking. The fiddlers I admired had an amazing, raw, spirited sound, and I was determined to figure it out. Because all of a sudden, here was a world of music where people hung out in bars, wore blue jeans, and stayed up until the crack of dawn, playing music on a front porch until the sun rose. And there was less "right and wrong" playing. Musicians all had a different style, and were free to interpret a tune however they wanted to.

You, dear reader, must be thinking along the same lines. Maybe you've enjoyed the fiddlers with the local bluegrass band. Or your favorite part of *Riverdance* was the fiddle solo. Perhaps you've envied those fiddlers sawing away in the corner of your local Irish bar. You might love the part in your favorite Lyle Lovett song when the fiddler takes off between verses. Perhaps the fact that Dave Matthews, a Top 40 artist, has violinist Boyd Tinsley in his band is what makes that band a little special. Or, you've got a soft spot for that infamous song featuring a fiddle— "The Devil Went Down to Georgia." One or all of these things makes you feel inspired to be a part of the strings section—the fiddlin' kind!

In this book, I'll introduce you to some Irish, Scottish, American old-time, and bluegrass music. While there's no end to the technical virtuosity of the master players from these genres, great fiddle music starts with *feel*. Most of the tunes are fairly simple, so you can learn them and have fun even if you're not that great, technically, yet. When you feel like pulling out the fiddle at family gatherings, you can do it—solo! Or you can find local music groups that sponsor musical get-togethers for learning or playing. Then the better you get, the more style and technique you can add to the melody you've played for months or years. I'll make sure to steer you toward some resources beyond this book to help you when you get there.

So whether you used to play violin as a kid, or have recently refused to let your family sell that old fiddle you just found buried in grandma's attic, or have never touched an instrument in your life, this book will give you a start in your quest to "saw away" at the fiddle.

How to Use This Book

This book has everything you need to know about the fiddle. There's some interesting facts and information, purchasing advice, and, of course, fiddle lessons. In the spirit of fiddling, I've tried to keep boring exercises to a minimum. That way, you can learn a technique while you also get to play a new tune. The book is divided up into four parts:

Part 1, "So You Wanna Play the Fiddle," goes through everything you ever wanted to know about the instrument itself. We cover the history of the instrument, as well as how fiddle music evolved. You'll get an anatomy lesson, so you'll know what I'm talking about when I tell you to grab the frog. I'll guide you through purchasing and maintaining your fiddle, and how to get it prepped to play. I'm also going to make sure you know how to stretch out your arms and hands.

Part 2, "Fiddling Around," starts off with a music theory lesson so you know what all that cryptic stuff on a music staff means—and don't worry, I'll let you cheat. You'll get a complete step-by-step on how to hold the fiddle and the bow and get them working together in harmony. (Actually, just melody.) Then I'll get you started with a few basic tunes while teaching you basic technique.

Part 3, "Fiddle Genres and Styles," is where you start exploring different fiddle styles. I'll explain a bit about each genre—the culture and the history behind it. You'll learn some of the easier tricks of the trade to each style, with your left hand and your bow hand. Each chapter will have plenty of tunes to try your hand(s) at.

Part 4, "Movin' on Up," has a few chapters demonstrating some of the more difficult fiddle stunts you can pull off as you progress. We discuss improvising, alternate tunings, and playing *really really fast*, among other things—all while learning actual fun music to play. The last chapter in the book discusses the different ways you can continue learning after you have finished the book and can no longer call yourself a complete idiot at the fiddle!

There are also a few appendixes at the end of the book that are chock-full of information. Appendix A contains a glossary, so even if you forget the meaning of a fiddle term, you can look it up in the back. Appendix B is a list of fiddle books, online resources, fiddle camps, music organizations, and retailers that will help you keep learning, listening, and playing. And, of course, you can't learn without hearing what you want to sound like. Appendix C discusses a few fiddle players who are either important historically, or really worth checking out for examples of what the best players sound like.

The Complete Idiot's Guide to Playing the Fiddle has made sure you can learn in every way possible: reading, hearing, and seeing. The enclosed DVD has a 30-minute beginner fiddle lesson that will allow me to work with you in person as you get started. I've also recorded every single tune featured in the book, slowly, so you can hear what it all should sound like. The contents of the DVD are outlined in Appendix D.

Extras

No one wants a book of dense information piled in endless paragraphs to plug through when they're just trying to learn a few tunes. I've included little boxes containing valuable tidbits of information useful for any new fiddler. These will pop up on the sides of your pages:

def•i•ni•tion

This sidebar explains the meanings of the new words that you'll encounter while learning about the fiddle.

Fiddle Facts

Look here for fun and interesting facts about the world of the fiddle, and for a few quotations from those in the know.

False Notes

Check out the advice here to avoid problems with your playing or your instrument.

Tune Up

Tips to help you keep your music, body, and fiddle in tip-top shape.

Acknowledgments

I'd like to thank everyone who helped me out as I put this book together—whether their contribution was large or small, it was invaluable!

To begin with, thanks go to my friend Eric Garland, for sharing the process from his own publishing experience, which greatly helped me to turn my idea into a reality. Thanks to my agent, Barbara Doyen, for all her advice. Also, many thanks go to my acquisitions editor, Paul Dinas, who has definitely understood the "baby vs. book" dilemma, while imposing deadlines at the same time. Many thanks go to Mike Wilkins and Alan Mattes for volunteering a little engineering after hours for the audio portion of the DVD. Thanks to Gaelic Storm, for four years of touring madness—and because I noticed the fact that no one had written this book yet while we were waiting to perform in a bookstore. Finally, thanks to the following people who lent me bits of advice, ideas, tunes, or other two cents that were useful: Eric Merrill, Mark Evitt, Hanneke Cassel, Ben Wang, Jackie Mow, Bob Jackson, Phillipe Varlet, Alan Kaufman, Peter Purvis, Chris Bell, Flynn Cohen, Lissa Schneckenberger, George Keith, and Rebecca Shannon. Thanks to Anne Bell and Jessica Cooper for taking the "Linkster" off my hands for a few hours.

Great thanks and love to Matthew Bell—the best husband in the world, for so many reasons. And to our Lincoln, who made getting this book done a real challenge, but was at least mighty cute and sweet about it.

Thanks to my family: Mom for encouragement, love, and babysitting; Dad, who is always supportive; Diane, an army major who was over in Iraq while I sat comfortably at home writing a fiddle book; Meghan for calling me between coffee customers; and Hudson, for being the baby bro.

Trademarks

All terms mentioned in this book that are known to be or are suspected of being trademarks or service marks have been appropriately capitalized. Alpha Books and Penguin Group (USA) Inc. cannot attest to the accuracy of this information. Use of a term in this book should not be regarded as affecting the validity of any trademark or service mark.

Part  1

So You Wanna Play the Fiddle

The fiddle is one of the most common instruments in the world, for good reason. Most people feel it is the instrument that sounds most like the human voice: it's emotional, dynamic, and versatile—and it can play both melodies and chords, too. We'll start off this book with a little background, explaining where the fiddle came from and how it spread far and wide.

As you learn the fiddle, you need to know the names of its different parts. This book covers all the ones you need to know. You also learn how the instrument actually works to make sound. If you feel clueless about how to buy a fiddle, the information in these chapters will enable you to go shopping with confidence. You learn the minimum amount you need to spend, and what factors influence a fiddle's value. Also, you need a few accessories for your fiddle—starting, of course, with a decent bow.

Any good craft needs some upkeep. You learn how to get your fiddle, and yourself, properly set up to play. You learn all about maintaining your fiddle, too—some things you can easily take care of yourself, and others need to be taken care of by the professionals.

"I'm fine carrying the flag. I'm just sayin' it would be a lot more fun with a fiddle."

The History of the Fiddle

In This Chapter

- ◆ The fiddle in its early forms
- ◆ How the Italians achieved perfection
- ◆ The fiddle's popularity spreads
- ◆ Two continents meet on one new one

Of course you want to play the fiddle! It is a great instrument—responsive, emotional, dynamic, and versatile. While in modern years it has lost some of its prominence to instruments like the electric guitar, it was for centuries *the* source of fun and entertainment for people of the Old World, and the New. People would dance all night to the sound of its sonorous strings. Before rock 'n' roll became the symbol of mischief, preachers would rail against the sin the fiddle inspired. Nowadays, the guitar probably does get the title of "most popular," but in the old days, when you rocked out, you did it on a fiddle. And you still can, of course!

The fiddle as we know it comes from a long line of instruments. This chapter begins in the early days of the fiddle, and follows from when it was perfected by eighteenth-century Italian craftsmen, all the way to the sound of lonesome fiddle notes crying out onstage at the Grand Ole Opry.

First Came Fire, Then the Fiddle

Okay, so I'm probably exaggerating the sequence of events. There was probably a wheel, and maybe even hieroglyphics, that came between fire and the fiddle. But the basic mechanism of the fiddle is a type of instrument that many different cultures did come up with independently of each other.

Even in the days before the drive-in movie and Internet chat rooms, people sought to entertain themselves. Music, of course, is one of the most basic forms of human interaction. So, first people started singing. Then they usually came up with stuff to bang on (percussion) and tubes with holes to blow into (flutes, etc.). Then, someone figured out that if you strung up a thin piece of animal gut, you could pluck it and make a note. Eventually, someone else discovered that if you wanted to sustain the note, you could use some type of bow implement to draw across the string. Voilà! The ancestor of the fiddle was born.

In Europe, it's hard to know exactly where the bow was developed and when. Some people think it was actually developed in central Asia, in places like Persia (now Iran) and Afghanistan. By the Middle Ages, however, it's fairly certain that Europeans were bowing to their hearts' content all over the continent.

The details of these early stringed instruments are fuzzy, because most of them were destroyed or lost. For clues on what they looked like, and how they were played, we more or less rely on written accounts and visual art. We *do* know that there were many forms of bowed string instruments across Europe. They varied in shape, size, manner of playing, and sound. The number of strings could even vary, from one to six. And it's a good bet that many of these instruments didn't sound so hot.

One form of string instrument was the crwth—a wooden rectangle, with a fiddle-esque construction suspended in the middle. This was used around the British Isles, and actually lasted in Wales for centuries after it had died out everywhere else. Then there was the viol de gamba, which was used for baroque music and was played on the knee. There was also a family of instruments called the "fiddle," or "fedyl." All of these names for the fiddle's ancestors had different forms in different regions and times. But basically we can rest assured that bowed instruments were popular all over Europe after about 1000 A.D.

There was good reason for the popularity of bowed instruments. They had great tone and rhythm, and their versatility meant that they were useful for all different types of music. People from all levels of social classes used the instruments for their events—from the peasants farming the fields, to the formal (and probably more boring) court shindigs.

Many of the first bowed instruments would have been used to accompany singing. Singers probably found that the sound of a bowed instrument matched their voice in a way that a plucked instrument or a wind instrument never could. Early fiddles might have had strings that simply droned under a singer's voice, as a form of one-note accompaniment, not unlike a bagpipe's drone. This means that the fiddle was probably the earliest form of the karaoke machine!

Much like computer software today, people continually experimented with the construction and design of bowed instruments. These changes often were made in response to changing needs for performance. First of all, when the instruments were initially changed from plucked to bowed, they needed some modifications. Instead of hooking a finger or a pick between the strings to make a note, you ran a bow across the top of the strings. The design had to accommodate the movement of the bow, so cutaways were added to the sides. Also, the bridge had to be raised. This would have increased string tension. As a result, the strings had to be more directly and securely attached to the body of the instrument itself. This is still the case with the violin today.

Fiddle Facts

The Chinese use a two-string fiddle called an ehru (pronounced *AR-hoo*), which evolved from an instrument created in Mongolia. There are also many forms of stringed instruments that are indigenous to African music.

Tune Up

The versatility of the fiddle includes the ability to play loudly or softly, notes that are short and harsh or long and sweet, and notes that are bendable, and therefore emotional.

Around the end of the fifteenth century, the present form of the violin was beginning to take shape. There were bigger court events down at the castle, and the emergence of high-pitched soprano singers down at the concert hall. People were trying to make the violin higher in pitch, and louder, too. This meant thicker strings, which again increased the tension on the instrument. It also called for more hair on the bow to pull out the sound, and the use of rosin to add a bit of stickiness. To protect the instrument from this new tension, supporting structure was added on the inside of the body of the fiddle. Instrument makers discovered that an arched body was better able to withstand tension, so they added curves to the fiddle instead of having to depend on a thicker cut (and therefore, less responsive) slice of wood. The curved body led to the evolution of f-shaped holes on the sides of the fiddle, as opposed to the circle or C shape that was prevalent on flat-surfaced instruments, like the guitar. The sides, or ribs, of the violin got shorter, too.

Early bows were different as well. In fact, the name "bow" actually comes from the early shape. Instead of being a relatively parallel duo of stick and hair, the wood of the early models of bows arched out over the hair—just like a bow used in archery. Eventually, the wood was made straighter as bow makers began experimenting with tension and carving. They got the stick straighter, and by doing so, improved the balance and action of the bow. They also made a handy gadget to hold the hair in at one end, and a screw so that the hair didn't have to be tight all the time. This allowed the wood to relax between playing.

> **Fiddle Facts**
>
> Some people believe that Leonardo da Vinci designed elements of the modern violin, due to the mathematics and engineering that went into it. However, there is no definitive proof of this.

Il Violino Magnifico!

The Italians definitely deserve some praise from all of us. For one, the world would definitely be a less tasty place without pizza, pasta, and cannoli. But great gastronomy isn't the only thing we have to thank Italy for. By the sixteenth century, the highest levels of violin craftsmanship definitely were being reached in that boot-shaped peninsula—specifically, in the two towns of Brescia and Cremona. In Brescia, there was a famous maker named Gasparo de Saló. For a while, he was credited with being the first maker to shape the violin into its modern form. However, scholars now doubt that this is the case (though de Saló's violins are still respected and sought after). In Cremona, the stage was being set for the emergence of the most famous fiddle maker in history (okay, so in Italy it was called the *violino*).

Here's how it all started: around 1520, a man named Andrea Amati was born. He is sort of the "godfather" of fiddle makers, because he went on to have a few sons and many grandsons who all worked as prized fiddle makers.

Most people agree that Andrea Amati was the first one to really figure out the elements that make up the modern form of the violin. Among other things, here's what he came up with:

♦ He curved the bridge, so that there was no more droning.

♦ He put the strings farther apart.

> **Fiddle Facts**
>
> The standard definition of the note A has risen steadily in pitch since the 1700s. That means the strings on antique fiddles are tighter and the instruments under more stress than they were designed for.

def•i•ni•tion

Varnish is the shiny coating of a fiddle. While it is important for color and appearance, its quality is also very important to a fiddle's sound. A poor varnish can stifle the sound, and a great varnish can allow a good instrument to sing like a canary (not the one in the coal mine).

- He made a body that was more resonant; that is, it vibrated as the strings were played.

- He used harder wood for the back of the fiddle, so it reflected the sound of the strings on the interior resonating chamber.

- He gave the fiddle the dainty, womanly shape that it still sports today.

- He perfected the *varnish*.

Not many of Amati's instruments survive today, but the few that do demonstrate these accomplishments.

At the same time that fiddle makers were experimenting with the shape and materials of violins, string technology was improving as well. Around the middle of the sixteenth century, strings were composed of two twisted strands. This improved clarity and sound. A hundred years later, a gut core was wrapped in a thin metal wire. This is pretty much the style of strings we use today.

Andrea Amati had two sons, who did some pretty nice work themselves. However, his grandson, Nicoló Amati, was actually the one that put Cremona on the prize spot of the violin-making map. His violins got an even better, larger tone as he made the arch of the fiddle more subtle and then made the ribs (the sides) of the violin a bit larger. He also made strides in choosing the correct types of wood to use in the violins, and he used some great varnishes.

One of Nicoló's apprentices was Andrea Guarneri. His violins are some of the most sought after, even today. As the years passed, and this dynasty of sons and apprentices grew in skill and stature, Cremona was built up as the center of violin craftsmanship perfection. But the best was yet to come.

The Stradivarius

While you may not have heard of the violin makers of Cremona, Italy, we've mentioned so far, there is one more that you probably have heard of: Antonio Stradivari. If you are carrying a fiddle case around, there is always some jokester that wants to know if you've got a "Strad" in there. Many people who don't know the first thing about fiddles or fiddle music still have heard of a Stradivarius. (This is the Latin version of his name, which is more familiar to most people.) That's pretty interesting, when you think about it. Can the average Joe name the famous maker from any other style of instrument? Probably not. Yet the name Stradivarius has managed to become well known around the world. This is a reflection of the fact that he was a great craftsman, but also that fiddles were such a part of daily life for centuries.

Fiddle Facts

Antonio Stradivari made over 1,100 instruments, 650 of which survive today. He also made cellos, violas, mandolins, and harps.

Antonio Stradivari was not born into a family of fiddle makers, but most people believe that he learned the craft when he apprenticed, along with his pal Guarneri, under Nicoló Amati. He applied mathematics and geometry to his craft, and pretty much clinched the perfection of the violin that the Amatis and Guarneri had been working on for over a hundred years. The golden age of Stradivari's fiddle making is pretty much considered to be 1700 to 1720. This is when Stradivari reached his 40s and started improving on Amati's design. Stradivari lived for 93 years and made fiddles for much of that time. Now here's the amazing thing: *no one* has really managed to improve the fiddle since Stradivari's day. In fact, how he made his varnishes is still a mystery.

It's hard to get your hands on one of Stradivari's instruments today, but they are still considered to be masterpieces. They are played by some of the most famous musicians in classical music. People who actually own Stradivari fiddles tend to be wealthy patrons who loan the instrument to a talented musician of their choice.

> **Fiddle Facts**
>
> The fiddle in the movie *The Red Violin* was based on a real-life 1720 Stradivarius violin known as "The Red Mendelssohn."

The Fiddle Travels Around the World

So in Italy, the violin was perfected by 1720. But the rest of Europe wasn't going to sit around and just let the Italians have all the glory. Soon, violin makers sprung up all over the continent—Belgium, France, Austria, and England. Joseph Hill was one of the more famous English violin makers. Mirecourt became the center of violin making in France, and Sudetan and Vogtland achieved some reputation in Germany.

For a while, the business of violin making worked like this: a talented craftsman would set up shop, work out his design, and start making high-quality, high-priced fiddles, with the help of a few apprentices. But the fiddle was becoming more and more popular, as people all over Europe began using it instead of their native bowed instruments. As demand increased, so did the clamor for cheaper models. Soon, entrepreneurs figured out a way to bring division of labor to the process of fiddle making. This enabled the instruments to be made more cheaply and in greater volume.

While the early "factories" were often just families churning out violins in assembly-line fashion, they had an impact. The fiddle spread all over the place. It was to be one of the most popular instruments for making music for centuries to come. No matter what type of music was being played, the fiddle's great tone and versatility meant that it was well suited for the local tunes.

In Central and Eastern Europe, Roma musicians became some of the most skillful fiddlers on the continent. Some countries and cultures adapted the shape of the fiddle to suit the local music even better. In Norway, a type of fiddle called the Hardanger fiddle was made with *sympathetic strings* that gave a fuller sound to the dark, chordal folk music of Scandinavia. Other cultures took the standard tuning intended for chamber music, and changed it so that it worked better with their own chords and melodies.

def•i•ni•tion

> **Sympathetic strings** are strings that are not played directly, but rather vibrate along with the strings that are being played.

Scotland

There were earlier forms of the fiddle in Scotland, but the minute the fiddle itself arrived, it was all the rage. There was a huge dancing culture in Scotland, whether among the rural folk of the Highlands or the gentry of the big cities of Glasgow and Edinburgh. The fiddle became a mainstay at dancing events all over the country.

The music of Scotland was influenced by the compositions of Europe. Great showman fiddle players emerged to perform in formal concert settings. Many fiddle books were published, containing thousands of compositions that are still played to this day.

Ireland

Whether or not there was a bowed instrument in Ireland before the Italian instrument arrived is in some dispute. However, the bagpipes and the harp were definitely used to play music in Ireland for centuries before the fiddle arrived. The new arrival was found to be perfect for the ornamentation of the native music, though, and became synonymous with Irish music. The influence of the pipes can be heard in Irish fiddling, because much of the music reflects the range of the pipes. This means that the G string isn't used as much in Irish traditional music.

Traditional Irish music was primarily for dancing. But in rural Ireland, dancing was usually done in people's homes, or, in nicer weather, outdoors at the cross-roads. The dance steps were taught by a dancing master—a man who typically traveled with a piper or a fiddler. He would come to a town or village for about six weeks, and teach. People didn't dance to a band as they do today. Rather, traditional fiddlers played solo.

Fiddle Facts
The fiddle has often been called "The Devil's Box," due to the fact that it got people dancing. It also has been said that the fiddle was the devil's preferred instrument.

The Fiddle in America

The fiddle was brought to colonial America by settlers from Scotland, Ireland, and England. Fiddle music was an extremely popular form of entertainment. People brought the tradition and love of dancing with them as well.

As in Scotland, music was a pastime of the gentry and of the common man. The music the settlers brought with them would be the foundation for two new styles of American-made music.

Europe Meets Africa

Fiddle Facts
Thomas Jefferson was an avid fiddler, and practiced up to three hours a day as a young man. He is said to have courted his future wife with it, too.

America has been a melting pot for centuries, either voluntarily or not. When people emigrated from Europe to live in the New World, they inevitably encountered people from Africa—mostly slaves. Due to the sheer volume of the slave trade in the very early days of the United States, slaves often outnumbered free citizens.

Of course, the legacy of the slave trade in America hasn't been pretty—from the Civil War to Civil Rights, it's definitely been the source of conflict. It can't be denied, though, that it caused two very different musical cultures to have continuing and great influence on each other for all of America's history. Much of the music that has emerged from America since before its founding wouldn't have existed without the interaction of both European and African music and culture. Old time, bluegrass, jazz, and rock 'n' roll are all products of an involuntary experiment—that of very different cultures suddenly finding themselves living together in very close proximity. Music is always changing, but it especially changes in these circumstances!

Many people of European descent learned the fiddle in early America, but they also loved to dance. One of the ways they assured themselves of music for a local event was to teach their slaves how to play their favorite tunes on the fiddle. This is indubitably one way that European fiddle tunes made their way into African American string band repertoire. The slaves brought their own music and traditions to the New World. The banjo is a descendant of several African instruments. It was a rhythm instrument, and gradually became used to back up fiddle tunes. The music that the European settlers brought with them was altered and adapted to these rhythms, probably both by the slaves themselves and musicians who were intrigued by the sounds they encountered. The most obvious example of this is that the music began to be played more on the *backbeat*.

From Appalachia to Grand Ole Opry

Eventually, people in the urban areas of America started dancing in crowded dance halls, instead of at smaller gatherings. The fiddle wasn't loud enough. So it was replaced—first by the louder piano, and then by wind instruments.

However, in the more rural South, where people were more spread out and isolated, the fiddle tradition remained strong. Different regions developed their own styles, all of which are lumped under the title "old time." The music to the east of and alongside the Appalachian mountains had one style, the music from the southern part of the Appalachian mountains another. A strong tradition developed in the Ozark Mountains of Missouri. And Western fiddlers of Texas and Oklahoma forged their own individual style as well.

Many of these traditions carried on for hundreds of years. Folklorists who ventured into some of the more isolated regions of the mountains would find songs that were direct descendents of, or even identical to, songs that were sung in England and Scotland hundreds of years before. Many of the fiddle tunes, though played in their funky new style and under different names, still could be traced directly back to Europe as well.

In the early part of this century, radio began entertaining people at home. Record labels began releasing music on 78s. And people began leaving rural areas to seek work in factories and cities.

Bill Monroe of Kentucky was one of them. He took the music of his native state and set it to fast-paced rhythms. Monroe formed his group, Bill Monroe and the Blue Grass Boys, in 1939. He pioneered the "high lonesome" style of singing. The band featured several harmonizing singers, and jazz-style improvisation. There was always a fiddle in the band. In bluegrass music, the fiddle didn't just

def•i•ni•tion

The **backbeat** refers to the second and fourth beats in a phrase of music; instead of counting ONE-two-three-four, one would count one-TWO-three-FOUR.

Fiddle Facts

Evidence of the fiddle's popularity in America can be found in the books of Laura Ingalls Wilder. Laura's "Pa" played the fiddle and sang to entertain the household.

repeat a tune over and over, as it did in Irish, Scottish, and old-time music. It ripped out fast melodies and haunting chords between song verses.

The fiddle always has been a strong part of American musical tradition. There's been old time and bluegrass, Western swing, and country and western. And, of course, everyone knows America's most famous song about the fiddle: Charlie Daniels' "The Devil Went Down to Georgia."

The Least You Need to Know

- ◆ The technique of playing stringed instruments with a bow was a worldwide phenomenon.

- ◆ The structure of the fiddle hasn't really improved since early eighteenth-century Italy.

- ◆ For centuries, the fiddle was the most popular instrument across Europe and America.

The Anatomy of a Fiddle

In This Chapter

♦ The difference between a fiddle and a violin

♦ All the fiddle and bow parts that you need to know

♦ How a fiddle actually works

Whenever you learn something new, you usually need some new vocabulary to go along with it, too. There are definitely some fiddle-specific terms that I'll use in this book. So take some time to get to know your instrument—its curves, its buttons, and how it is all strung together.

This chapter starts off by clearing up the confusion over the terms "fiddle" and "violin." Then we introduce you to the various parts of your fiddle and the bow. Finally, you learn exactly how all these parts work together to produce the sonorous, beautiful sound of the fiddle.

So What *Is* the Difference, Anyway?

Your first question upon seeing the title of this book was probably something along the lines of, "Gee, that sounds great … but what is a fiddle anyway? Is it the same thing as a violin, or what?" You're not alone in wondering—most professional fiddle players are asked that question all the time. The simple answer is: *yup, it is!* There is no difference. A fiddle and a violin are the same instrument.

Here's the deal. Mere terminology, and nothing more, is at the root of the confusion. The *kind* of music that you play dictates what you call your "axe." A classical violinist doesn't sit in the fiddle section in the orchestra. An Irish fiddler would never say they played the Irish violin. Either way would just be kind of, well … not so cool.

Musicians who use the term "fiddle" play all the types of music you'll find in this book—such as folk, traditional, or country music. This includes Irish,

Scottish, old-time American string band, and bluegrass fiddling. This is music that comes from "the people."

The musicians who play "fiddle" music tend to be scruffier, more rebellious types than their classical buddies. (Dare we say, more fun, too? Okay, I'll let you decide about that.) But for years, it's true, many classical players didn't consider fiddle music to be *real* music. In their minds, the rough and passionate tunes of the common people were no match for the grandeur of sonatas, symphonies, and concertos. Okay, we won't start singing workers' anthems or anything here. But as fiddle music has become more popular in the mainstream, classical musicians and their fans have begun appreciating the fact that fiddle music is complex, and not as easy to master as they originally thought. In fact, in recent years, classical orchestras and musicians have begun collaborating with fiddlers. These endeavors have done well, and created some lovely music.

But I digress. Basically, when people start asking you what the difference is, you can say, "It's the *attitude*, dude!"

Okay, so it's the same instrument. But people do look for very different sounds out of the same instrument. A fiddler and a classical player often will demand very different *qualities* from their fiddle, qualities that best complement the style of music they play.

This is because a fiddler and a violinist have different goals for their sound. A classical musician needs an instrument that is made to show off great technical work in a concert hall, with a silent audience listening rapturously. Their music often is played up in very high registers, with complex and intricate runs and chords that need a crystal clear sound to show them off. They also are made to blend in well with the other stringed instruments—whether in the orchestra, a string quartet, or singing solo in a concerto.

A fiddler, on the other hand, plays in quite different settings. A fiddler often is playing in places that are noisy and rambunctious. Their music might be the background to a bar full of people who are swilling a few beers while they enjoy the music. Or, they'll be hanging out in the kitchen on a Sunday afternoon playing a few tunes. They might even be fiddling to a room of hundreds of dancers stomping their feet. The sound might be cutting through the noise of a crowd with the crackle of an in-house sound system. They don't necessarily need an instrument that is crystal clear and beautiful. They want something that complements the earthier style of music that they play.

So besides the obvious fact that the two types of musicians play differently, how might their instruments differ? Here are some of the ways that the instrument played by a concert violinist can vary from the one played in your local bluegrass band:

- ◆ A classical player usually wants his violin to be made by a respected, sought-after maker of violins, often one from previous centuries. That player will seek out the highest level of craftsmanship he can get. A fiddler isn't as concerned with who made it. She just wants to know if she can wail on it! A Stradivarius, set up to play a concerto in Carnegie Hall, might actually be terrible for fiddle music. It might just be *too* nice-sounding. A less expensive instrument can actually be more desirable to a fiddler than a cherished masterpiece. (That's a sales pitch everyone likes to hear!) Some types of fiddlers actually aim to get a mushier sound—a purposeful sloppiness that is full of character and personality. So a $3 million Stradivarius just won't do!

♦ A violinist might use a rounder-cut *bridge*, which keeps the bow on one string and yields a clear distinction. A fiddler, especially when playing more chord-driven old-time and bluegrass music, might want a flatter-cut bridge so that playing more than one string at once—known as double stopping—comes more naturally.

♦ A classical player would make sure to use strings that yield a clear, sweet sound. These are usually gut-style strings (see Chapter 3). A fiddler often, though not always, uses steel strings, which give a brassier, straighter sound. These are often cheaper, too!

♦ The other thing that you may notice is that two players might hold their "violin" and "fiddle" very differently. In classical music, there is one standard. Holding your violin or bow any other way than that standard is considered just plain wrong. However, among fiddlers, the only thing that is wrong is what doesn't work for you. Trying to achieve a certain sound, a fiddler might find that the standard violin or bow hold (again, meant for one type of music) just doesn't cut it. Or, they just don't like holding it that way. In the fiddle world, no one will tell you that you are holding your fiddle wrong. (They might, however, still gently suggest that you may be better off trying it a different way, if it seems you are having trouble.) So you'll see fiddlers with fingers hanging off the bow, or with their left thumb protruding way above the neck of the fiddle. It's all good, my fiddling friend!

♦ Last but not least, sometimes you'll see fiddlers drinking beer or smoking while playing. This is not recommended by the surgeon general or myself in any way, shape, or form—but let's just say, you wouldn't see *that* at Carnegie Hall!

def•i•ni•tion

The **bridge** is the carved-out piece of wood toward the middle of the fiddle or violin that holds up the four strings.

But this is all anthropological window dressing. The answer to the question, "So what *is* the difference, anyway?" is still "Nothing!" The next time someone hands you a violin and asks you to play a fiddle tune on it, there's nothing stopping you—except perhaps that you've still got to work your way through this book first.

The Strings Are Connected to the ... Tailpiece

With any new skill, there's some new terminology. You're going to be shopping for a fiddle. You're also going to be maintaining and playing it. So you'll need to know a little bit about it first. After all, you don't want to be stuck at the repair shop saying, "Can you replace the thingymajob on this fiddle?"

Fiddle Facts

The fiddle is a deceptively complex instrument. It is made up of around 70 different pieces!

You'd rather be showing off your new vocabulary to all your non-fiddle-playing friends, whether they're interested or not!

So before you start learning how to play, I'll introduce you to the fiddle, bow, and all their parts.

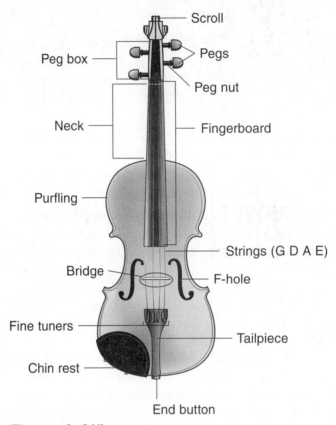

The parts of a fiddle.

Fiddle Facts

The f-holes of a fiddle often are intentionally not made to be completely symmetrical.

The body of the fiddle itself is made of hardwood, usually European spruce and maple. The spruce is used for the front, or *belly*, of the fiddle, and the maple is used for the back and the sides, otherwise known as the *ribs*. On the front of the fiddle are two holes shaped like two reverse images of the calligraphic letter f, which are called, obviously enough, *f-holes*. These holes allow the sound of the fiddle to emerge from where it has been resonating inside the body. They are, in effect, the speakers of the instrument.

Along the edge of the fiddle are two decorative lines outlining the shape of the instrument. This is *purfling*. It may appear that the lines are just painted on there to "look purty" (and in cheaply made instruments, that can be the case). But purfling is actually thin, carved-out notches that are filled in with a thin strip of a different shade of wood.

While it does add to the visual elegance of a fiddle, purfling also serves a protective purpose. It helps prevent cracks from spreading from the edge of the fiddle (which can get bumped now and again) to the center of the fiddle, where they can cause serious problems with structure and sound. They are the fiddle precursor to the airbag.

At the top of the fiddle is the *scroll*. This is a decorative part of the instrument and usually is shaped like a swirl when the fiddle is viewed from the side. The scroll can be used to hang an instrument as well, from a hook on the wall or a music stand. Just make sure it's secure if you do that.

Just below the scroll is the *peg box*, which contains four holes. Into these holes are inserted the fiddle's four, usually black *pegs*. Each of the fiddle's four strings is wrapped around one peg. The end of the string is threaded through a small hole in the peg itself, secured in place before it is wound up tight. The peg is turned in order to loosen or tighten the strings, which changes their pitch. Moving clockwise from the lower-left peg, the pegs hold the strings in this order: G, D, A, and E.

The *neck* is the long and thin section of the fiddle that is held with your left hand. It actually starts with the scroll and ends where it meets the body of the fiddle. The neck consists of two layers, seen from the side. The bottom layer is hardwood, part of the body of the instrument.

The top section of the neck is usually made from a dense, dark wood called ebony. The ebony is carved into a long black strip known as the *fingerboard*. The fingerboard extends beyond the neck, so that the bottom half is suspended above the belly. The strings then hover above the fingerboard. This, obviously, is where your fingers go when you play the fiddle.

Unlike a guitar, or mandolin or banjo, there are no frets on the fingerboard of the fiddle. This means that placing the fingers precisely in the right position is very important when playing. It is also what allows the expressiveness of the fiddle to shine through, because notes can be bent and slid into, adding a lot of color to the sound.

Sitting atop the fingerboard is a raised, thin wooden block of matching ebony black, called the *peg nut*. This is what elevates the strings and spaces them evenly apart once they leave the peg box. The peg nut is intrinsic to the *action* of a fiddle. Action basically refers to how hard it is to press a string down with your finger.

Just after the space at the end of the fingerboard, the strings rest upon the four notches on the *curve* of the *bridge*. Here, they sit up a bit higher than at the peg nut. They also are spaced a little wider. This means that the distance from G to E is greater at the bridge than where they emerge from the peg box.

The tension of the strings is the only thing holding the bridge in place. So if all four strings were to come loose at once, the bridge would fall down. The bridge is more than just a fancy place for the strings to sit pretty, though. It is the second step in the process that makes the violin's sound. When a fiddle is played, the bridge transfers the vibrations of the strings to the rest of the fiddle, where it is amplified by the body and resonates in the interior space.

Fiddle Facts

The scroll shape of the fiddle is just a tradition, and isn't related to the sound. Occasionally, you can find a fiddle scroll that has been carved into an animal head or some other creative shape.

The wood used to make a fiddle has to be aged for almost 10 years before it is used. This helps give it the strength it needs to withstand all the pressure it will endure.

False Notes

Action can be high or low. If action is too high, it can be painful for your fingertips and make playing more difficult. This can often be fixed by lowering the height of the peg nut.

Tune Up

A good violin shop will be able to tell whether the bridge's feet are sitting in the correct spot, and can carve the bottom of the feet so they are, in effect, molded to the surface of the belly.

The bridge's two *feet* have to be precisely placed on the surface of the fiddle. The feet of the bridge usually, but not always, are placed exactly between the notches in the middle of the f-holes. This placement is important because the bridge works with two important parts that are on the inside of the fiddle: the *bass bar* and the *sound post*. These have two purposes. Both help support the belly of the fiddle. The belly can use this support, because it is experiencing a tremendous amount of pressure from the strings and the bridge—almost 40 pounds, in fact! They also continue the transfer of vibrations that the bridge is transmitting from the strings.

The bass bar, as you might guess from its name, is a bar placed under the foot of the bridge that holds the lower-pitched G and D strings. It is fixed in place and can't really be accessed once the belly is sealed on the fiddle.

The sound post, on the other hand, is a movable dowel that is wedged underneath the higher-register A and E strings. The position of the sound post can be changed to improve the sound of your fiddle.

At the bottom end of each string is either a loop or a small metal ball, which attaches the string to the *tailpiece*. The strings are either looped around or inserted into the tailpiece. The tailpiece, which secures the end of the strings, is held in place itself by a strong loop called the *tail gut*, which goes around an *end button*. The end button holds the whole string/bridge/tailpiece connection in place. This has to be tightly secured into the fiddle, or things will come flying apart. (Refer back to that 40 pounds of pressure.)

Where the strings connect to the tailpiece, you often find *fine tuners*, which are used to change the pitch of the string in smaller increments than the pegs. The fine tuners can be made as part of the tailpiece, or as separate parts that are inserted into the tailpiece.

To the left of the tailpiece is another black piece of wood, the wedge-shaped *chin rest*. Aptly named, this is where you rest your chin while playing. The chin rest is attached to the fiddle by means of a metal bracket that can be tightened or loosened with a small tool.

The Bow: Not Just Any Old Stick

The bow is often underestimated. Though it may seem like a basic stick with some hair on it, it's really an intrinsic part of the fiddle. It is a blend of grace, balance, and strength. A badly made bow can make playing a fiddle a very frustrating experience. A great bow can make you feel like your playing is worth a million bucks. Many professional players can have a bow that costs as much or more than their fiddle itself!

The tip of the bow also can be called the head. At the tip, the stick becomes very thin and narrow. It ends in an L-shape wedge. On the underside of the wedge is a small ivory facing, or plate, which is partly decoration, but mostly it protects the delicate tip from the accidental drops and blows caused by the bow's owner. (More contemporary-made bows often substitute some other kinder, gentler material for the ivory.)

Fiddle Facts

While the best violins are often Italian, many high-quality bows are of French origin.

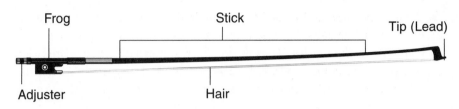

The parts of the bow.

In the middle of the ivory plate is an opening where the hair of the bow is held in place with a well-fitted wooden plug. The plug sits underneath the hair and out of view when the hair is tight. This plug says a lot about the skill of the bow maker, because if it is not done right, it can pop out. The hair of the bow is horsehair. The hair is usually a pale white or blond color. Black hair, which can provide a coarser surface, is also available. This type is most often used in bows meant for the thick strings of upright basses, though.

The wood of the bow is called the stick. The stick is made to curve downwards, toward the hair. This is known as *camber*. The camber of the bow is one of its most important features, as it affects the bow's balance and movement across the strings.

The handle of the bow is called the *frog*. The frog holds the hair in place at the other end of the stick. At the end of the frog, there is a small metal *adjuster*, composed of a *screw* and a *button*. This can be turned away from you or toward you, to make the hair tighter or looser, respectively. Just up the stick from the frog there is usually a leather band called the *grip*, which can help you hold the slick wood of the bow more easily.

Physics Makes Music

You've now completed the VIP tour of the fiddle and the bow. But the whole mechanism of the fiddle may still seem a little confusing to you. After all, how, exactly, does a ribbon of horsehair running across a string make sound, or, music, in fact?! Plucking a string, like on a guitar or harp, might seem more obvious. You pull on the string, let go with a snap, and the string vibrates. It makes sound.

Here's what's happening when you pluck a string and make it vibrate: you've created a *standing wave* that is the source of the sound. The length and width of the string, as well as the material it is made from, all affect the vibration and the sound that you get from it.

Believe it or not, a similar thing is happening when you run the bow over the strings. The horsehair may appear to have a smooth surface. However, under a microscope, it can be seen that the surface of the hairs is covered with very fine scales. When *rosin* is put on the bow, it adheres to the scales, making the bow sticky.

def•i•ni•tion

You might vaguely remember the term **standing wave** from high school physics class. This is a wave that doesn't move (as opposed to, say, an ocean wave). A standing wave oscillates—moves back and forth—between two fixed points.

Rosin is a substance made from the resin, or sap, of pine trees. It is molded into a cake or little wooden box, which is then used to rub on bow hair.

Here's what happens when you use the bow: the scales catch on the string, then release. This is like a "minipluck"—it causes the string to vibrate. As long as the bow continues to move, this event happens repeatedly. The string vibrates continuously and without fading. It is being "plucked," by the bow, over and over. Amazing … and much easier than trying to achieve that sound with a pick in your hand.

This is only the beginning of the sound, though. A string itself actually makes very little noise when vibrating. If it did, there would be no reason for the beauty and variety of stringed instruments. You could rig up some strings on an old coat hanger and play away! But the instrument is not just for looks. It is a resonator and an amplifier.

As we already learned, the bridge transmits the vibrations of the strings to the rest of the body with the help of the bass bar and sound post. Once that happens, the belly and the back of the fiddle then all vibrate with the sound waves that the bow hairs have produced, thereby amplifying the sound. This vibration of the body sends the standing waves into the air inside the fiddle, where it resonates. It's a little echo chamber in there, basically. We then hear this coming out of the f-holes as sound.

The construction of the fiddle is made to be a perfect balance of wood—in the bridge and the body. It is an amazing feat of engineering. The wood must be thick enough to withstand the enormous amount of pressure being exerted by the strings, but it can't be too thick. It has to also be thin enough to transmit the strings' vibrations into the air to be heard as sound. This perfect balance of thinness and strength is the result of generations of fine-tuning by violin craftsmen. All in all, it's a pretty fantastic little machine, and not bad lookin' either!

> ### Fiddle Facts
>
> A table, a chair, a bowl of fruit, and a violin; what else does a man need to be happy?
>
> —Albert Einstein

The Least You Need to Know

- A fiddle *is* a violin.

- A fiddler and a violinist often will want different sounds from the same instrument, and will achieve this through different features on the instruments, as well as different playing styles.

- The fiddle's strings, bridge, and body are all necessary parts of an elaborately engineered system that produces the sound you hear.

- The rough surface of the bow, coated in rosin, is what sticks to the string and makes it vibrate.

Obtaining a Fiddle

In This Chapter

♦ Avoid wasting money on a poor-quality instrument

♦ Where to find a good fiddle

♦ The various kinds of fiddles and bows available

♦ How much you can expect to spend

♦ Whether or not to go electric

The first step in learning the fiddle is, of course, to get yourself one. This can seem like an overwhelming prospect at first. After all, fiddles aren't just lying around like ants at a picnic. You've got to know where to go to get one, and how to decide on an instrument once you get there. There is a range of choices. Like anything, you can overpay for a mediocre instrument, but you also can score a deal on a real gem. It boils down to what you want and what you are willing to spend.

This chapter walks you through your quest to find a fiddle. We cover where you should buy the instrument, what you should be looking for in an instrument, what you can expect to spend, and what kind of accessories are an absolute "must-have" for this season (and for all seasons).

On the Search for a Fiddle

Finding the perfect fiddle is something you do want to put a little thought and effort into. It's not quite the quest for the Holy Grail, but getting this part right is important. You do want to have a decent enough instrument, not a piece of (fill in your own colorful noun here). It means the difference between enjoying practicing regularly, and ending up letting the fiddle sit in the corner, unloved and unplayed. It means that you will be able to tell when your playing is improving. With a lesser-quality instrument, you can end up fighting the instrument more than playing it. Having a good instrument also means that other people will want to listen to you and play with you, instead of running away—with the dogs howling alongside!

Buyer Beware

It does pay to be cautious as you search. Looking on the Internet, it may seem that there are actually great bargain fiddles to be had everywhere. A quick search on eBay or some other Internet auction site will bring up a slew of violin and bow packages for under $100. This may look like a great deal, but you should think twice before slapping down a hundred bucks on a fiddle you've never seen or played.

There are some reputable sellers and decent deals on auction sites, and if you are careful and know what you are doing, you could do okay. However, the truth is that most fiddles available so cheaply are badly constructed factory-made instruments, or ones that are in poor condition. A fiddle like that would be difficult and frustrating to play, and would make practicing a chore.

Let's say you did buy one of these fiddles. To make it playable, a fiddle shop might have to do work on the body, fingerboard, bridge, sound post, or peg nut. Any or all of these might have to be adjusted, repaired, or replaced. This easily can cost you $100 or even more—double or triple what you originally paid! If it's really a doozey, the fiddle might not really even be worth the effort, making your original investment a waste of your money. And let's face it: there is hair from Napoleon's head being sold on eBay. Anyone can put anything up for sale. (There is a chance that perhaps it *could* be his real hair … just "use your head"!)

There are some other ways people have been known to find a bargain. Decent fiddles have been found at resale locations like yard and estate sales, antique shops, and flea markets. Sometimes a friend or family member has an old fiddle sitting in the attic. If you are looking at getting a private teacher, ask them if they know anyone looking to get rid of an instrument.

Sometimes you can score. But then again, sometimes not! In these situations, though, you aren't completely at the mercy of the seller. At least you can pick the fiddle up, look it over, perhaps try to eke a few notes out of it before you take your gamble!

Generally, if you come across a fiddle that is very cheap, on cyberspace or real space, here is what you should keep in mind:

- The fiddle should be free of major cracks and dents, and generally should have a solid body of wood. Make sure nothing is warped, like the fingerboard and the scroll.

- A fiddle with the bridge standing and holding all four strings is probably in much better shape than one lacking these features.

- Can you return the fiddle if you find out it's not up to snuff? Then you can better afford the risk of purchasing it as a "bargain."

Tune Up

Look through the f-holes to the inside of the fiddle, and you will most likely find a label there. This label will be printed with the name of the maker and the year it was made. This information is usually truthful—but there are thousands of fiddles that claim "Stradivarius."

Fiddle Facts

A century ago in Ireland, way before today's "Celtic Tiger" economic comeback, aspiring and thrifty fiddlers in County Donegal, Ireland, came up with a version of the fiddle made from tin.

Finding a Good Fiddle Shop

Whether you already own or are hoping to own a fiddle, you need to know where your closest violin shop is. Fiddles, being such a complex and specialty instrument, aren't just sold and maintained anywhere. No fiddler will recommend that you stroll into the general music shop that sells drums, guitars, and keyboards and purchase a fiddle there. That shop might have one lonely looking, suspiciously shiny fiddle hanging forlornly on the wall. In general, however, you should resist the urge to adopt it and give it a better home. The fiddles are usually slightly overpriced and the salespeople usually don't have a clue about bowed-string instruments, no matter how much they know about drums and guitars.

Yes, sir, only your local violin shop will do. Here's the scoop: most violin shops are not stuffed in between the Applebee's and the Gap at your local mall. Locating one usually takes a little bit more detective work if you are starting your search cold. But they are around.

Every major city (and "sorta major" cities, too!) should have at least one or more quality violin shop. Sometimes they are located near the local orchestra's performance site. Then there are also fiddle shops scattered around in small towns that serve a larger geographic area. Down south, fiddle makers can be found at bluegrass and old-time music festivals, selling reasonably priced fiddles directly to musicians.

There are also shops that bill themselves as "acoustic" or "folk" music shops. These places are worth a try. They often focus on the fiddle's more fretted friends, such as guitars, banjos, and mandolins, but sometimes they will have an in-house "fiddle guy" who knows what he is doing. Sometimes they also team up with a local *luthier* to outsource any fiddle work that comes their way. They also might be willing and able to refer you to the right fellow (or gal).

The most important thing is to find a shop whose people are qualified and experienced in working in violins. This may sound a little daunting ("How am I supposed to know?") Just ask a few conversational questions about where they studied, and if they play violin themselves. And honestly, there isn't the biggest market for fiddles in the general population, so if you walk into a store and it's nothing but fiddles hanging from the walls (and maybe cellos and basses, too), you probably are in the right place.

Here are several ways you can find your friendly neighborhood violin shop:

◆ Look in the phone book under "violins" (you could look under "fiddle," too, but most shops will use the more formal name for the instrument). If you don't find a violin shop, look under stringed instruments or musical instruments). A violin shop will almost always contain the word "violin" or "strings."

◆ Ask the salespeople at the general music shop, the one that *doesn't* really sell fiddles, if they know of a good violin shop in town. They'll most likely understand that their fiddle inventory is sub-par. Hopefully, they'll be willing to direct you to a good shop if they know of one.

def•i•ni•tion

A **luthier** is a skilled craftsperson who builds or repairs stringed instruments, such as guitars, fiddles. Originally these craftsmen worked on lutes, and they kept their title as the instruments changed.

- If you have a private teacher, she will certainly be willing to help you find a good shop (and should be able to offer some comments on an instrument you are trying out, too).

- Next time you go out to hear a local band, feel free to ask the fiddler where he takes his instrument to be worked on. This can be especially good when you need some work done yourself, as he also could direct you to one of many luthiers who work out of a small, unobtrusive workshop without an obvious storefront. This type of workshop usually is harder to find if you are just starting out in the music world.

- Go onto the Internet and search for violin retailers. There are a few good shops online. (Some actual physical violin shops also have an online presence with a good website, and operate nationally.) Buying an instrument and a bow is a little more arduous when you can't actually try out the instrument in person. However, if you find that you live in an area far from a good violin shop, it's an option. Online retailers often have good deals on strings and a good selection of accessories as well.

One nice thing about violin shops is that they will often let you take an instrument to try out for a few days. You will have to leave a deposit or working credit card number, of course. But then you can take that fiddle home and play on it in your own kitchen. Just ask what the shop's policy is.

Renting Is an Option

Let's be honest: the fiddle isn't the very cheapest instrument to start out with. You can get a kazoo for $3, a harmonica for $20, a guitar for a hundred … for a decent violin, you usually have to spend a bit more than that, unless you're lucky. And if you are just dabbling with the idea of fiddling as a fun little hobby, you might be starting to wonder if you should find another dream that isn't so heavy on your wallet.

Don't despair yet! There is a way to avoid spending all that money right off the bat. Many violin shops will rent a violin to you for a fairly reasonable monthly fee. That way you can spend less, and experiment for a few months. If the fiddle isn't for you, then you aren't stuck with an instrument you spent a fair bit of money on. If you find you love playing the fiddle (and why wouldn't you?!) and want to go on to purchase one, the same store will often issue you some credit based on the money you have spent renting. Some stores also have a rent-to-own system where you can decide to buy the fiddle you are renting, and apply the rental money to the price. This latter option can work out well, though it also can constrain you in your choice of instrument.

Choosing a Fiddle That Works for You

Once you've found a fiddle shop, you can start shopping. There are a variety of levels of violins to choose from, and many different factors you need to take into account when choosing an instrument. If you are completely new to the instrument, ask lots of questions and find the deal that works best for you. As you become more accomplished on the fiddle, you will find that you develop preferences. It will become clearer what you are looking for in *your* instrument.

Price

As in most things you purchase, cost is often the first thing you need to take into account. Everyone has a different budget and has to set their own limit for what price of instrument they can afford. You also have to decide how important this new hobby is to you and weigh your budget that way.

Violins come in a huge range of prices, and the sky is the limit. You can spend anywhere from just over $100 to a cool $3.5 million for a Stradivarius. (I'm going to assume that your budget is a little lower than that.)

Here's one thing to remember: while you may think a more expensive instrument is a better instrument, this isn't always the case.

Here's the thing: violin prices are a little like prices of wines. Seriously! They are made by highly skilled craftsmen and priced at all different levels. But prices aren't easily tied to one factor. You can find good wine for under $10, and you can pay hundreds of dollars for a mediocre vintage, just because it got kinda popular in Hollywood last year. The same works for fiddles: the maker, age, condition, sound quality, appearance, where it was made—these are all things that can affect the price of an instrument. Rarity and popularity of a certain type of fiddle can jack up the price. Certain individual makers are especially prized. And other fiddles can be seen as "investment" instruments—ones that will keep going up in value.

> **Fiddle Facts**
>
> The Stradivarius violin known as "The Hammer," built in 1707, set the record for the highest price ever bid for a musical instrument when Christie's auctioned and sold it in 2006 for $3,544,000.

But if you go into a shop looking for your dream fiddle, there are many that will fit the bill and your budget. A $300 fiddle could be music to your ears compared to the $3,000 instrument hanging down the rack. If that's the case, don't doubt your judgment—trust your ears and go for the bargain! If you've got some money to spend, keep your allowance in mind, but don't discount a cheaper instrument thinking that it must be better to spend more. On the other hand, if your budget is smaller, feel confident that it's possible to find a good instrument that won't break your bank.

Levels of Craftsmanship

One reason fiddles are priced differently is that they are built through three different styles of manufacture.

◆ **Fiddles can be made in a factory, much as any other modern item.** These types of fiddles are generally the cheapest as they are mass-produced. The cheapest factory-made fiddles are to be avoided—especially older models made in China. In more recent years, however, China has greatly improved its process and has been turning out some very decent instruments made in factories. These can be a very good deal and a great

False Notes

If you're buying a fiddle, make sure you buy one that you like playing. However, also aim to buy a decent instrument—no matter the price range—that won't lose value because it is in marginal condition. The vast majority of instruments, when well maintained, should stay at around the same value that you paid for it.

way to start out. One hundred years ago, Germany was producing many factory violins, and these older instruments can be found for a very decent price today as well.

◆ **Many fiddles are made in a workshop setting.** There may be a master luthier directing the process, but the fiddle is put together by many different people. This type of fiddle tends to be in an average price range.

◆ **The most expensive category of fiddle is one made by an individual maker, who puts together every bit of the fiddle him- or herself.** The more well-known luthiers may have a distinctive and consistent quality to their instrument that musicians seek out. Many fiddles by current American makers sell for between $10,000 and $20,000.

Prices from these three categories may overlap. Some workshop-made fiddles are more expensive than one from an individual maker. And vice versa. But certainly the method by which a fiddle was made is a factor in the cost and is worth taking into consideration.

Whatever way a fiddle is made, age often increases the quality of the sound. A well-made fiddle especially will ripen with age, so often people will seek out an older fiddle. However, buying a quality instrument that is straight off the workbench is better than an old one that hasn't been well maintained.

Tone and Feel

def•i•ni•tion

The **tone** of a violin is the quality of the sound: whether it is loud or soft, has more emphasis on the low or high notes, is scratchy or smooth, and so on.

The *tone* of the fiddle is one of the most important factors when buying a fiddle. Tone is an amalgam of many different things. You are looking for a fiddle with a full, rich, and clear sound. The sound should be pleasant to listen to—not too scratchy or fuzzy in quality. The fiddle should play equally loudly on all strings, and not seem louder on the D string than the A string, for example. Pay attention to how long the string rings after you play a note and then lift the bow.

The feel of the fiddle is just that—how it feels to hold and play. Some fiddles are larger than others. Some necks are thicker than others. Some fiddles are heavier than others.

Basically, this part of picking out your instrument is where things often get objective and personal. Try out different instruments and see what suits you. A fiddle might be attractive, well made, and a decent price to boot. But if it's just not *you*, then you should pass. Try at least four or five fiddles at a time; you will often find that you quickly narrow it down to one or two that you like more than the others. You will find a certain sound that you like and a certain feel that you like.

If possible, listen while someone else plays the instrument, as fiddles sound very different when they are not blaring right into your ear.

... And There's the Bow, Too!

Once you've picked out your fiddle, you're not done. You can only pluck at it if you don't have a bow. Most people are a little shocked when they first realize that a decent bow will cost them a little money, too. If you have gone and bought yourself a really nice fiddle, you should do it justice by getting a decent bow as well!

The best bow is a combination of balance and weight. Balance is in part a reflection of where the center of the bow's weight is. If you were to rest the stick on your finger, with it laying horizontally, your finger would lie much closer to the heavy frog than the tip. You can feel this as you hold the bow: the whole stick should feel good from the vantage of your right hand. A bow with good balance makes playing easier. A bow that is too light can be harder to control, and a bow that is too heavy can be a bit unwieldy and tiring for your right hand, as well. A bow can vary in stiffness as well, with some sticks being more supple than others. All this can affect your sound.

Many professional fiddle players will spend over $1,000 on a good bow. However, when you are first starting out, a fairly inexpensive bow should do just fine. A violin shop should be able to help you, and might even just throw a bow in with a cheaper fiddle. Nowadays inexpensive bows made of fiberglass are decent enough for a beginner's needs, and they can run under $50. There are some bows made out of carbon, as well.

You may find that as you improve, you will get a sense of what a good bow is. You'll begin to feel like you are struggling to get the sound you want with the bow you have. Then you'll know it's time to go shopping for a truly well-made bow. It is easy enough to play basic tunes with a cheaper bow, but more advanced playing will need the freedom that a good bow brings.

Again, when picking out a bow, take your time and try out a batch at a time. You will start to see the differences between them, narrow it down to two or three, and eventually find the one that you think suits you the best.

Tune Up

If you find you "outgrow" the first instrument you picked out, keep in mind that many violin stores will let you trade in your well-maintained instrument for a better one, at the same price that they sold it to you for.

All the Accoutrements

If you are buying a fiddle from a violin shop, the instrument almost certainly has been *set up* well and is ready to take home. If you already have a fiddle, or found yourself what looks like a bargain, you will want to make sure it is set up correctly. To some extent, if you put new strings on it and start playing, you can tell if the instrument is in good shape yourself. If you take it to the experts, though, they might be able to improve the instrument's sound significantly with a few small expert changes. The better set up an instrument is, the easier and more satisfying you will find playing. There are also a couple of personal choices you can make when setting up an instrument.

def•i•ni•tion

To **set up** an instrument is to make sure it is at its greatest playing potential. When setting up a fiddle, a luthier will play the instrument, examining the bridge, the fingerboard, the height of the strings, the pegs, the sound post, the tailpiece, and the neck to make sure they are all in ideal shape.

A Case

Many people refer to their fiddle as their "baby." The difference is, you are *legally* allowed to walk out of the fiddle shop without a safe contraption to transport the fiddle in ... but you'll still probably get some pretty skeptical looks from the guy behind the counter.

The truth is, you really should have a case, both to store the violin in when you're not using it and to carry it around in when you go outside. The case will protect your fiddle from bumps or falls, as well as changes in the temperature and humidity, and will make it easier to put your fiddle somewhere in the house, too. (Especially if you've got pets or children!)

There is quite a range of choices available. The best advice is just to correlate the price of your new fiddle with the price of the case. If you bought the cheapest fiddle you could tolerate, then there are simple and functional cases available for $25 that will do the basic job. Most cases under $100 are the most familiar ones, shaped like a violin (and often used in the 1920s by Tommy-gun-toting gangsters!)

If you've spent a little more money, you might want a slightly better product to protect your new "baby." Spending a hundred dollars or more usually gets you a rectangular-shaped case. Added options include more cushioning, better design, a strap to fasten the fiddle into its hollow, outer waterproof covers with zips and pockets, backpack-style straps, and better shock resistance. Then, of course, there are always the really pricey ones that are advertised through stories of forgotten fiddles falling off car roofs at 60 mph and surviving. As you are trying to decide on a case, don't be afraid to ask your salesperson what he or she recommends for you and your violin.

The Strings Section

Once you start playing the fiddle, you will start on a journey of string exploration. It's kind of fun to try out different strings and find what works for you and for your fiddle. You can find that certain brands just don't fit the sound of your fiddle at all. Most established players have a brand of string that they swear by and wouldn't use anything else, and have a few that they wouldn't touch with a 10-foot pole! The type of string you use does have a great effect on your sound. Some strings have a quicker *response* than others. Some are thicker and some are thinner. They are made of a variety of metals, such as nickel or aluminum.

There are basically two types of strings used by fiddlers: steel-core strings and synthetic-core strings. Each type of string has a main core of material running up the center, and is completely covered by a very thin ribbon of metal that wraps around the outside. The E string is simply a thin strand of metal. There are cheap strings and very expensive strings, but as with everything else in fiddles, it is largely what you like and desire that should dictate what type of string you use.

Fiddle Facts

A good and true woman is said to resemble a Cremona fiddle: age but increases its worth and sweetens its tone.

—Oliver Wendell Holmes

---

def•i•ni•tion

Response is a term used to describe how quickly an instrument or string sounds the note after you move the bow. A quick response means you feel no delay when you play.

◆ *Steel strings* often are favored by bluegrass players because they have a brassier sound. Being 100 percent metal, they aren't affected by changes in the weather or temperature. As a result, they tend to stay in tune between playings very well. They respond very quickly as well.

◆ *Synthetic-core strings* were invented in the 1970s and are made with perlon. They are basically an artificial gut string, but without the disadvantages of gut, such as easily going out of tune. They are now made by many different makers from a variety of substances. Different brands have different rates of response, sound, and feel, so you'll want to experiment with what you like.

Fiddle Facts

Before this century, the only strings available were gut-core strings, made from sheep or lamb intestines.

Bridge Cut

The fiddles in the store will obviously already have a bridge fit to them. As a fiddler, you have a choice when having your bridge put on your instrument. The curve of the bridge can be done with a higher or flatter arch, depending on the style of music you play. If you are very interested in old-time, American string-band music, then you might want to ask your luthier if he or she could make the bridge a little flatter. This will make playing *double stops* or drones easier, obtaining that country sound.

Most violin shops will automatically have a more pronounced curve on their bridges. If you are interested in playing different types of music or just want to play a few tunes for fun, this is the way to go. As your style and musical preferences grow, along with your familiarity with your own playing, you will probably feel more confident knowing which type of bridge you would like to have on your fiddle.

def•i•ni•tion

A **double stop** means playing two strings at one time.

Chin Rests

Most fiddles already have a chin rest on them. If you don't like the feel of the one on there, it's simple to change it. When you are in the violin shop, you might look down and be amazed at the variety of chin rests that are available to you. There are large ones, small ones, round ones, ones ending in a pointed shape, ones that sit in the center of the fiddle instead of on the left side.

The best thing to do is ask the violin shop which ones they recommend or are most popular. They will have a good idea of which ones are more standard, and which ones cater to people with specific tastes in chin rests. You can try a few on, too. A friendly violin shop should be willing to change out a few for you to try before you buy. Don't feel like you are stuck with what you pick forever, either. Most chin rests are between $10 and $30, so if you decide you want to try a new one later on, it's no big deal.

What About Electric Fiddles?

Acoustic certainly isn't the only choice in the instrument world. There are electric fiddles around—players like Boyd Tinsley from Dave Matthews and jazz violinist Jean-Luc Ponty are well-known examples. You might be considering going for an electric fiddle instead of an acoustic. However, you'd be better off not doing that.

Why? An electric violin is pretty much just that—an electrified version of the acoustic instrument. Compare that to the electric guitar. There, you're almost talking about a different instrument from the acoustic version. In an acoustic guitar, as with the violin, a wooden body sends the energy of a vibrating string into the air. In an electric guitar, the strings of an electric guitar pass over a magnetic *pickup*, which senses the vibrations and transfers the signal to an amplifier. In one, the bridge transmits the vibrations, in the other a magnet. The two types of guitars sound completely different. The technique for playing them is really quite different as well. In an electric violin, the pickups are usually little piezo crystals that sit in the bridge, pick up the bridge's vibrations, and send them to an amplifier.

An electric violin usually is built out of a solid body. Remember that bit about standing waves and vibrations in the last chapter? Well, without the f-holes and meticulous craftsmanship of wooden bars and plates around an open body, the electric violin becomes basically a stand for a vibrating string—which, as you remember, makes very little sound. There is also very little tone quality to an electric violin. The sound from the strings is amplified with electronics, and has to be made to sound natural electronically with EQ, reverb, foot pedals, and other effects. They are best in bands that are really loud, where they have to compete with drums and electric guitars—although a regular fiddle still can be used in this setting.

None of this is a bad thing, of course. But if you really want to learn the instrument, it's better to start on the acoustic version. That way, you learn how to work with the deep emotion and human qualities that make the fiddle such a unique and versatile instrument. Later, if you find yourself playing in a band or situation where an electric fiddle would come in handy, you will be better equipped to demand the best sound out of it that you can get.

def•i•ni•tion

A **pickup** is a device that translates the vibration of a moving string into a signal of electric current that can be sent to an amplifier.

Fiddle Facts

Swing violinist Stuff Smith invented the electric violin in the 1930s, so he could be heard over the horn players in his band.

The Least You Need to Know

- Buyer beware. Make sure that a "bargain" fiddle isn't going to cost you more than your initial investment in repairs and set-up costs.

- Purchase a fiddle at a reputable violin shop, or at least a folk or acoustic music shop that has an experienced luthier working for them. This is where you should take your fiddle for any repair or adjustment you can't do yourself as well.

- Whether you like a fiddle or not is the best indicator of whether or not you should buy it.

- A cheaper bow is fine for a beginner, but you will want to upgrade as you become a better player.

- You should buy a case to protect your fiddle from bumps or falls, and to store it in safely.

- It's better not to buy an electric fiddle if you are just starting out.

Chapter 4

Preparing to Play

In This Chapter

- ◆ Tuning up your fiddle
- ◆ Rosining the bow
- ◆ Making your fiddle more comfortable—or quieter
- ◆ Warming up before playing
- ◆ Exercising your body, arms, and hands

Before you just start playing the fiddle, you've got to have the thing in tune! On top of that, an in-tune fiddle also should be a comfortable fiddle. Being comfortable will ultimately mean that you want to practice more often—and can do so for longer.

Playing music is a form of physical exercise. Though it's not really strenuous enough to take off those few pounds you gained over the winter holidays, it does make demands on your muscles and joints. It is also a form of repetitive motion. As a result, if you play a lot, you can be susceptible to many of the same ailments that can strike the modern office worker or ice-cream scooper. So it's good to form a habit of warming up to play from the beginning.

This chapter gives you a quick primer on getting your fiddle comfortably set up to play, in tune, as well as how to get some volume control, should you need it. We also cover a few ways to prepare your physical self for fiddle playing. As an added bonus, these few stretches and circles definitely will take some stress out of your day!

Tuning Up

Many people find tuning their instrument one of the hardest, and most annoying, things about their new hobby. After all, being able to hear the correct pitch is a skill. If you're not previously experienced in music, it takes some time to learn. You've got to be able to recognize whether a string needs to be tuned up or down. Then of course, you've got to turn the pegs and/or fine tuners in order to get the string to the proper tension. *And* you've got to get all four strings tuned up to *each other!* You have to learn all that before you can even start making one note.

Fortunately, you've got this book to take you through the whole procedure. It's really not that bad. First, let's go over *what* exactly you need to tune on the violin.

The four strings on the fiddle are the notes G, D, A, and E, from lowest to highest. These strings are tuned in *fifths* according to the musical scale. This means that there are five notes from one string to the next.

This concept is illustrated best by looking at a piano keyboard (and if you have one of these that's in tune, they're very handy for tuning fiddles). The fiddle, being fretless, provides no hints as to where all the notes are on the fingerboard. Only the four strings are a clear indicator of what notes go where.

The piano, on the other hand, is an instrument that illustrates very clearly the position of every single note of the Western musical scale. It's basically a handy map of what you are hearing when you listen to music. The *white* keys of the piano correspond to each basic note of the scale, which is A, B, C, D, E, F, and G. The *black* keys are the notes in between these notes. The black note to the left of A is both an A flat and a G sharp. We'll explain all this in Chapter 6. For now, let's just find the four notes that represent our four fiddle strings.

Looking at the diagram below, we've marked the keys corresponding to the G, D, A, and E. As you can see, the G is the lowest string of the fiddle. Starting at the G, count five white keys up the scale, and you will land on the D. Starting with the D, count five white keys up and you are at A. Continue the same pattern and you'll end up at the E string. That, my friend, is what a fifth is!

> **Fiddle Facts**
>
> The note known as "middle C" is between the G and D strings.

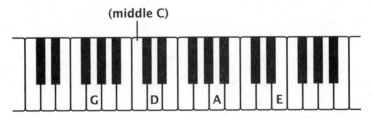

(middle C)

The strings of the fiddle, as seen on a piano keyboard.

As we've mentioned, before playing, a musician must tune. No ifs, ands, or buts. (If you are in a nonsmoking room, no butts, either!) Without tuning, a pleasant musical experience is pretty hard to come by. And frankly, audiences are, too!

Some days, it may seem that just getting your instrument tuned can take up half of your practice time. But the more often you tune up your instrument, the more quickly the whole process will happen. Your ears will sharpen. You will begin to hear instinctively whether a string is *sharp* or *flat*. You also will know

> **def•i•ni•tion**
>
> When talking about tuning, **sharp** means a string is too high, so you have to *lower* its pitch to get it in tune. **Flat** means the note is too low, so you have to *raise* it.

which way to turn the peg or fine tuner to fix the problem. You will begin to feel like the Jedi master of tuning. You will realize that you are ready, at last, to make some music.

Electronic Tuners

Unless you are one of those lucky people blessed with what is known as *perfect pitch*, you'll need some help from some kind of device in order to tune your fiddle. Electronic tuners are one such device. They are very accurate and most are very easy to use.

Electronic tuners work in two ways. Some will play the note you need in an electronic tone. Others will register the pitch as you play your string. These let you know what you need to do to get your instrument tuned, with either a digital readout or a needle pointing to a spectrum. Here's how they work: when you play your A string, the tuner will register "A," and indicate whether or not you are sharp, flat, or right on the money. If you play your A and the tuner reads G or B, then you know that your string is really low or high and needs to be turned up or down a whole note!

Some models are designed only to read the pitches from your four fiddle strings. Others are *chromatic*, so you can get a reading on any pitch in any normal scale. This type is handy, as they also can be used to gauge whether you are playing a fingered note correctly on your fretless fiddle. Just don't get obsessed with doing that, as there are far better ways to work on improving your *intonation*.

Some tuners are made so you can clip them right onto the end of your fiddle. They read the pitch using the fiddle's bodily vibrations. This can prove handy if you are fighting interference from a noisy room.

Others are freestanding little gadgets. A fiddle shop or online retailer usually will stock a variety of these devices, at a range of prices. They all take batteries; some take AA or AAA, and others, the more-annoying-to-replace-but-longer-lasting lithium watch–battery type. When choosing a tuner, just try out the ones in the store, or ask for a demonstration of how they work. You'll find the one that seems most intuitive to you.

Tuning Forks and Pitch Pipes

A tuning fork is a simple, rudimentary tool. Shaped like a long wishbone, it is a one-note wonder, ringing out with the note A. To use a tuning fork, therefore, you have to be able to tune all of the strings from only one good note. You strike one prong of the fork gently against a hard surface (your knee bone, the edge of a table …). Once it is vibrating, you place the balled end on top of the bridge, or the fiddle's belly. The fiddle will then amplify the A note that is vibrating in the fork.

A pitch pipe is a small little harmonica-like device with four pipes sticking out. Each of the four pipes matches one fiddle string, so that you can tune each

def•i•ni•tion

Perfect pitch is the ability to tell what note is what just by hearing it. People can also sing the note needed to tune without having to get it from some contraption.

Chromatic means a scale that contains every single note in a Western musical scale.

Intonation means the degree to which a player is in tune. "Good" intonation means one is in tune, and "bad" intonation means one is out of tune.

Tune Up

When having trouble tuning, try singing "Twinkle, Twinkle Little Star." The first four notes of that song ("Twinkle, twinkle") are a fifth apart. For example, you should be able to hear Twinkle when you play the G, then the D string; same with the D and A, or the A and E strings.

string individually. This is useful if you still have trouble tuning and need to hear the pitch for each note. However, you have to be careful not to overblow, as they can go sharp on you.

Both of these options have their drawbacks if tuning is still a challenge for you. But they are quite inexpensive, around $5 a pop for either of them. They are also quite small. So there's no reason not to have one or the other sitting in your case. You might say they are "travel tuners for the fiddler on the go."

The Internet

Tuning has also entered cyberspace. In a pinch, you can turn on your computer and with a bit of searching, find websites where people have recorded the notes you need to tune, or even videos of themselves tuning fiddles. A simple search for "fiddle tuning" usually brings up one or two results. I include one website in Appendix B.

The Fine Tuners

The fine tuners aren't called "fine" because they're incredibly good looking. Rather, it is because the fine tuners are used to make small adjustments to the pitch of your strings. As long as your fiddle is in reasonably good tune to begin with, they take less finagling and are easier to use than the tuning pegs.

To make the string go higher in pitch, turn the knob on the top of the fine tuner to the right (clockwise). Turning to the left (counterclockwise), then, will lower the pitch. If your string is sharp, turn the knob to the left; if flat, turn to the right.

A fiddle that has been sitting around usually is going to go flat, not sharp. The result is that after repeatedly tuning up, your fine tuner will be maxed out. You may notice that the tuner doesn't turn any more to the right. Look underneath the tailpiece at the bottom of the fine tuner, and you will see the tuner's lever getting close to the belly of the fiddle. When this happens, you should turn the fine tuner counterclockwise until it is *almost* to the beginning of its thread. If you unscrew the tuner all the way, you will feel it go loose. Screwing it back in a tiny bit will allow you some leeway if you need to tune down a little. Then retune the string with the tuning pegs.

The Tuning Pegs

Sometimes the fine tuners aren't enough. If a string has really gone out of whack, it is necessary to tune using the tuning pegs. Turning the peg *toward* you will lower the pitch of the string. Turning it *away* from you will raise the pitch (unless someone has put the string on backwards, of course). While you are turning the peg, keep some counterpressure on it with either your other hand, or your fingers otherwise, it can spring loose on you and you'll have to restring your string.

False Notes

Keep an eye on the bottom lever of your fine tuner. Make sure that it doesn't actually reach the belly of your fiddle. This can cause damage to the varnish—or possibly even dent or tear into the wood of the belly. Many tuners aren't able to reach that far, but it's better to make sure.

When you tune with a peg, it's easier to tune up to the pitch you need. Turn the string down first. Then ease your way back up, aiming for the pitch you want. Once you are at the right note, you'll have to exert a little pressure to get the peg to stick in place.

It is possible to turn the peg with one hand while bowing. This is the best method if you don't have fine tuners. Sometimes climate can make this difficult. If it is humid, the peg may be particularly sticky and won't want to move. If it's dry, the peg will be loose and won't stay in the place where you want it. In these cases, you can pluck the string to tune, and use two hands on the peg to tune as best you can. Fine tuners will get the exact result you want.

If your fiddle doesn't have all four fine tuners, you'll always need to use the pegs, of course. Some people get used to tuning with the pegs instead of the fine tuners and actually prefer that method.

Prepping the Bow

And then, of course, there's the bow. The first thing you have to do is make sure the hair is tight enough. It should be tightened just enough so that the hair isn't dragging against the wood of the bow when in use. If the hair doesn't have any give against the strings, then it is on too tight. The exact tightness is your preference.

Next, you've got to make sure there is rosin on the bow. Using rosin often provokes the question from observing nonplayers, "What is that?" After all, most other instruments don't get involved with pine sap in any way. Before you play the fiddle, though, you need to rub a little rosin on the bow hair to get the stickiness you need.

To apply rosin, simply place the bow hair onto the top of the rosin. Using approximately the same amount of pressure that you use when playing a string, rub the hair from tip to frog, coating the hair with a dusty layer of rosin.

While it is important to rosin the bow, make sure you don't overdo it. You don't need much more than a couple strokes across the cake. You don't need to rosin the bow every time you take out your fiddle, either, unless you really played the heck out of it the last time you played. Too much rosin can interfere with the action of the bow on the string.

Using a Shoulder Rest

Some people play the fiddle with a chin rest and not much more. However, most people find this awkward and uncomfortable. The violin is thinner than the length of most people's necks—and also, it's made of hard wood that can bite into your shoulder or chinbone. Playing without a shoulder rest can make you feel like your neck is being crunched. So, most players like to use a *shoulder rest*—a cushioned strip that is placed on the bottom of your fiddle.

False Notes

To tune with the peg, always start by loosening the peg by turning it *toward* you. That way if the peg is stuck, you won't break a string in a sudden release.

Tune Up

Almost every violin has a fine tuner for the E string. It is very thin, so small adjustments using the fine tuner go a long way—a tuning peg usually overdoes it.

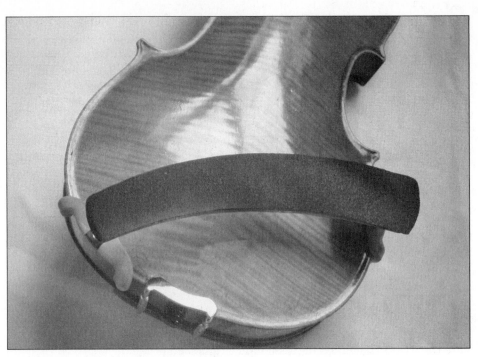

A shoulder rest placed correctly on the fiddle.

The shoulder rest should curve away from you when it is being used. This is so your shoulder can fit right into the semicircle. If you are not quite comfortable, you can adjust the height of the shoulder rest, depending on the length of your neck, or just your own preferences. This is done by screwing or unscrewing the two sides of the rest.

Mutes

If you are all set to go, but worried about bothering someone with your playing—your neighbors, the sleeping baby, and so on, there is a solution. A small violin *mute* will do the trick.

There are several different types of mutes, but the most basic type is a little, solid, circular black-rubber device with two slots on the bottom and a notch on the side. You place the mute on the strings between the bridge and the tailpiece, then slide the notch over the bridge. This will dampen the bridge's ability to transfer all the strings' vibrations to the rest of the fiddle body. The result is a thin, trumpetlike sound that lacks the full ring of an unmuted violin, and it is much quieter. So now you have no excuse not to practice!

The Importance of Warm-Up

Okay, so now you've got your fiddle all tuned up and it feels good to go. However, it's never really a good idea to start playing the fiddle "cold." Even if you are only going to be playing for a short while, try to give your muscles a little stretching and warming. This helps to prevent the strain on your muscles and

def•i•ni•tion

A **mute** is a device that dampens the natural vibrations of an instrument.

joints that can eventually turn into long-term damage. Just as you shouldn't start running or exercising without a little warm-up, you shouldn't begin playing without one.

There are many stories of people who had to stop playing because of problems such as *carpal tunnel syndrome*, tendonitis, and other less commonly known ailments involving shoulder or back problems. Your whole body is connected. Not paying attention to your hands and arms can lead to problems there, and further up into your shoulder and back.

Sometimes these things are inevitable, or at least more likely in some people than others due to genetics or fate. But prevention is always the best cure. Proper stretching and warming up is a major part of that. By giving your muscles a chance to warm up, you help avoid strain and swelling that can lead to those chronic problems.

There are both general warm-up and specific, hand- and arm-centered exercises you can do. Both are important.

The Whole of You

Everything in your body is connected. It's not really far out to suggest that there is a mind-body connection that influences strain and injury. When you are stressed out from daily life and work, it will manifest itself through tightness in your shoulders, back, and hips. This will affect your playing if you don't address it before your daily practicing.

Holding the fiddle under your chin, and moving your left fingers while swinging with your right bow arm is, to be honest, not such a natural way to just hang out. Your position can be affected by tension in your body. It also can exacerbate that tension if you don't check in with yourself and make sure that you're always relaxed.

Here are some basic exercises that will help you loosen up before playing. Most of them are pretty basic—you've probably done these before. They won't take more than a few minutes, but you'll feel so much better!

- Taking a few deep breaths is a good way to start out. We take breathing for granted, but we often forget to breathe properly with the stress of the day, or when concentrating hard on learning to play the fiddle!

- Stand up and stretch. Reach your arms to the ceiling, taking care to relax your shoulder blades and stretch gently up through your spine and arms.

- Circle your arms in a big circle, first forward, then backward. This will get the blood flowing into those extremities. Next, hold them out to the side and swing them forward and back.

- Look all the way to the right, then slowly bring your head all the way to the left. Repeat this a few times. Next, drop your head onto your chest, then move it in a circle slowly and gently a few times. This will ease tension in your neck and shoulders. Reverse direction.

def•i•ni•tion

Carpal tunnel syndrome is compression of the median nerve, which runs from your neck all the way down to your hand. It is very common in musicians, who often overuse some or all of the muscles surrounding that nerve. Symptoms include pain in the joints, swelling, and numbness and tingling in the hand and fingers.

False Notes

Forgetting to breathe, or breathing shallowly—often a result of stress—can lead to lower oxygen levels in the blood. This, in turn, leads to more tense muscles, and more stress! Break this cycle and breathe.

◆ Shrug your shoulders, bringing them up to your ears. Then circle them forward, down, and back until they are back up to your ears again. Reverse direction.

◆ Reach your hands out in front of you, palms facing out. Grab one hand with the other and stretch out your arms. You should feel a good stretch in your back and shoulders.

Aaaaah! Breathe again a few times.

Take Your Hands to the Spa

One of the easiest ways to get blood flowing in your hand is through a little massage. Hold one hand with the other, massaging all around and in the palm with your thumb. Once the palm is feeling good, work your way up each finger. Pay some attention to the knuckles. The nice part of this is that it feels pretty good, so you'll want to keep doing it! Those hands of yours, after all, work hard for you all day—picking things up, typing, holding forks, and so on. Give them a little treat before you make them do something crazy like play the fiddle.

Once you give your hands a good massage, work your way up your forearm a bit as well, massaging the underside of the arm and those muscles in there.

All that massaging will get the blood flowing, warm up your muscles, and loosen up the joints. The added benefits aren't just physical, either: a relaxed hand always makes better music. Do what is comfortable and don't get too aggressive with yourself. Be gentle.

Arm and Hand Stretches

Once you've gotten a little blood flowing and warmed up your body and hands, you should do a few exercises more specific to the arms and hands to get them stretched out.

◆ Reach your arms out in front of you. Raise your hands, as if you were signaling "stop!" to someone. Hold for 10 seconds, then, with your arms still outstretched, drop your hands all the way down—kind of like a dog would hold an injured paw.

Tune Up

If you feel tightness or tiredness in either of your arms while you play, stop and shake the hand and arm out completely, letting the wrist flop around loosely.

Hold the hands up, arms outstretched.

Then lower the hands, stretching the other side of the arm.

◆ Hold your hands in prayer position in front of your chest (hands flat and palm to palm, not clasped together). *Slowly* raise your elbows until you feel a hint of stretching. Don't overdo this stretch by pulling hard. Once you have a gentle stretch going, hold for 10 seconds. Release, shake your hands out, and repeat.

Holding your hands in prayer position, gently raise your elbows.

◆ Make a fist. Then bend your wrist down until you feel a mild stretch in the top of your forearm. Stretch gently for 10 seconds, then take a break and repeat.

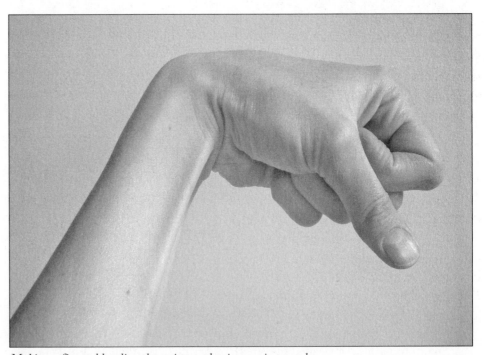

Making a fist and bending the wrist gently gives a nice stretch.

There you have it—a basic routine that shouldn't take you more than a few minutes. Stretching and warming up is a great habit to get into. Even if you think that you don't need it because you are only beginning, getting into the habit is a good idea.

After You Play

It's good to stretch out after you play, not just before. Stretching after you play will help cool down muscles that have been worked out. Specifically, if you can only do them once, do the previously described hand exercises afterward, not before. If you do skip stretching at the start, try to at least warm up by playing something easy first.

It's also good to pay attention to how you feel after you play. Do you feel any tension or pain in your arm, elbow joint, fingers, or shoulders? If so, think about your position the next time you are playing the fiddle. Do you notice an aspect of your fiddle or bow hold that might be causing that strain? Taking time to think about your position and pinpointing any small problems early will prevent them from ballooning into larger issues. Many people have had to take a break from or even give up beloved hobbies and successful careers because of repetitive strain injuries. With a little effort, you can help avoid this being you.

The Least You Need to Know

- Tuning is necessary every time you play. There is a variety of tuning equipment that can help you tune your instrument, including electronic tuners, tuning forks, pitch pipes, the Internet, and a piano keyboard.

- The fine tuners are best for small adjustments to your strings, and the pegs are best for larger adjustments.

- Add some tension to the bow before playing, and make sure there is some rosin on there, too.

- A shoulder rest will make playing more comfortable for you, and a mute can make your fiddle quieter.

- Playing the fiddle makes demands on your fingers, hands, wrist, and body, so it's worth starting off with the habit of warming up and stretching and finishing off your practice session with a good stretch as well.

- You want to ease your muscles into relaxing, not injure them, so make sure to stretch gently—don't overdo it.

Chapter 5

Caring for a Fiddle

In This Chapter

- Storing the fiddle
- Keeping it clean
- Changing the strings
- Checking the bridge
- When to take it in for professional maintenance

You're now the proud owner of a fiddle. It can sound a *bit* like a dying cat in the hands of a beginner—but fortunately, it won't need any food and water, or those expensive pet-sitting services. But it will need some basic, tender loving care to keep it in good working order. The better maintained your fiddle, the easier it is to play—and the better you sound.

For the most part, because a fiddle is a very complicated and delicate instrument, some routine maintenance needs to be done by a professional, at a reputable violin or strings shop. But there are also a few things that you can learn to do so you can maintain your instrument at home.

Where Should I Keep It?

Fiddles are engineering marvels, built with balances of tension and pressure. That same instrument is also built of wood—once a living, breathing thing. So the first rule of maintaining your violin is to store it in livable conditions.

You'll notice the fiddle reacting to subtle changes in its environment, usually by going out of tune. If your fiddle spends some time in a cold place, like in a car during autumn or winter, you might find your pegs have shrunk and slipped, loosening the strings. This means time spent restringing your fiddle, and sometimes coaxing your out-of-whack and annoyed fiddle back into tune.

Tune Up

A simple rule of storage is that a room that is always too hot or too cold for people will be the same way for your fiddle. To help avoid temperature extremes, store your fiddle under the bed, or in a closet.

The dry air that comes with a severe cold snap can result in cracks. Extreme heat and humidity, like that of a summer afternoon in a sunny car or a summer spent in your attic, can cause the fiddle's seams to separate.

All this damage is easily avoided, of course. Store the fiddle in a temperature-controlled room—the ones you live comfortably in. In general, don't leave your fiddle sitting in the car, especially on hot and sunny or very cold days. This is also a good idea if you don't feel like donating your instrument to an opportunistic thief, either.

In colder climates, try not to keep the fiddle next to a thin outside wall in the winter. This will greatly decrease problems and increase your fiddle's well-being.

If your fiddle does end up in an environment where it has become hot or cold, it's best to open the case and let it adjust to room temperature for a little while before tuning or playing it. (If you've *really* cooked or deep-frozen your poor instrument, then you might want to let it adjust in the case for a bit before opening it as well.)

Pay attention to the humidity of the air, too. Some cases come with a "hygrometer"—a little gauge that shows you how humid the air is. In a dry climate like Arizona, or a cold dry winter month, it can help to put a humidifier in your fiddle to keep some moisture in the wood. This will prevent cracking. The fiddle also tends to sound less brittle if it's been around some humidity. You can find inexpensive gadgets to accomplish this task at your local violin store. The simplest is called a "Dampit." It is a small sponge tube that is encased in porous rubber. You immerse the Dampit in water, and the sponge soaks up the water. You then insert the Dampit into the circular end of your F hole, sending out moisture into the fiddle's middle.

Snug as a Bug

Here's another good habit: after playing the fiddle, put it back in its case. Aside from being a handy storage space, the case is good for general protection against bumps and falls, as well as the antics of curious children and high-energy pets. It is also a "coat" so to speak—clothing for the fiddle that renders changes in humidity and temperature in the outside world a little more gradual. Your fiddle will thank you for all this good care. It will often be easier to tune and generally less "cranky" when it's been protected from the outside world.

Tune Up

Humidity and dryness in the air definitely have an effect on your bow. You'll find your bow gets tighter if the air is drier, and can go completely floppy if playing outside in dewy evening air.

Before placing the bow back in the case, make sure to loosen the hair tension. It should reach the point where it looks pretty relaxed, but not to the point where individual hairs start hanging free of each other willy-nilly. This gives the bow a breather from tension between your (frequent!) practice sessions. Just like you, a bow needs to stretch out and take it easy after a good workout! Loosening the bow in this way also will prevent tightening if the humidity should drop.

A Clean Fiddle Is a Happy Fiddle

Now that you are getting into the habit of always putting your violin back in the case, you also should know that the violin should be cleaned before you put it away. Unlike many instruments, violin playing can get a *little* dirty! After you've spent some time rubbing a rosin-caked ribbon of horsehair across your strings, you'll find rosin dust sprayed over the surface of your fiddle. (Hopefully, it is focused around the space between the bridge and the fingerboard!) While you'll find some fiddlers like to let this collect on the surface of the fiddle (lending it a dusty, old and wise appearance) it's generally recommended that you wipe this off. As rosin dust builds up, it becomes harder to get off and can melt onto the surface in hot, humid weather. The dust can affect the varnish and dampen the tone of your fiddle as well. You probably enjoy a good shower after lots of exercise. Your fiddle also will appreciate being cleaned of its workout grime layer.

Any soft cloth will do—a cotton diaper works well, or an old T-shirt. Again, use the "fiddle as human" method of choosing: if you wouldn't enjoy rubbing it on your own skin, you probably don't want to subject your fiddle's varnish to it, either.

Wipe under the bridge and fingerboard, around the f-holes, on top of the fingerboard under the strings, and anywhere else you've managed to get rosin dust in your musical enthusiasm! Also, run the cloth on the undersurface of the wood of your bow, as rosin will have sprayed up from the hair. Remember not to touch your fingers directly to the bow hair or the area of the strings where the bow runs across them.

After wiping the fiddle down, place the fiddle back in the case.

That's pretty much it for day-to-day care of the fiddle. But over time, you'll have to do a few more things to keep your fiddle as "fit as a fiddle"!

False Notes

You might see "cleaner" products for sale that are meant to polish your violin. It's best to avoid these products as they're not always good for varnish.

Tune Up

If your fiddle is covered with rosin dust or dirt that is caked on, it often will take a professional cleaning at the violin shop to get back its shiny self.

Keeping the Bridge Upright

With regular tuning and playing, or after you change the strings, you might find you've knocked your bridge off its feet. Sometimes it becomes tilted a little in either direction. This is something you should check on regularly. The bridge needs to stand up straight for the same reason you do: if it keeps slouching, eventually it will curve. A curved bridge will need to be replaced—and that's $50 or so you can put off spending, as long as you are diligent about checking and correcting. At least it's cheaper than back surgery!

To check, examine the bridge in profile. Hold the fiddle sideways up in front of you, with the G string closest to you. Is the bridge standing straight up under the strings, or is it leaning? The side of the bridge closest to the tailpiece should be vertical and parallel to the joint of the rib. If it's crooked, remember what your mother used to say: "Stand up straight!" Check the feet, too. The bottom feet of the bridge should conform to the arch of the belly, not lift off the surface.

If they are, that's a sure sign the bridge needs to be straightened. You can also take a birds-eye view of the bridge to make sure it is still parallel to the fingerboard.

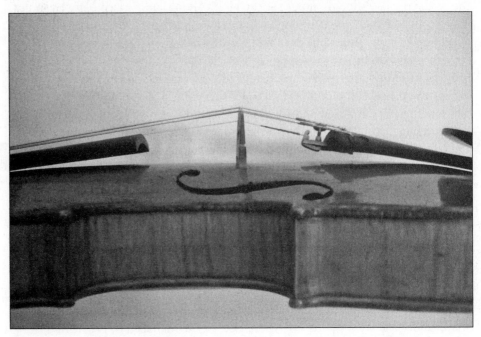

A bridge that is standing correctly.

Pulling the bridge back into place can feel a little daunting at first. But if you take it nice and easy, it's not too hard to do.

Tune Up

Every time you change your strings, rub a little graphite on the four notches of the bridge. This eases the friction from tuning or bridge adjustment, resulting in a longer string life.

◆ Sit down. Don't loosen the strings—the bridge should be adjusted with the strings at full tension. Put the fiddle in your lap, the bridge parallel to the wall in front of you. Grasp the corners of the bridge with your thumbs and forefingers.

◆ If the bridge is leaning away from you, make sure your forefingers are above your thumbs. (They will be on opposite sides of the bridge from each other.) Place some pressure on the center of the bridge with your thumbs (for counter-support) and *gently* pull the bridge toward you with your fingers. You usually don't have to move the bridge more than a millimeter or two.

◆ If the bridge is leaning toward you, make sure your thumbs are sitting above your forefingers. Place pressure on the bridge with your fingers (for counter-support) and gently push the bridge away from you with your thumbs. Do this a little at a time, checking after you move the bridge to see if it is now straight in profile. You'll find that this is routine and easy after a few times of trying it. Seeing a newly straightened bridge is very satisfying!

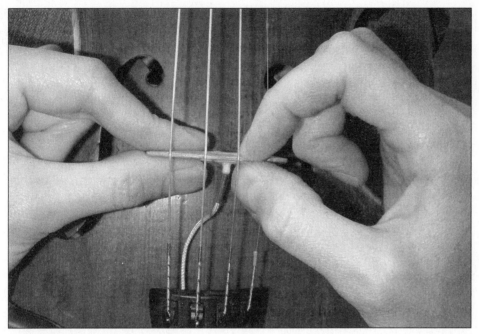

Using the fingers to adjust the bridge.

The Pegs

The tuning pegs sometimes can be problematic. The fact that the fiddle hasn't changed much since the eighteenth century also means that the tuning system is old-fashioned. Violin pegs are simple friction pegs. In other words, they are held in place only with pressure. There are no fancy metal parts to hold them or gears to turn them. Their tapered shape means that the further you push them into the holes, the tighter they are.

Because they are made of wood, the pegs are also sensitive to climate and changes in the weather. As spring and summer hit, often the pegs swell and all of a sudden you will find that they are stuck fast in their holes. Then as winter rears its cold and ugly head, your pegs can shrink in the drier weather. This can cause slippage in the case or, more frustratingly, while you are trying to tune.

These issues are usually easy to deal with. When the pegs are stuck, just loosen them, tune, and make sure not to jam the peg in too hard when fixing the peg in place. When the pegs are slipping, just push them in tighter.

A Change of Strings Is Gonna Come

Strings should be changed every so often. How often depends on how much you play. It can range from every few weeks for a regular professional player, to every four to six or even twelve months for someone who plays less often. Sure signs that it's time to change strings include frayed or splitting strings, discoloration, or, obviously enough, a broken string!

Tune Up

If you simply cannot get a peg to stop slipping, you can buy a compound or paste from a violin retailer to help hold it in place. If the problem is severe, the pegs might need to be "re-rounded" by a violin shop to keep them in place. You also can buy compounds that will lubricate the pegs if they don't easily loosen.

A **false string** is one that can no longer hold its pitch properly.

Fortunately, unlike guitar strings, violin strings don't randomly break too often. It's up to you to detect that time when an old string's life has come to a well-played end. An older string often loses tone, and sounds lifeless. Another sign is what's known as a *false string*. You'll especially hear that your string has gone false when you are tuning it. Play the string with a good strong tone, then lift the bow off the string, letting the note continue to ring. A false string will go up in pitch a small bit from the original tone, so that it can never be completely in tune.

Finding it harder to play—or feeling like you're playing worse than usual—also can be a sign that strings are beyond their prime. (It also simply may be a sign that you need to practice more, of course!) But sometimes, simply changing your strings does make you feel like a much better player.

The Technique

Changing the strings is—again!—like riding a bicycle. A little tricky at first, but once you've got it, you'll never forget. Here is how you do it:

1. Pick a string—starting with the high E or the low G is the simplest option. Grasp the tuning peg, and turn it toward you to loosen and unwind it. (If you have to turn it away to unwind it, someone put the string on backwards!) When the string is loosened, gently pull it free from the peg and out of the tailpiece. You can wind it into a coil and put it in the new string's empty packet, marking it "Used!" to save for emergencies—or just throw it away. If you've got a graphite pencil ready to rub on the exposed bridge notch, now is a good time to use it.

2. Unwrap the new string, making sure you've got the right one! Uncoil it. The top of the string is the colored end *without* the loop or metal bead. Stick that end through the hole in the tuning peg. Allow the end to poke through the other side of the hole, about a millimeter or two. Then, holding the string just below the peg, turn the peg so the string kinks and is secured in place.

3. Carefully start turning the peg *away* from you, wrapping the string around the tuning peg. Start right next to the hole and move outwards. Make sure each wrap of string sits right next to the next snugly, without overlapping.

4. When an inch or so of the colored end is still visible, you're ready to connect the other end to the tailpiece. If you've wound too far, just hold the string firmly as you unwind it a bit. This will keep the tension on the coil you've made.

5. If the other end is a metal bead, tuck it in at the bottom of the corresponding tailpiece string slot. The slots are made so they are wider at the bottom for insertion and narrower at the top. Pull the bead upward, so it's nestled in snugly at the top of the slot. While you're doing this, don't forget to keep the tension steady on the nice tight coil you've made on the peg above. This is accomplished by pulling the string away from the fingerboard somewhere in the middle of the string.

False Notes

Only change one string at a time. That way, you won't knock the bridge and/or the sound post out of place. That will change the tension that holds the fiddle together and can affect your sound ... and will mean a trip to the violin shop for a paid adjustment.

The string is kinked at the end, and it is being tightly wrapped around the peg.

Hold the string tight while you tighten it.

Tune Up _____

If your strings are breaking often, investigate. The grooves in the bridge can get too deep and pinch your string, causing it to break. You can use a metal nail file to make it shallower. A groove can get too deep in the peg nut, too, but have the violin shop deal with that problem.

Tune Up _____

If your string height is too high, one culprit might be that the neck has gradually "fallen" back. The bridge height can be adjusted to compensate, or the neck may have to be professionally reset.

6. Once you've gotten the bead tucked into its new home, continue holding the string there in the middle while winding the string up the rest of the way. Tighten until you don't need your other finger to hold it anymore. Gently disengage, and get that string nice and taut.

7. Finally, tune that string up to its proper pitch. Make sure the tuning peg is in nice and snug. Also, check to make sure the string coil on the peg isn't pressed right up against the side of the peg box, or the peg will tend to pop out.

8. Repeat for the other three strings.

Check the bridge in between each string change to make sure it's still upright, and give it a little tug to stand up straight if it's trying to lean over!

Breaking In Your Strings

After you put on a new set of strings, they will take a while to break in. This means that they will sound a little green. They just need to stretch and settle into their new home. How long this takes depends on the type of string you've bought—a day or so should do it.

You can help the new strings break in with a gentle stretch. Place your finger under one string somewhere near the bottom of the fingerboard. Gently tug so that the string is experiencing a little extra tension, but not so much that you're going to yank the string right back out of the peg. Run your finger up and down a few inches, then gently let go. After you've given your new string this little massage, tune again. Play your fiddle with some vigor for a few minutes, then tune again. You might find it's a little more out of tune than usual the next time you take it out of the case, too. But once the strings have broken in, your fiddle will sound refreshed, with a better tone for your playing enjoyment.

We've Done All We Can Do

Following the basic maintenance techniques we just covered generally will keep your fiddle in good running order. However, here's what you should leave to the professionals.

Bow Rehairs

After you've been playing for a while, you might find that your bow is "going bald"—that is, it is missing some of its hair. Even if all the hair is there, it pays to rehair the bow once in a while. That's because those small scales, the ones that provide a rough surface to "catch" the string, start to wear off. If this happens, the bow just won't work as well as it used to. A bow rehair costs around $45 and has to be done by an expert. At a violin shop, there is usually one person that is the "bow guy."

How often does this have to be done? An amateur player probably only has to do this once a year or less often. For a professional musician, touring on the road and playing a crazy, two-hour show every night, that rehair can come every three or four weeks! If you feel like your bow just isn't "grabbing" the way it used to, try a rehair.

If you open your case after a while away and find that a great deal of bow hairs have broken in the case without your playing them, you may have a case of "bow bugs." These are little critters that for some reason actually like to eat bow hair. One way to prevent these pests from settling in is to practice often, as they hate light. If you've got them, you can try thoroughly vacuuming out your case and leaving it open for a day or two. Fortunately, aside from reminding you that you really ought to practice a bit more, they won't hurt the instrument or bow themselves.

Recambering the Bow

Once in a while, check to make sure the stick of your bow hasn't warped. You can do this by closing one eye and holding the frog in front of your open eye, looking straight down the stick. If the tip is curving to the right or the left, the bow might have to be recambered.

When the bow was made, the luthier heated up the stick until it was red hot and then got it nice and straight from top to bottom, and curved toward the hair. If a bow goes off its natural shape, then it needs to be heated again to fix this.

A New Bridge

If your bridge seems to stay curved even though the feet are firmly sitting on the arch, it is warped—despite your excellent vigilance in keeping it straight, I'm sure! It will have to be professionally straightened or replaced.

Just find a reputable strings or violin shop and have them examine it. They'll tell you whether they should fit you with a new bridge. This usually costs around $75. If you vigilantly maintain your bridge, it can last over 30 years.

Crack Repair

Keep an eye out for cracks and open seams in your fiddle. They can occur when the fiddle has gotten too dry or cold. Sometimes, like when your car gets towed, these things happen despite your best efforts to avoid them.

One sign of a crack might be a buzzing sound that you can't find. If you do hear a buzz, check a few things before you freak out about a possible crack. Some possible buzz culprits: the chin rest has come a little loose; your big earrings, necklace, or zipper are touching the violin surface when you play; or one of your fine tuners has got a screw loose. Or there is just a mosquito in your ear. (You'll need bug repellent for that.)

Tune Up

It can also be time for a rehair when the hair near the frog is completely dirty and doesn't "catch" on the string anymore.

False Notes

Need to take the fiddle on a plane? There are, unfortunately, too many stories about heartbroken musicians finding damaged or destroyed instruments at the baggage claim. Don't check your instrument; fiddles usually fit in the overhead compartment just fine.

Cracks often will be very thin and hard to spot yourself. Again, a reputable violin shop, with a trained violin repair person, is the only place to take a violin with a crack. The price for the fix varies. It's like a tooth cavity, though—don't put off repairing the crack for fear of cost! It's only going to get more expensive—and damaging to your instrument if you delay fixing it.

Check the Sound Post

If your fiddle has experienced a nasty knock or fall, you may want to ask a violin repair person to check the state of the sound post. Lots of changes in temperature or humidity can nudge the sound post from its best position as well. If the sound post is not positioned properly, your fiddle will not sound as good as it can. Your helpful violin repair person can use a special tool made just for sound posts to move the post to a better place. There is usually a small charge for this service. But it's worth doing, because a badly placed sound post can make you feel like you're playing badly due to the inferior sound that often results. Of course, that inferior sound often is solved with more practice, too.

If the sound post has fallen completely down in your fiddle, unwind the strings and place a cloth underneath the fingerboard and tailpiece, and take it to a professional right away.

> **False Notes**
>
> Never try to adjust the sound post yourself. There is a very specific tool for this purpose, and it is easy to damage the fiddle if you don't know what you are doing.

Bow Trauma

Try your best not to drop your bow or plunge the tip into a low ceiling as you play. Its construction of grace and balance also means that it is very delicate. If you do drop it, look it over and make sure it's okay, especially the tip.

If you do manage to break off the tip, get that fixed right away. It's an inexpensive fix that will save the head of the bow.

A bow that is split in the middle is also something that it's better not to try fixing with your home stash of Gorilla Glue. Take it to a professional.

No matter what happens to your bow, you will be amazed at what amount of damage is actually repairable by the masters at your local violin shop.

> **Fiddle Facts**
>
> One of the ironies of violins is that often the more expensive the bow, the more easily it breaks—they're sensitive, okay?

Planing the Fingerboard

Sometimes your fingerboard will develop grooves from fingernails digging into the surface. Eventually these can interfere with the pitch of the note you are trying to play. An experienced luthier can "plane" the fingerboard, rendering it smooth and accurate once again.

The Least You Need to Know

◆ Store your fiddle in its case, in a temperate, humane environment.

◆ Always wipe your fiddle down and loosen the bow after you play.

- You can change your own strings, keep your bridge straight, and maintain your pegs yourself.

- Cracked, warped, or damaged fiddles and bows, bow rehairs, bridge replacement, and sound post adjustments should be left to the professionals.

Part 2

Fiddling Around

Reading music is one way of learning tunes. In this part, you are introduced to the basics of music theory. At the same time, you learn a helpful system of hints, so you don't have to sweat this too much while using this book—instead, you can just play music.

You also learn the standard methods of holding the fiddle and the bow. Then you'll find out how to use them together. After that, you learn more basic and essential techniques. But instead of using endless boring exercises to learn these, you can start playing some fun and familiar tunes right away.

"Sorry, Maestro. I don't speak music."

Chapter 6

Reading Music

In This Chapter

- The musical staff: its symbols, spaces, and lines
- The different lengths of notes and rests
- Key signatures, scales, and modes
- A handy "cheating" guide to make reading music easier
- Musical markings just for the bow

First things first: fiddle music is not written music. It is almost always learned by ear. Each style of fiddling comes from a region and its history and culture, not printed pages. When people say the music was passed down through their family, they don't mean that Gramps handed his kids his personal music notebook! Rather, Gramps' children and grandchildren learned his music from hearing him play.

Fiddle music is complex. It is made up of elements that are hard to write using music notation. For one thing, different players almost always interpret the same tune differently. Also, fiddle tunes are repeated several times when they are played and the player won't play them the same way twice in a row. Fiddle players add flourishes, bends, and other ornaments that are tricky to put into symbols.

That being said, we aren't all lucky enough to have a grandfather, or grandmother, who is versed in a traditional fiddle style. When you are learning from a book, it is logical to have some written music. It's also just a handy skill to have at your fingertips, as it is the most universal way of sharing music on paper.

However, I'm not going to ask too much of you! In this book, I'm not giving you a complete tutorial on music theory—just what you need to know to learn a few fiddle tunes. I let you cheat a bit, too, by using a numbering system to make reading music easier for you. You also learn the symbols that represent what your bow is doing. This, along with the audio portion of the accompanying DVD, will set you up to learn all the music in this book.

The Structure

As I've said, we're learning fiddle music here. And I'm a fiddler, of course. So I don't view music notation as being "the music" itself. For a fiddler, written music is only a kind of shorthand for the tune. You can never write down everything that is going on in a fiddle tune. First of all, every fiddler has his or her own version of a tune. The way I might play "Turkey in the Straw" is not the way, say, Bob or Nancy would play it. The notes are different. We structure the tune slightly differently. And I play chords where Bob doesn't, and vice versa. There's improvisation, ornamentation, and variation, little accents that come from the bow, and it's different from player to player. Heck, I might play a tune differently depending on my mood. All we can really do when we write a fiddle tune down is write down the bare bones of the melody—the skeleton of the tune. It's up to you to add the meat, the hide, and the hair.

I guess you could say that written fiddle music is like a road map: you have a line that signifies the road on the paper, and it shows where it goes and how big or small it is. But you don't have the McDonald's, the potholes, and the crosswalks on that map. So that line on the paper can never really show you what actually being on that road is like. You've got to go there to check it out for yourself. And the more often you go down the road (or listen to fiddlers play a tune), the more often you will be able to remember everything that, in reality, is on the road, not just on paper! And, of course, as time goes by, the markers will change as people try new things, add things, take them away ….

Many people get nervous when they look at music for the first time. It seems like a baffling code of sticks, dots, and lines. They assume that it is a difficult code that only extremely talented musicians could ever hope to master. But this is an unfounded assumption. Music notation is a fairly simple and logical system. (Music theory, however, can be a dense topic when you really get into it.) If you can learn a few place markers for yourself, then you can always figure out how to play the tune.

So with all that said, I'm going to give you a basic overview of all this, but explained in layman's terms. I'm not going to get too obsessed with music theory, at least any more than I have to. This is all merely a means to an end. We've got fiddling to get to, after all!

Staff and Bars

The foundation of music notation is the set of five lines that stretch across the page, over and over. This is the *staff*. It is the canvas on which the little dots are waiting to be drawn. There are five lines, with an empty space between each line. Each line and space of the staff represents one, and only one, note of music. When a note is drawn into that space or onto that line, this indicates there is a note to be played.

Tune Up

Remember, you've got tunes in these pages, but you should always listen to the audio on the DVD. Try to learn the melody as much from listening as looking at the page. This is called "learning by ear," and the more you do this, the easier it gets.

The staff is then divided into little boxes, which are called *measures*, or bars. The lines dividing the measures are vertical lines called *bar lines*. We use measures so we can divide the staff into smaller sections that contain the exact same length of music. They are also handy for talking about the music. You count measures starting with the first measure, called measure one. Then you can say things like "Look at measure five" when you need to ask a question about it or tell someone where to start playing.

The bar lines can also contain some information for you. A *double bar line* indicates that you are leaving one section and starting another section. A thicker double bar line, known as a *final bar line*, means the song is over. A bar line also can indicate that you are supposed to repeat a section, as follows:

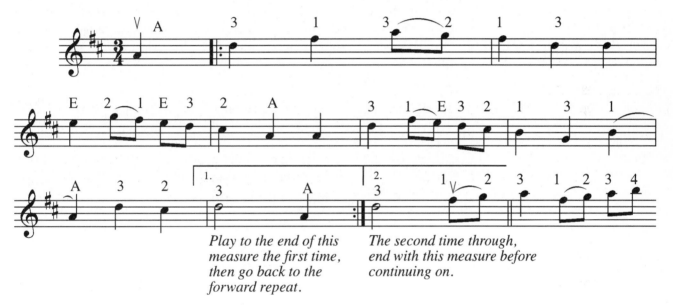

Play to the end of this measure the first time, then go back to the forward repeat.

The second time through, end with this measure before continuing on.

The melody should be played twice, but with a different ending each time.

The *forward repeat* bar indicates the start of the section that you will repeat. The *backward repeat* means that at the end of that measure, you need to go back to the forward repeat bar. Basically, when you see these, just play everything within them twice before going on to the next section.

Sometimes you will see two backward repeat bars. These are *first and second endings*. When you see this, first play the first ending, and at the repeat markings, go back to the forward repeat. Play the section again, but this time *skip* the first ending and go straight to the second ending. This should make even more sense once you are playing the melody.

Clef

Music is made up of notes that are very high, and very low, and everything in between. The mere five lines and four spaces that make up the staff can only contain so many notes out of the vast scale that humans use to compose music. So whoever made up this fancy little notation system for us also designed something called *clefs*. These designate whether the staff you're looking at represents notes from the lower registers or higher registers.

The two most common clefs are called *treble clef* and *bass clef*. Treble is used for music that uses the higher notes, and bass is used for music that uses the lower notes. Instruments like the piano and harp that go from very low notes all the way up to very high notes use both clefs together in a set of two *staves* (plural of staff) called the grand staff. A treble clef staff is on top, and a bass is on the bottom. You can write a *scale* from the bottom of the bass clef that will continue on up the treble clef, as they meet in the middle of the scale. That's handy for a pianist, because they tend to use the whole keyboard! The lines and spaces on the bass clef do not signify the same notes as the treble clef.

Now for the fiddle. It uses only the treble clef, because it only produces medium to high notes. (If your fiddle is playing bass notes, you might want to tighten your strings up a bit!) So let's just forget about the bass clef now. As a fiddler, you'll probably never need to think about it much again. It's merely good to know it exists.

At the very left of the staff is a fancy-looking squiggle that vaguely resembles the symbol for the word "and," as found on the number seven on your computer keyboard. That is your treble clef. It is your stalwart, the thing you can always count on to be there as we proceed through this book. Everything else sitting on the staff will be different from tune to tune, but the treble clef will always be there. Here's a picture of the staff with a treble clef.

The treble clef.

So look at it, notice it, and now, no need to linger! Let's move on and let the treble clef do what it does best—hang out at the left of your music, making no fuss.

The Notes

So now you've got a staff, and a treble clef that lets you know that you're in the upper registers of notes. So, what about the notes? Well, first of all, let's establish which notes on the staff match the open strings of your fiddle. This is what they are:

The four strings of the fiddle, as written on a treble clef staff.

The first thing you'll notice is that the G note of the G string isn't even on the staff. When you stop to think about it, the reason for this is obvious, really. As I said, each line and space represents one note. Well, the staff only has four spaces and five lines … which is only nine notes. So, the ingenious designer of this system gave us a way to put notes above or below the limits of the staff, too. When you get to the top or the bottom of the staff, you can keep going!

This is accomplished with the use of *ledger lines*, which are little dashes placed above or below the staff. They're kind of like a temporary staff, there only when you need it. When you think about it, this is a great way of doing things. If you just made the staff a nine-line behemoth, your brain would swim looking at the mess on the page.

Here is the entire scale of notes you can play with your hand in the basic position on the fiddle neck—we won't be going up the neck for quite a while.

All the notes you can play on the fiddle (without moving your hand up the fingerboard.)

As you can see, the G starts two ledger lines below the staff and the B on the E string is just one ledger line above the staff.

Eight Is Enough

As you look at the scale in the previous figure, you will see that the alphabet letters used for notes repeat themselves over and over. After G comes A, not H. This goes on endlessly. The seven notes' values in music are A, B, C, D, E, F, and G—over and over and over, up and down the musical scale.

Once you get to the eighth note, you have gone a full *octave*. This means that you get two of the "same" notes, but an octave apart. If you sing them together, they seem to match. That is why they have the same name. Start on an A, go up eight notes, and you're on another A. Sing them together, and it sounds pretty good! Two people can sing the same melody at the same time an octave apart—it is a kind of unison.

In Western music, when you go up or down notes in a scale, you have two choices. You can move either a *whole step* or a *half step*. There are two half steps in one whole step. These half steps make up all the keys of a piano keyboard. So if you play both the black and white keys consecutively, you are playing a series of half steps, also known as a chromatic scale. Usually, the half step is from a white key to a black key (though B to C is one case where you go white key to white key in a half step). A to B, C to D, D to E … these are all whole steps.

Fiddle Facts

The eight-note scale that begins and ends on an octave is illustrated quite well by Maria, the nanny in *The Sound of Music*. She uses the pan-scale syllables "do, re, mi, fa, so, la, and ti" for her little ditty, but it's the same idea: once you use seven notes, at eight you're back to square one … "do!"

The black keys of a piano are the *sharps* and *flats* of music. To explain these two words, let's start with the note A. The white key that is A is known as "A natural." Take it down a half step, which is the black key to the left, and you've got "A flat." When you're in a car, this is a serious problem and demands a call to AAA. In music, it's just another note, though if you meant to play A natural and got A flat, that can be somewhat of a problem, too.

Let's go back to the piano. If you play the black note to the left of A natural, you're playing A flat. The white key to the left of A flat is G. So what happens if we were discussing G, and not A, here? The A flat would be a G sharp instead. The two names share the same note. D sharp and E flat are the same note. F sharp and G flat are the same note, too. (B sharp is a C natural, though, because B and C are only a half step apart. Inversely, C flat would be a B.)

However, this is getting very descriptive. To summarize: you've got a half step above and below every note. If you include all the half steps in a scale, you have a lot more than eight notes. However, all the notes in that scale are still just sharps or flats of your basic notes, A through G.

Your fiddle neck is related to the piano keyboard, except instead of piano keys, you use specific finger positions on the strings. You start from the low G string and move on up to the E string. With each finger you press down on the string, you make the string shorter and therefore a different, higher pitch. You can make the string shorter by a whole step, half step, or even less. Here are the notes, as you play them on your fiddle neck.

The notes of the fiddle, on the fingerboard of the fiddle.

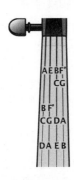

Notice that one note on each string—the spot where your pinky finger sits—matches the pitch of the next string. So the D that is played on the G string matches the pitch of the D string.

All Notes Have Value

We've now established that the position of a note on the staff determines what pitch you have to play on your fiddle. But there is also another component to written music, and that's time or how long you play the note. The note can be either short or long, and we've got to be able to pin down exactly *how* long. This is accomplished through the shape of the note.

Here are the ones we'll see most often in fiddle music:

- Quarter note: We'll start here. The quarter note is your most basic note, the beat you often are tapping your foot to.

- Eighth note: Any note shorter than a quarter note will have a little *flag* on it. The eighth note is half the length of a quarter note. When you have two or more eighth notes together, they often are connected with a bar that replaces the flag.

- Sixteenth note: This is half of an eighth note. There are four sixteenth notes in one quarter note.

Then there are the longer notes, which you see in fiddle music less often. You will find them in slow songs.

- Half note: This is a long note, consisting of two quarter notes. It is shaped like the quarter note, but it is hollow.

- Whole note: This is an even longer note, consisting of four quarter notes in length. (Four one-quarters equals a whole—hence, the two names have meaning.) It is shaped like a hollow oval.

Here's a "one of these is not like the others" situation.

- Triplets: This is technically not a type of note, but more a way to tweak the use of one of the above types of notes. A triplet is when you replace two of one kind of note with *three*, in the same amount of time. So instead of going "du-du" in one beat, you go "du-du-du."

- And lastly, we've got dotted notes. A dot next to a note means that you add half its value to itself. For example, a "dotted quarter" lasts for the same time as three eighth notes. A dotted eighth lasts for three sixteenth notes.

The different lengths of notes.

You'll also see *rests* written into the music. A rest is just that—when you take a moment of silence, and don't play a note. The rests you'll see most often in this book are the quarter rest and eighth rest. There are also whole rests, which look like a little box suspended from the top of a staff space. Half rests are that same box, but "dropped" so that it sits on top of the line at the bottom of that space.

Sixteenth rests look like eighth rests, but with two flags instead of one. Here's a picture of them all:

QUARTER RESTS	EIGHTH AND SIXTEENTH RESTS	HALF RESTS	WHOLE REST

The different lengths of rests.

Time Signatures

Just to the right of your treble clef will be two numbers stacked on top of each other. This is your *time signature*. Remember how I said that every measure in a staff contains exactly the same length of music? The time signature lets you know what that length of music is. It indicates how many beats are in a measure.

The time signature can be thought of as a kind of fraction.

◆ The bottom number on the time signature indicates what *kind* of note you are counting as a beat. If it is 4, it is a quarter note (i.e., 1/4!). If it is an eighth note, the bottom note is an 8. These are the two numbers you'll see most often on the bottom of the time signature in this book.

◆ The top number of the time signature indicates how *many* of that kind of note are going to be in each measure.

So if you have a 4/4 time signature, that means you have four quarter notes in each measure. When you hear the rock singer scream out, *"One, two, three, four!"* before the band kicks into the song, then that song is likely in 4/4. If you have a 2/4 time signature, that means you have two quarter notes in each measure. 6/8 means six eighth notes in each measure. 3/4, which is the time signature of waltzes, is three quarter notes per measure. And so on.

Don't Forget the Keys!

You might remember when Nigel Tufnel of the band and movie *Spinal Tap* called D minor "the saddest of all keys." But what does it mean for a song to be "in the key of __"? Basically, this is what tells you which of the basic notes (A, B, C, etc.) are sharp or flat in a particular song.

The Symbols

To figure out what notes are sharp or flat, just look at the key signature. The key signature is on the staff, between the treble clef and the time signature. It is made up of a cluster of one of two types of symbols there. The sharp symbol looks like "pound" on your telephone keypad. The flat looks sort of like a medieval letter "b." The notes that are sharp or flat in the tune are indicated with the appropriate symbol placed in the space (or on the line) of its corresponding pitch on the staff.

The key signatures you'll find in this book.

Check out the key of G—it has one sharp. It's sitting on the line where the note F goes. Therefore, all the Fs are sharp in this song. Whenever you play an F on the fiddle, you'll have to make sure those fingers are in the appropriate place on the fingerboard when you play these notes.

So why do we need all these different keys? The simplest key, you'll notice, is the key of C. This is the key that uses *no* sharps and *no* flats (to reference our piano keyboard again, this would mean using only white keys—no black ones). If we used only this scale to make all our songs, it would make music kind of limited. By using different keys, we allow our music to have different moods and colors—so in a way, Nigel is actually on to something.

A La Mode

Okay, now I'm going to make things a little more complicated for you. When you have a key signature on a staff, you then know what notes are sharp or flat. The key signature usually is labeled by the name of its major scale: key of C, key of D, key of G, and so on.

Here's the complicated part, though: the key of the tune actually will be one of many that are based on that key signature. Which of these key signatures this is depends on what scale is the backbone of the melody. Two of these types of keys might sound familiar to you: these are *major* and *minor.* When trying to figure out what key a song is in, your key signature is one clue. Then you have to look at the melody itself and see whether it seems to be working from the major or minor scale for that key signature.

First off, let's look at the major key. When a melody is in a major key, the scale the melody is based on actually starts and ends on the note that the key signature is named for. For example, a scale in the key of C would start on C and end on C. This looks like the following:

> **Fiddle Facts**
>
> Scales are made up of ascending and descending half steps (H) or whole steps (W). A major scale goes like this: W W H W W W H. A minor scale goes like this: W H W W H W W. Another "rule"? Major sounds happy. Minor sounds sad.

The key signature is C, and we've got a C major scale.

When a melody is constructed from this scale, the song is in the key of C major.

However, scales can be played around with, too. You can start and end the scale on a different note—in fact, any note of the major scale. For instance, if you start and end the scale on the *sixth* note of the major scale, the key is then a minor key. For a C major scale, the sixth note is an A. The key signature is our "key of C," but the song is said to be in the key of A minor.

The key signature is C, but we've got an A minor scale.

The notes are all the same as in a C major scale, but because the scale starts and ends on the sixth note of the C major scale (i.e., A), the music doesn't sound the same. It's eerier, because you've moved the order of the whole and half steps around.

Major to minor is only *one* way of tweaking the major scale to get a new sound. In fact, in traditional music you often will encounter some of these different sounds—otherwise known as *modes*. The most common modes in traditional music are *Mixolydian* and *Dorian*. (You might hear about the Ionian and Aeolian modes, but these are effectively the same as major and minor.)

I don't want to get too into this here—just be aware that these exist, and are ways of playing around with the ordinary major scale to yield yet another, different sound. These modal keys are the reason traditional music often can sound haunting or mysterious!

Here's how these modes work:

def•i•ni•tion

A **mode** is a scale composed of notes from the major scale, but starting on a different note. Take the G major scale—it starts and ends on G. Now use the same eight notes, but start and end on a different note than G. You'll end up with a very different-sounding scale.

- ◆ **Mixolydian**—start and end your scale with the fifth note of the major scale. So a key signature of D will be in the key of A Mixolydian.

- ◆ **Dorian**—start and end your scale with the second note of your major scale. So a key signature of G will be in the key of A Dorian.

Tune Up

This all might seem confusing to you. You might not want to puzzle over a tune trying to figure out what scale it is based on. So … don't! When you are learning a tune, whether or not it is major or minor is kind of an academic question. Don't get too hung up on all this if it all feels a bit vexing to you now.

Using Numbers with the Notes

So now you've been introduced to the basic system here. It's not so unfamiliar to you anymore. You've got a grasp on treble clef, key signatures, time signatures, and what notes are signified by the little lines and spaces of the staff line.

So even if your head is spinning, you can continue on with this book, and the fiddle. That's because (shhh …) I've got a little system that will help you cheat! This way, you don't have to waste time and energy feeling stressed trying to figure out what notes are what, and where the fingers then go on the fingerboard, and what key you are in, and all that jazz (or, fiddle music …?) We're going to use music notation to learn these tunes, but I'll be giving you some clues as well.

The System

You'll have a tune in front of you—a staff with a time signature, a key, and a bunch of notes on it. To get help with the time signature, your best bet is still just to listen to the music on the DVD. The key signature, same thing.

However, I'll give you help with the notes you need to play. Above the staff, you'll actually have a label for each note that yours truly will provide for you. This label will be one of two symbols: a letter or a number.

♦ The letter will be one of four choices: G, D, A, or E. This means that you are on an *open string*. If you see a note with an A above it, play the A string. Simple!

♦ If you see a number above the note, it will be one of four choices: 1, 2, 3, or 4. The 1 means your index finger, the 2 your second finger, the 3 your ring finger, and the 4 your pinky finger. When you see the number 1 above a note, press the first finger down.

There will be a little bit of figuring out that you'll have to do. When you see the number, how do you know which string you are supposed to be on? To some extent, you will have to remember the spaces that are open strings, and figure out whether the note with the number is above or below the closest open string. If it is above it, it is on the string. If it is below it, then it's on the string below.

The Fretless Fiddle

If only we could just leave it at that. Numbers, letters, great, let's go! There is one other thing that has to be reckoned with, though: your fretless fingerboard.

Frets provide an advantage for newbie musicians, since the fixed metal bar does the work of finding the proper pitch for you. Two frets make one space that is one note. You put your finger anywhere between those frets, and it's still the same note.

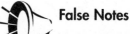

False Notes

You won't get better at reading music if you depend too much on the numbering system. Focus your eyes on the staff and notes first, only using the numbers and letters above when you really need to.

def•i•ni•tion

An **open string** is a string that is being played without any fingers pressing it down—it just rings free.

Fiddlers, however, are far too sophisticated creatures to rely on such a simple method. No, no. We have no such thing as frets. You get to make great music, brimming with the breathtaking expressiveness that a fretless instrument is capable of. So instead of frets, you get a black expanse of smooth ebony fingerboard. This is a minefield of out-of-tune notes that surround a few exact positions that make the notes you need. Trust me, you'll learn where these positions are soon enough.

But until then, you probably need a little help. So before every tune, I'm going to place a little drawing of your fiddle neck and the four strings. The picture will also be labeled with what key the tune is in, so you don't have to keep coming back to this chapter to figure it out from how many sharps or flats there are in the staff. On the fiddle neck, I'll write where your fingers go in that key. For example, here's the key of G.

Key of G

In the key of G, you can see that your second finger will be next to the third finger on the bottom two strings, but next to the first finger on the top two strings. This might be hard to remember on your own, but with our handy little drawing, you'll have it right there by the tune you're playing.

Bow Markings

As the fiddle is an instrument with moving parts, there are ways to mark the bow movements onto the written music as well. I'll use some of these bow markings on the tune to suggest ways that you can bow the tune.

I say "suggest" because as I've mentioned several times, fiddling is an individually interpreted craft. So I only put these bowings in as a way for you to try out what I might do. If you saw me play these tunes, you'd see that I might duplicate the bowings I put in this book, I might not. I certainly would never use the same bowings the first and second time I play a tune through. And two different fiddlers most likely would not bow the tune the same way. With an orchestra, you see entire string sections moving their bows in tandem. It's kind of a pretty sight, but the wildly flying bows of a gaggle of fiddlers sawing out a tune together is pretty cool-looking, too.

As far as learning how to bow fiddle music goes, here is the procedure I'd follow if I were you.

- First, learn the tune from the DVD and the music. Just get the notes and the rhythm down right. Pay no attention to bowing markings.

- Once you've got the tune up and running under your fingers, slow it down again and try to use the bowings I've marked.

- Finally, after you've mastered the bowings in this book, try experimenting with your own bowings and see what you can come up with yourself.

Tune Up

The rule of bowing in fiddling is this: there might be a wrong way to bow, but there are many right ways. And "wrong" is a somewhat fuzzy definition, as two fiddlers might not agree on what that is.

The first markings we'll encounter in bowing are the "up" and "down" bows. They look like this:

The "V" marks an up-bow; the upside down, square "U" marks a down-bow.

It looks like the up-bow marking is pointing down. However, just think of the direction of the open space. The down-bow marking's opening faces down, and the up-bow marking faces up.

We also will have what are called *slurs*. In the fiddle, this means that you connect two or more notes onto one bow stroke. A related concept is that of the *tie*. This is not what you might get your Dad for Christmas or Father's Day. A musical tie is when two of the same notes are connected to make a longer note, especially across bar lines. We mark these with a little curved line.

Three slurs and one tie.

The Least You Need to Know

- Learning by ear is the traditional, and best, way of learning fiddle music.

- Written music is a way to sketch out the basic melody of a tune, and is necessary when learning fiddle tunes from a book.

- The lines and spaces of the staff each symbolize a specific pitch.

- A key signature shows you which notes of a scale are sharp or flat in a particular tune, and a time signature shows you how many beats are in a measure.

- In this book, letters above the notes represent the open string, and numbers represent which finger you should use to play a note.

- Bowing markings are written on the tunes to help you learn a style, but they are by no means definitive.

Chapter 7

Fiddle and Bow Technique

In This Chapter

- How to hold the fiddle and the bow
- Exercises for the bow hold
- Understanding how the bow arm works
- Coordinating the left hand with the bow
- Getting started with a few easy tunes

So you've got a fiddle, a shoulder rest, and a bow that's nicely and lightly dusted with rosin. Everything is tuned and tightened up and ready to go. You're rarin' to start playing that fiddle.

Unfortunately, this often isn't the easiest part. Unlike a guitar, or a saxophone, or a kazoo, holding the instrument is a bit awkward at first. But so is learning to ride a bicycle, and you did that, right? Once you learn, you won't forget. In fact, after you get through that new and exciting awkward phase with your fiddle, holding it on your shoulder should feel completely natural. So lift up your chin, and I'll help you put a fiddle under it. (And a bow in your hand, too.) And then we'll play a few little songs.

Using the Chin to Hold the Fiddle

As you are an observant person, you have of course noticed by now that the fiddle has *two* parts to it: the fiddle and the bow. Both need to be held in a somewhat specific way.

Let's outline the process of learning to hold your fiddle. We won't concern ourselves with the moving parts of this instrument yet. For now, just put the bow down in a safe place. This way, you can concentrate on the fiddle itself.

False Notes

It's important to stay relaxed. A tense fiddle or bow hold can lead to neck, arm, or wrist troubles. Also, that tension often can be heard in your playing.

1. Hold the fiddle in front of you. The f-holes should be facing the ceiling. The chin rest should be pointed at your chin, the scroll directed away from you.

2. Grasp the top right-hand curve with your left hand. Your palm should be on the back of the instrument, your fingers gripping the belly. This will give you a good hold on the instrument as you start "fiddlin' around" with finding a good resting spot for the chin rest end.

3. The chin rest will go, obviously, under your chin. But your chin doesn't go straight down on it. Rather, lean your head to the left side. Center the fiddle over your left shoulder. Drop your chin onto the rest. It's a bit like a romantic nuzzle. (I'm sure you're getting fond of your fiddle by now.) Your head will end up tilted to the left just a bit.

Holding the fiddle so you can put it under your chin.

4. Make small adjustments until you feel the fiddle is in a spot that is secure. It should end up angled about 30 degrees, following the line of your collarbone area.

5. Finally, let go of the fiddle with your left hand. Are you able to hold it comfortably using only your chin and shoulder?

Fiddle Facts

You sometimes can find old-time players holding the fiddle by balancing it on their chest instead of under their chin.

If this feels awkward, remember that it is a new skill. Holding the fiddle will feel easier and more natural with time and practice. At the same time, don't be afraid to play with your position for a while until you find what works and, most importantly, is comfortable for you. There shouldn't ever be any tension in your neck or shoulder. If there is, don't get all "high strung" about it—just keep playing around! If mere fidgeting fails you, try adjusting the height or angle of your shoulder rest.

Tune Up

I'm teaching the standard holds for the instrument here. But as I explained in Chapter 2, anything goes in fiddle music, so modify this to your liking (or not) as you progress.

The fiddle tucked correctly under the chin and over the left shoulder.

As you develop comfort and skill with your instrument, you might find that you prefer working with variations on the standard fiddle or bow holds. As long as you keep the mantra of "no strain or pain" going, that's fine. Remember—in fiddle music, anything goes.

Using Your Left Hand

The left hand on the fiddle is responsible for the pitch of the notes you play. That's why you've spent the time to get the other end of your fiddle tucked firmly under your chin. This enables you to take some of the pressure— literally!—off your left hand. That hand is then free to produce crystal-clear notes, and easily create the various effects needed for fiddle sounds.

How the Left Hand Sits

The position of the left hand is derived straight from its natural form. To demonstrate this, I'll have you put the fiddle in your lap for a moment.

1. Hold your left arm straight out in front of you, palm up—and of course, relaxed! Notice that your fingers naturally curl up and over toward your palm.

2. Next, bend the elbow toward you. Let your wrist follow—relaxed, but keeping the palm on the same plane as your arm. Stop when the arm is bent just about 45 degrees. Your thumb should be sticking up, your fingers curled toward your palm.

That is pretty much how your hand should look when playing the fiddle— except there will be a fiddle neck inserted under the fingers! So let's put one there.

1. Place your fiddle under your chin as you already learned. Hold it there, leaving your left hand free.

> **False Notes**
>
> Avoid supporting the neck of the fiddle with the palm of your left hand. This is one way to encourage carpal tunnel syndrome. Keep your wrist unbent and let your chin do the work.

2. Straighten your left arm out underneath the fiddle, then bend it in the same way as before.

3. This time, tuck the fingerboard between your thumb and your four fingers. Your thumb should be on the left side, while your four fingers curl up and over the right side.

The fingers naturally curl in the shape you use to hold the fiddle.

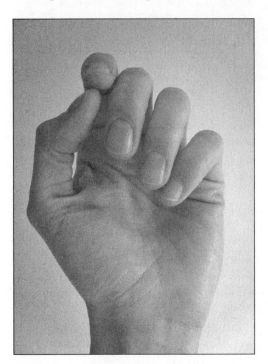

Just like any good relationship, there should be a bit of space in this arrangement or it will start to feel cramped. The right side of the fingerboard should meet your index finger between the knuckle and the middle joint. The left side of the fingerboard should gently rest against the top part of your thumb. The length of your hand from your thumb to your index finger should be open, creating a nice, round space. Your fingers will arch over the fingerboard. You should be impressed with the elegance of it!

The left hand should curl naturally around the top of the fingerboard.

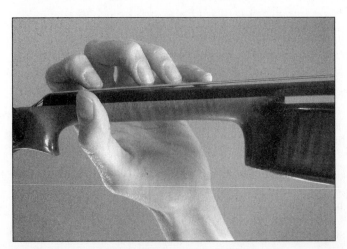

How the Fingers Sit

Now that your hand is sitting in the correct position, you might be wondering where to put your fingers on the fingerboard. This is where things get a bit tricky. As we've said, there are no frets. With a fiddle, the placement of the fingers has to be exact, or the note will be sharp or flat.

Eventually, where to place your fingers will become automatic thanks to muscle memory. Concentrate the most on the position of your first finger. In basic fiddle scales and in the first tunes in this book, the first finger always will be in the same place. Once you figure out where that should go, you can gain a feel for where the rest of the fingers go. (Think "riding a bicycle" again.)

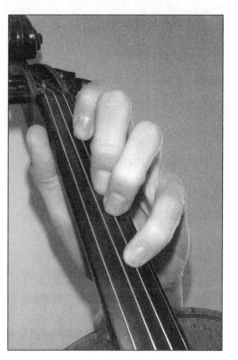

It might help to hold your fiddle like a guitar for a minute so you can see where your fingers need to go. The first finger will sit on the string about one and a quarter inch from the nut. The third finger will be placed about two inches up from the first finger. The second finger will sit snugly next to the third finger. This is what might be referred to as the "basic" position.

We'll have a chance to practice getting those notes out once you learn your first scales, but first we need to learn how to hold the bow.

Holding the Bow

I often get a chuckle when I see a publicity shot of a fiddler without his or her bow. You know that some photo director insisted that they lose it, thinking it will result in a better shot, but forgetting that the bow is part of the instrument as well. One can look fabulous, with a fiddle wonderfully tucked under

The basic position of the fingers on the fingerboard.

Tune Up

If you are having trouble with your finger positions, a violin shop can place strips of colored tape to mark where your fingers should go.

your chin, left hand gracefully at the top of the fingerboard ... but it's just not a fiddle without the bow. By now, you've sensed this and are starting to wonder if we're ever going to put "one and one" together. Never fear! You're now ready to install the moving parts in this fabulous machine.

When handling a bow or the fiddle, there are two areas you should always avoid touching with your fingers:

◆ The horsehair of the bow.

◆ The area of the strings that the bow runs across—that is, between the bridge and the fingerboard.

This is because the natural oils on your hands will coat the bow, and the rosin won't stick as well. This can affect your sound and make it harder to play the instrument. Handle the wooden parts of the instrument only, and make sure others do as well (you'll find that sometimes people, curious about your instrument, will try to grab your whole bow with their fist!)

As with your left hand, the position of your bow hand is conveniently based on the hand's natural relaxed curl. Your hand should feel almost as relaxed when holding the bow as when not holding it. The trick is to wield grip and pressure just firm enough to end up with a bold, strong tone.

So let's get started! Take the frog of the bow with your right hand.

1. Use your left hand to hold the bow steady, holding it by the stick somewhere in the middle horizontally, so that it is parallel to your torso.

2. Approach the frog with your right hand, which should naturally sit in that relaxed curl, fingers facing down this time.

3. Place your thumb in the opening of the frog. The index finger goes on top of the bow, leaning on its left side, between the first and second knuckle. The middle and ring fingers creep down the far side of the frog, curled over the top. The tip of the pinky sits right on top of the bow.

The standard bow hold.

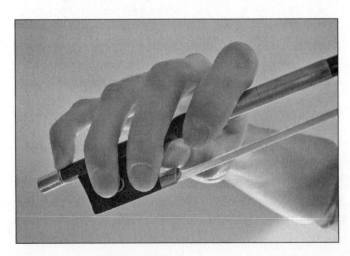

There is a reason behind the rhyming here. (Okay, so there wasn't any rhyming.) But there *is* a reason that each finger is placed in a specific position. All the fingers of your right hand work together in different ways. The index finger provides pressure on the bow. The middle and ring fingers work with the thumb to provide the main "gripping" forces. The pinky finger, meanwhile, provides a bit of delicate balance on the end.

Bowing Finger Exercises

Getting your fingers to relax while holding a bow is a key component to getting the strong but fluid movement that is needed for the fiddle. Here're a couple of exercises to make sure your bow fingers are smooth, strong, and relaxed all at the same time.

Finger Curls

This exercise will make sure you've got a strong yet at-ease grip on the bow. You certainly don't need to hold your stick like you would a motorcycle handlebar while driving 80 mph!

1. Hold the bow as we just learned.

2. Try extending your fingers until they are straight, and then, reversing, curl them as round as possible.

At first you might find it pretty tricky to hold on to the bow as you straighten. Eventually, though, you'll have that bow in an unshakeable yet friendly grip, while your loose and limber fingers curl and uncurl. Down the line, this means you can hold on to your bow while you're letting loose on a wild and crazy tune.

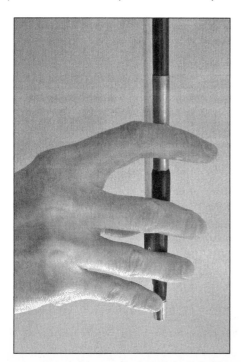 

Extend your fingers until straight (left). Then curl them as round as possible (right).

Bow Crawls

See if you can't use your fingers to "crawl" up and back down the wood of the bow, following the instructions below.

1. Hold the bow as just described.

2. Rotate the bow to a vertical position—with the tip pointed at the ceiling.

3. Start "crawling" up the bow—as if your fingers were a spider, moving away from the frog and up the stick. (As usual, try not to touch the bow hair.)

4. Once you've gone a little under halfway, "crawl" back down to the frog.

Doing this exercise allows you to become more comfortable holding and working with this little stick of wood that's so vital to a good fiddle sound. If you are able to crawl up and down the stick with your fingers, then you have a strong grip that is also flexible and relaxed. You won't drop the bow, either.

The Graceful Bow Arm

At last! You can hold the fiddle under your chin and the bow in your right hand. While you may feel a *bit* like you're in a weird juggling and balancing act, you're actually on your way to making some noise—and eventually, even some music! But first, let's cover a bit of how the bow actually should work.

There is graceful flexibility in every stroke of the bow. The bow moves across the string by bending your fingers, wrist, arm, and shoulders in a related set of motions. This cooperation of the various parts of your arm allows a smooth and straight bowing motion. Let's try it!

Place the bow on the A string of the fiddle, somewhere in the middle of the stick. The ribbon of hair should be placed squarely onto the string. It shouldn't lean toward or away from you, as this will result in undue pressure being placed on one side of the bow, straining the hairs.

Your arm should be on the same plane as the stick of the bow. Make sure your right shoulder is relaxed and not crunched up against your innocent right ear. Your wrist should be a nice flat surface leading from your hand to your arm.

I'm going to have you experiment so you can find the arm/bow connection. (Not quite the song sung by Kermit, but there's a ring to that phrase, isn't there?)

The elbow controls the movement from string to string. With your bow sitting on the A string, lift up your elbow. Don't bend the nice flat surface of your wrist—keep it nice and even with your arm. This will allow your arm to move as a cohesive unit. The bow will lower onto the string to the left of the one you were sitting on—so now it should be on the D. If you keep lifting the elbow, the bow will end up sitting on G. (Conversely, start down on the G string. Drop your elbow and arm, and watch the bow move onto the D, then the A, and finally, the E string.) Now, try going back and forth from the G to the E; doing it smoothly is what enables you to jump from one string to another as you play—in other words, crossing strings.

The elbow, wrist, and bow should all rest on the same plane—here on the A string.

The same bow arm plane, angled to reach the G string.

The Long and Short of It

There are some good terms to know when talking about bow technique.

- An *up-bow* is when the frog moves toward the fiddle, the tip heading toward the ceiling. (Sit down if the tip's going to make contact!)

- A *down-bow* is when the frog is moving away from the fiddle. When you're playing a down-bow on the E string, the frog will move *down* toward the floor!

- A *long* bow is one that uses much of the length of the bow as you play.

- A *short* bow is one that uses only a small part of the length of the bow.

The bow should remain parallel to the bridge and the edge of the fingerboard.

Here's how you keep your bow nice and straight. As you bow, it should stay parallel to the bridge and the edge of the fingerboard. It also should be somewhere equidistant between the two. The *wrist*, not the elbow, will lead this movement. It should bend first.

Try making a note while experimenting with this concept—just play an open string or two. I'm not playing favorites, but the A string is a great place to start—not too high, not too low. Start with a down-bow, somewhere in the center of the stick. As the bow moves, the elbow should bend. As you reach the tip of the bow, the wrist and fingers should extend.

Try an up-bow next, starting from the tip. Bend the wrist and fingers, then the elbow, and finally the shoulder as you approach the frog. Don't bow from the shoulder first, as it's the least efficient—and incorrect. Not to mention that if your entire arm is flapping back and forth like a chicken's, you won't look so dignified!

The result of this is that when you are at the frog, your wrist should be bent *toward* you. When your bow is at the tip, your wrist is bent *away* from you. In the middle of the bow, the wrist is pretty much straight and on an even plane with your arm.

Work in the middle of the bow, executing some small bow movements back and forth on the strings. Try short up- and down-bows. Is your sound a bit "crunchy"? If you are hearing screeches and grunts from the bow, you're probably pressing down too hard. Keep experimenting until you hear a few nice notes coming from the fiddle.

Next, try lengthening your strokes. Sing out with a couple long, sweet-sounding (as sweet as you can manage, anyway!) bows, and some medium-length bows.

As you play, watch what the bow is doing. Is it moving in an arclike motion, or a straight back-and-forth trajectory? If the former, see what bending your wrist and elbow more will do for you. The shoulder should move only as a last resort to keep that bow moving.

Tune Up

If getting that "arm/bow connection" feels difficult or awkward, try practicing while looking at yourself in the mirror. It's great for your technique (as well as admiring just how totally *smokin'* you look when playing the fiddle!)

Tune Up

It's easy to get frustrated when learning the fiddle. Just remember to take a deep breath and let go of the tension once in a while.

Proper position of the wrist at the end of an up-bow (left). The arm extended at the end of a down-bow (right).

Under Some Pressure

The bow is a three-dimensional tool. Not only do you move the bow back and forth, and up and down, but there is an element of movement (although much smaller) perpendicular to the sawing motion. This is how you control your tone. A bow stroke needs the right amount of pressure for the perfect sound.

What is the "perfect" sound? This all depends on the moment … much like conversation. Light pressure equals a breathier sound. You almost always want to avoid sounding breathy except for occasional effect. Heavy pressure yields a loud, scratchy sound. Again, a truly scratchy sound is pretty much reserved for special occasions. Most of the time, you want enough pressure on the bow to yield a clear, steady tone that rings out sweet and strong.

The secret to manipulating your fiddle tone is in your index finger. This doesn't lie across the frog just to relax and take it easy. As you play, you'll constantly be using it to apply pressure to the bow.

Try it out. Start bowing and making a few notes. Now, press so hard with your index finger that you produce a strained, scratchy sound. Next, ease up completely—give your bow a "floating" feeling—and the result should be a light, breathy note … kind of a wussy sound, actually. Finally, go for the average, and see if you can't get a nice, even, pleasant tone as you move the bow across the strings.

Fiddle Facts
It is the tone that makes the music. —Proverb

 Tune Up

Your bow is heaviest at the frog. To keep a steady tone, you'll need more pressure from your index finger as you move toward the tip on a down-bow.

The Left Hand

By now I'm sure you've got some beautiful tones coming out of your fiddle with your elegant bow strokes. But you are probably getting tired of playing only G, D, A, and E notes. (If your open strings are yielding different pitches, you might want to tune up before continuing!)

Your left hand, of course, is the tool you use to make all the different notes in those melodic fiddle tunes. But once again, the fiddle can be trickier than most stringed instruments to make notes on. This is because there are no *frets* like those on a guitar or a mandolin. Those instruments come with a built-in "cheat sheet"—the frets clearly mark where you put your finger to make a note. With a fiddle, you actually have to develop some *muscle memory*—that is, a feel for where the notes are. Depending on which notes are sharp, flat, or natural, you have to move the position of each finger up or down the unmarked fingerboard. This is a little more difficult, but it also makes you look pretty darn cool among your fair "fretted" friends! And though it sounds daunting, there's nothing a little practice won't make instinctive.

Take a Number

You're used to calling your fingers various names—index, ring, etc. When playing the fiddle, the fingers lose these names and they get a number. It's just easier that way. It isn't meant to make your fingers feel less like fingers with their own special identity! Basically, your index finger becomes the first finger, your middle finger becomes the second finger, and the ring finger becomes the third finger. Any guesses on what we call your pinky finger? If you guessed the fourth finger, you are correct.

Play Some Notes

Let's put fiddle and bow together again—and this time, we'll add your left hand to the mix. If we were to play a simple scale in the key of D, here's how your fingers should be placed: first finger plays the E, second finger a F♯, right next to the third finger, which plays a G. The fingers follow the same pattern when playing the B, C♯, and D on the A string. Following is how that eight-note scale looks written.

def•i•ni•tion

A **fret** is a metal bar embedded into the fingerboard. It creates a wide space where you can place your finger to make a note.

Fiddle Facts

There is nothing, I think, in which the power of art is shown so much as in playing on the fiddle. … Any man will forge a bar of iron, if you give him a hammer; not so well as a smith, but tolerably. A man will saw a piece of wood, and make a box, though a clumsy one; but give him a fiddle and a fiddle-stick, and he can do nothing.

—Samuel Johnson

Key of D

The D scale.

The A scale, starting on the A string, is on the same pattern. Give this a try:

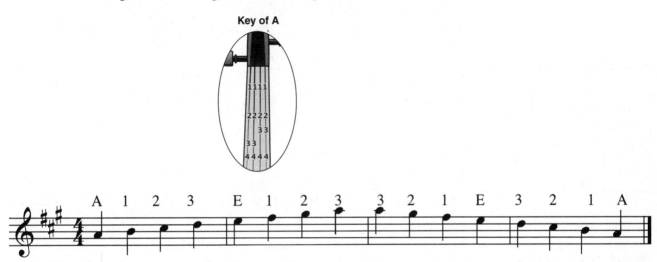

The A scale.

A one-octave G scale, starting on the G string, has the same fingering pattern. However, when we go up to two octaves, now you've got to think a little harder. The second finger on the A and E strings, playing a C♮ and a G, respectively, sit next to the first finger, not the third finger. Give this a try:

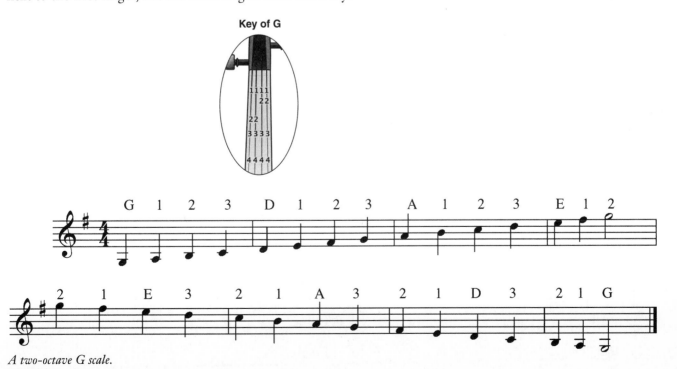

A two-octave G scale.

Coordinating the Left Hand with the Bow

One constant challenge with the fiddle is making sure your bow strokes are properly synchronized with your left hand's finger movements. One way to make sure you do this is to take it easy—slow down. As you learn tunes and tricks on the fiddle, it's tempting to speed up and "play a few licks." But make sure that as you speed up and start having fun, you give yourself the proper time to get all the moving parts working together. Otherwise, the effect is somewhat like watching one of those old Godzilla films badly dubbed into English—the words and the sound just aren't lining up right, and the effect is a little disconcerting. That same effect can be produced when the bow strokes don't quite line up with what the left hand is doing. A tune played slowly and well is *always* much more pleasant to listen to than a fast lick with sloppy changes.

Separate Notes

So you have played a few scales. Try them again a few times, this time concentrating on lining up your bow's change in direction with your left-hand fingers. Any slips or hiccups? Practice more slowly!

Now let's try an actual song. (Finally, you say!) How about the golden oldie "Mary Had a Little Lamb"? This is a five-note wonder of a tune that can be played on one string. Here it is in the key of D.

Once you master the fingerings, give it a shot on the A string and the G string. Try to notice the different tensions and responses of the strings as you do so. For example, the G string takes a little more pressure than the A, and responds a little more slowly.

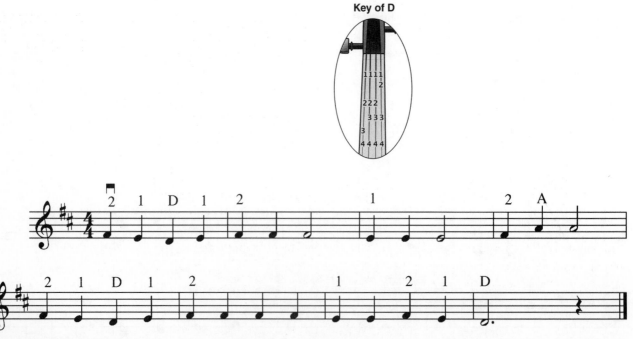

Mary Had a Little Lamb.

Slurs

One of the great defining characteristics of bowed instruments is that you can play an almost unlimited number of notes on one bow stroke. With plucked instruments like guitars, mandolins, banjos, and lutes, you are pretty much limited to one note per pluck. But with a fiddle, the bow sustains the note from frog to tip. Combining notes on a bow is called a *slur*. This is quite different from the term meaning "to speak insultingly of someone." In fact, a fiddle slur should result in pleasant feelings on the part of the listener and player alike!

Here's a couple different patterns to try out using the same two-octave G scales we just played: two-note slurs and three-note slurs.

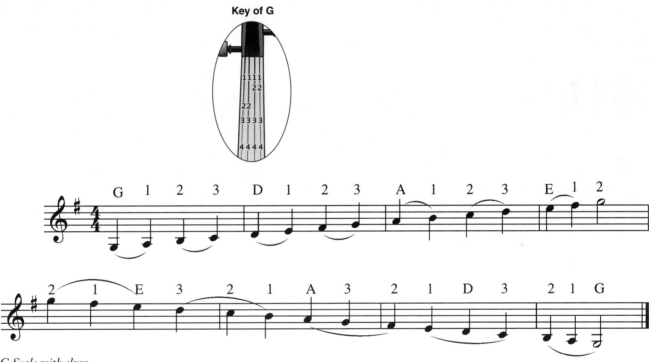

G Scale with slurs.

Experiment with slurs. Try slurring in fours. Try slurring a whole scale together, quickly and slowly, and see if you can't get it to sound good the whole way.

First Tunes

Take a moment and pat yourself on the back. You have now mastered holding and using the fiddle and the bow, and learned to coordinate your movements and play separate notes and slurs. That's all you need to start playing some actual music! Let's try a few more of your childhood favorites.

Here's another tune that might seem familiar. It is a simple tune, but it takes two strings to pull it off, so you'll have to cross strings a few times.

Key of A

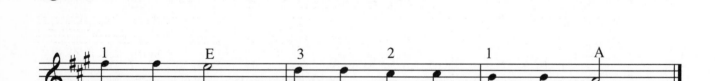

Twinkle, Twinkle Little Star.

The little ditty "Shortnin' Bread" is an easy tune. The tune will start on a down-bow, and then the pattern will reverse direction naturally. Try to get the same sound whether you are starting on a down- or up-bow. Then try putting a little Southern swing into it!

Key of D

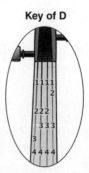

Shortnin' Bread.

The old standby "Row, Row, Row Your Boat" will give you a chance to try two different rhythms in a tune. It has triplets and dotted rhythms … but it's still pretty simple.

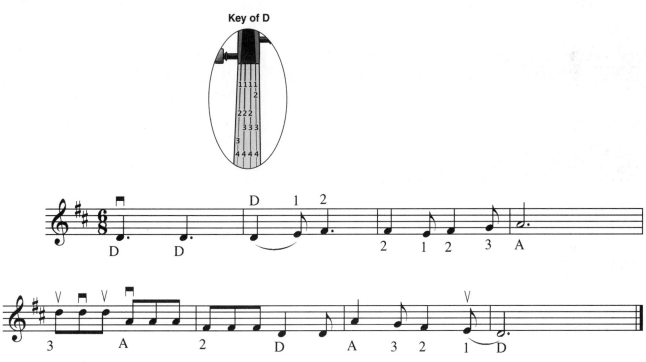

Row, Row, Row Your Boat.

If you've mastered these four numbers, you've got a good introduction to using your fingers and moving the bow. From here, it's only going to get more fun!

Fiddle Facts
Did you ever notice that "Twinkle, Twinkle Little Star," "Baa, Baa, Black Sheep," and "The Alphabet Song" are the same melody?

The Least You Need to Know

- Always stay relaxed in order to stave off problems with your body and your sound.

- Keep the fiddle tucked under your chin to take the pressure off your left hand.

- The positions of both fiddle hands are based on the natural curl of a hand at rest.

- A smooth combination of bending your wrist, elbow, and shoulder will move the bow across the strings in a straight direction.

- Maintaining the right amount of pressure with your bow hand will yield the tone you are looking for.

- Careful synchronization of bow and left-hand fingering will yield clear and separate notes.

Chapter 8

Simple Tunes

In This Chapter

- Working on good tone
- Fiddling around with some easy tunes
- Refining your long notes, short notes, and slurs
- Crossing strings

You're now on your way to becoming a fiddler! This chapter is where the fun finally begins. We're not going to waste too much time doing boring exercises and rote examples. Instead, we'll introduce techniques specific to the fiddle, while learning to play some simple, fun melodies.

Each song in this chapter allows you to concentrate on some technique that you need to master. Many of the melodies are probably already familiar to you. This means you can concentrate on playing the fiddle, instead of trying to learn new music *and* techniques at the same time. You get some tips and pointers to think about, while you fiddle to your heart's content on some fairly simple songs.

Good Bow, Good Tone

The fact that the fiddle is bowed means that it isn't limited by airflow (as in a flute) or by the natural waning of a string's vibrations (as in a guitar). The bow is a versatile tool that, as you master it, will allow you to produce a vast palette of sounds. Knowing how to take full advantage of the bow is one sign of a great fiddle player. Here's why the bow is so great:

- You can play a note as long as you'd like. If you've got great, smooth control of the bow, you can create an endless note.
- You can slur many notes together to create a smooth sound.
- Or you can play shorter, choppier notes and even bounce the bow around to get a percussive sound.

Learning to manipulate the bow tastefully and skillfully is how you will become a more expressive player. As you improve with the bow, you will develop the ability to evoke very human emotions and moods from your fiddle.

In the last chapter, you started experimenting with crunchy and breathy tones on the fiddle. This chapter expands on this. Some of the tunes in this chapter are made up of short notes, others of long ones. You also learn to use slurs of varying lengths. The location of slurs in a tune determines much of its sound, and tunes in this chapter make use of that, too.

Here are a few more pointers on using the bow well, and getting a better tone out of your fiddle:

♦ Make sure that your left-hand fingers are pressing down firmly on the fingerboard. You don't need to turn your knuckles white, but make sure you don't get any buzzing or "fuzzy"-sounding notes.

♦ Practice bow strokes that begin and end at the tip or the frog. They should travel the whole length of the bow. Then practice shorter, faster bow strokes that only use an inch or so. How is your tone as you play both of these?

♦ Use the structure and balance of the bow to get a solid, even sound. At one end, the natural weight of the frog will provide steady pressure on the string. As you bow down toward the tip, there will be less weight. As the bow becomes lighter, compensate with some pressure from your index finger. Make sure you are able to sound the same whether at the tip of the frog. This is a subtle dance, but it will eventually become second nature to you.

♦ Continue to think about the "arm/bow connection." There is a lot to think about with bowing (and the fiddle in general), so keep coming back to check on the basics. Your arm should be relaxed. Your wrist should be flexible and bend back and forth as you play.

Short Notes and Long Notes

When a song is made up of shorter notes, you need to concentrate on getting the same tone on both the up- and down-bows. Also, make sure that all the finger movements of your left hand are in sync with your bow hand. There shouldn't be any hiccups! Finally, keep your bow arm flowing smoothly. Don't stiffen up your elbow just because you've encountered faster notes.

Good rhythm is also important to develop early on in your playing. If you find that you are having trouble counting your beats and playing at the same time, you can get assistance from a *metronome*. In fact, owning a metronome can only help improve your sense of rhythm and keeping time.

Try the old Irish children's song, "I'll Tell Me Ma." Its melody is based largely around scales, with some different bowing patterns and rhythms.

def•i•ni•tion

A **metronome** is a device that will count steady beats for you. You can buy an electronic one that clicks along with flashing lights, or a mechanical one with a gear-driven pendulum.

I'll Tell Me Ma.

The next tune, "Amazing Grace," demonstrates the effect of the tie (two notes strung together to make a longer note). It can be tricky to figure out how a tie sounds just by looking at the music, but you should be familiar with these songs already (if not, listen to the DVD first).

In "Amazing Grace," you should strive to play the different lengths of notes with the same length of the bow. The challenge here is to keep an even tone, even as you use the different speeds and directions in your bow strokes.

On the two-beat long down-bows, don't use too much bow. Next, bow a little faster on the one-beat up-bows. At the end of the measure, you should be back in relatively the same place on the stick. In the middle of the tune, the long E will have to be played especially slowly—but still with a good balance of pressure and steadiness.

Tune Up

In the beginning, if you find it frustrating to follow the bow markings as you play, just play the notes first. You can pay attention to up- or down-bow markings and which notes are slurred later.

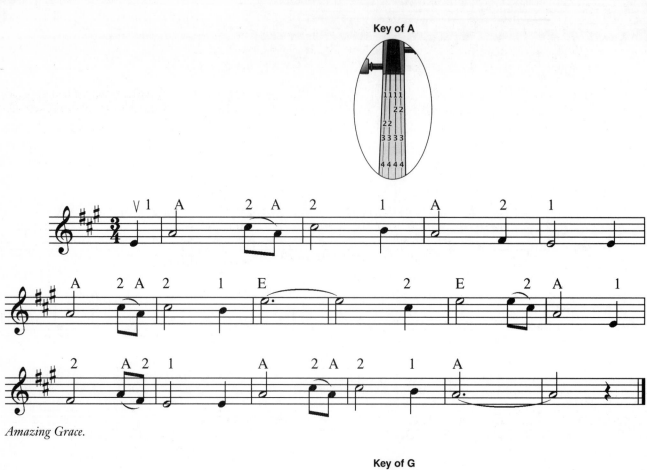

Amazing Grace.

Red River Valley.

"Red River Valley" is in the key of G. Take a minute to refresh yourself with the two-octave G scale from the last chapter. Then take note—your second finger is going to be high on the D string (F♯), and low on the A string (C♮).

In the fifth full bar of "Home on the Range," a D jumps to a G—and these are both notes that use the third finger. The best way to approach this is through a little "hop." Once you are done playing the D, lift the finger from the A string, and set it down quickly again on the G string.

In fact, first try this trick without playing a note. Place your first finger on the A string, and then hop back and forth from A to D, D to G, and so on. Try this with your second and third fingers. Then add the bow. Play a finger on one string, then on one next to it. By hopping back and forth you will be able to get a good clean sound (no buzzing or squawking from your fiddle.).

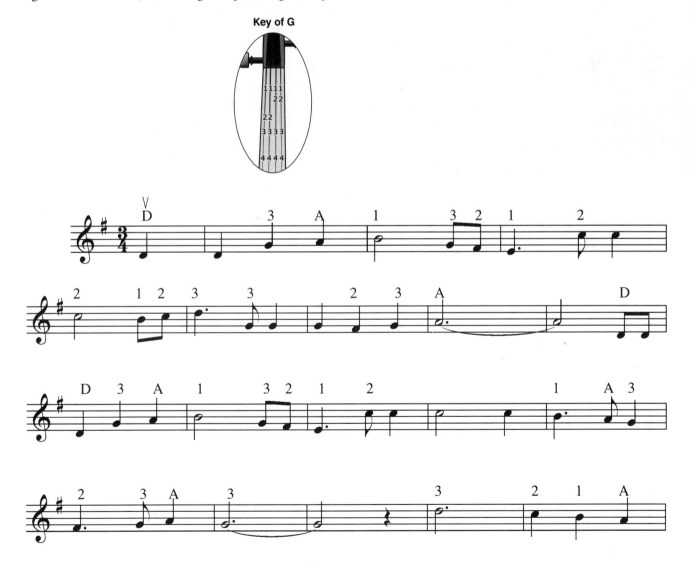

Key of G

Home on the Range.

The Fourth Finger

"The Parting Glass" is an old Irish and Scottish song that was sung by the Clancy Brothers. It is steady in rhythm, but slow. However, there is another challenge in this tune. Sometimes the melody reaches the E string, but it doesn't actually go above it. Instead, the notes head back down the A string. In these cases, you might want to try using your fourth finger to play the E instead of having to move the bow to play the E string, and then back again.

If you hadn't noticed yet, the fourth finger plays the exact same pitch as the next string up. The very first note of "The Parting Glass" is an E and you should try to play it with the fourth finger. Before you start, check it against the open E string to make sure it's in tune.

There are a lot of notes on the E string in this one, too. Make 'em pretty!

Key of C

The Parting Glass.

The E string easily can become squawky if not played right. When you are on this thin string, aim for a nice clear sound. You might not need as much pressure on the E string as you would use on the other strings. The next few songs will help you practice a nice, clear tone on the E string.

You can impress everyone at the party next New Year's Eve, when you pull out your fiddle and offer a rendition of "Auld Lange Syne" (which in the Scots language loosely means "the good old days"). The key signature is C, so your second finger will be low on both the A and E strings. It should be good friends with your first finger.

Key of C

Auld Lange Syne.

"The Ash Grove" is an old Welsh song. Look out for the *accidental* in the second half, when you play a G♯ in the key of D.

def•i•ni•tion

An **accidental** is a sharp, flat, or natural note that is not in the key signature. When written, an accidental is only good for one measure.

Key of D

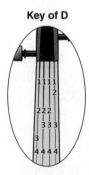

The Ash Grove.

More Work on Slurs

The Irish tune "Ryan's Polka" is a fairly basic melody. However, many of the slurs you'll use are not right on the beat. Rather, you'll slur into the beats. Slurring this way is the key to developing an authentic style later on, because many fiddle tunes use this sort of off-beat bowing.

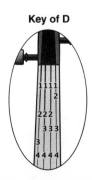

Key of D

Ryan's Polka.

Here it is—the famous and dramatic ballad "Danny Boy." Danny will provide you with another chance to practice good steady tone on long bows—especially on those upper high notes.

Fiddle Facts
The words to "Danny Boy," set to the older melody "Londonderry Air," were actually written in 1910 by an English lawyer and songwriter who had never even visited Ireland. The song became popular—and after Bing Crosby recorded it, was linked forever to Ireland in people's minds.

The high B, played with your fourth finger, is the ultimate test of good tone and tuning. Reach for it and let your pinky be firm on the fingerboard!

Key of G

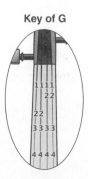

Danny Boy.

Take It Easy

If you want to become a really good fiddle player, here's one important point to remember: *Don't work more than you have to.* This may seem paradoxical. After all, don't you have to practice in order to improve? Of course.

But the key question is, *how* are you practicing? There are two ways of playing your instrument:

- You can make it difficult for yourself.
- You can make it simple for yourself.

The choice seems easy: why would anyone choose to make playing difficult? However, the paradox of the fiddle is that people often don't *notice* they are making things more difficult for themselves. It's very easy to acquire a bad habit that will actually hinder your playing. This, in turn, greatly affects your sound.

> **Fiddle Facts**
>
> Life is like learning a violin in public and learning as one goes along.
> —Samuel Butler

One example is in the left hand. In Chapter 7, I showed you the proper way to hold the neck with your left hand. This isn't just to impose random rules for the heck of it. Rather, there is a reason for everything. By resting the neck on the top half of the thumb, and keeping that thumb leaning away from you, you leave an easy, relaxed curl in your fingers. That way they don't have to cramp up when making a note.

Another example is in your fingers. When a finger is not being used, it should still remain curled *over* the fingerboard. This goes for all the fingers. Once a finger finishes playing a note, it should move no more than a half an inch from the strings.

The fingers themselves should stay spread out and open. Your third finger, for example, should sit above the D note on the A string. Don't let it spring back to form a cluster next to your index finger. Give the index finger some breathing room.

Your playing will be more efficient with these points in mind. And your fingers will be always at the ready to play a note. Instead of flicking from the side like a lizard's tongue to haphazardly land somewhere in the vicinity of the proper pitch, your finger will simply lower down a short distance onto the note that it was, in effect, targeting from above.

Before going on to the next section, go back and play all the tunes you've just learned, but keeping these points in mind. The less movement you see in your fingers as you play, the closer to an ideal left-hand position you probably are.

Finally, here's another good example of how to make things easier: be lazy! When you play the fiddle, don't lift a finger if you don't have to.

Here's what I mean by this. Take the tune "Ryan's Polka," for example. In the fourth bar of the B part, the melody goes "D-E-F-D." This phrase starts and ends on a third-finger D note.

When you play the E and F, there is actually no reason to lift your third finger—the D—off the fingerboard. Let it relax and stay where it is. That way, it will already be in place as you come back to play it again. You'll also need to make sure that you've got that third finger in just the right place so it doesn't buzz against the E string.

This is a great habit to master. Instinctively, most fiddlers want to lift a finger off the fingerboard when they're done with a note. But it's better not to.

This is what I mean when I say that it is easy to make things more difficult. Instinct on the fiddle isn't always the most natural thing. Instead, go for deliberate simplicity. So keep that third finger down until the end of the phrase, and that's one less thing you have to think about moving around as you play.

"The Girl I Left Behind Me" is a tune familiar to those in military settings. It came from Britain and has been played in this country (often on the fife) since before the days of the Revolutionary War.

Tune Up

In traditional music, sections of a song are often labeled as the "A Part" (first section), the "B Part" (second section), and perhaps even a C or D part.

Tune Up

There's another reason to work on not lifting up your fingers when you don't have to. Later on, it will make it much easier to impulsively play harmonies with yourself!

This ditty is in the key of D, but you will venture down onto the G string. So watch out. For the first time, your third finger will be in a higher slot on the fingerboard. On the G string, it needs an extra half step for the C♯.

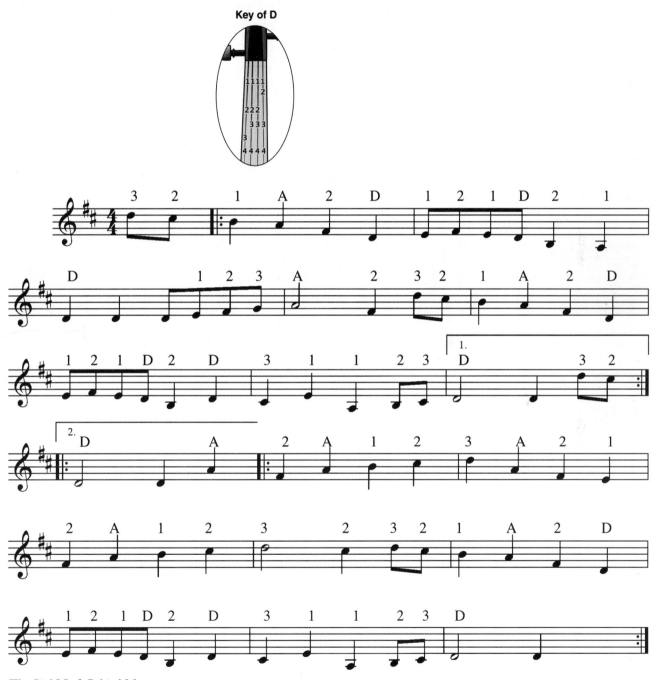

The Girl I Left Behind Me.

Crossing Strings

You just learned about keeping your fingers down when you don't have to lift them. With the next tune, you'll try keeping a finger down on *two* strings at the same time!

You have so far been "crossing strings" every time you move from one string to another. You've hopped the same finger across strings to play two or more consecutive notes that happen to be a fifth apart (for example, the notes B to F, or D to A, or C to G).

Following is the popular American tune "Devil's Dream." The patterns repeated over and over in this tune are the same as in many other Irish, Scottish, and bluegrass tunes. However, nailing this particular pattern of string crossing might take a bit of practice! So you might as well start working on it right now. We do a lot more of this in the next few chapters.

Look at the third measure of the tune, where you will find a D-F-B-F pattern. This is the pattern that will repeat itself throughout the tune.

To pull this off, you need to use the first finger on two strings *at the same time*, as you cross strings. To play this, carefully and firmly place the first finger across the two strings. Hold both notes firmly.

False Notes

When you learn a new tune, it is tempting to play fast ... but don't. Play slowly and take the time to concentrate on your rhythm, intonation, and bow coordination. Otherwise, you will end up with some sloppy habits.

The first finger holding down both the B and the F notes of the top two strings.

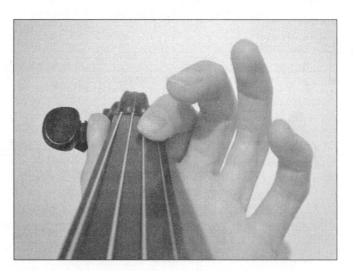

At first, play this tune very slowly. Once you are sure you are playing every single note well, then you can gradually start speeding up. This tune should be played fast once you have the rudiments down pat.

If there are any buzzing, scratching, or out-of-tune sounds, keep adjusting. Once you've got one finger holding down two good notes, you can bow from one note to the other with ease. Here are some pointers on playing the D-F-B-F pattern:

◆ Avoid that "chicken-flapping" look: don't move your elbow up and down too much. While it's good to raise and lower your elbow as you move across strings, it's not necessary when playing a passage like this. Instead, try to bend your wrist to move back and forth from string to string.

◆ Make sure you hold the first finger down constantly on both strings. The third finger should be the only one that moves.

Devil's Dream.

The Least You Need to Know

- Always listen to the music first, so that you develop your ability to learn fiddle tunes by ear.

- In order to get a good tone, you'll need to master a balance of pressure from your index finger and arm and speed of your bow.

- Slurring across the beat is a major characteristic of fiddle music.

- Avoid extra movements—clean and clear fiddling often means finding ways to simplify your playing.

Part 3

Fiddle Genres and Styles

Once you've got some basic melodies under your belt, there's a world of music to try. The melodies of Scotland, Shetland, Ireland, Cape Breton, Appalachia, the South, and the Grand Ole Opry await you! Each chapter in this part introduces you to a bit of the culture and history behind each region or type of music, and then gets you going on some great, but not too difficult, tunes.

Each chapter fills you in on the basic techniques and tricks that characterize each genre, then follows this with a selection of tunes to play. They are all about the same difficulty, so there is no need to work through Part 3 chronologically. Pick a tune, or a genre, and try it out.

"Nurse said it's always like this after the Scottish Music Festival. She said fiddles, reels, and whiskey always means trouble. Lucky you didn't poke your eye out."

Chapter 9

Scottish Music and the Relatives

In This Chapter

◆ The different branches of "Scottish" music

◆ Understanding Scottish rhythm

◆ An introduction to ornamenting your playing

◆ Playing some Scottish tunes

Often, when people think of Scottish music, they picture the Highland bag-pipes. The pipes often can be seen at parades, funerals—and, you know, those weddings where the groom and his men are wearing kilts.

Fiddles may be less exotic than the pipes, and they certainly are much quieter. (They are much easier to tune up, too.) However, they are just as important in Scottish traditional music as their "overblown" cousins. The fiddle has been a main feature in Scottish music for centuries. The weather is horrible in Scotland—you've got to have *something* people are willing to listen to indoors over there!

In this chapter, I take you through a little history, and give you a lesson about the culture that surrounds the music. Then I introduce different Scottish tune types. You also learn the left-hand ornamentation that Scottish and other Celtic traditions use to embellish their melodies.

"If It Ain't Scottish ..."

This book uses a very broad umbrella to include many different (though related) genres under the term "Scottish" music. There are many different types of music that are related to that of Scotland, and even vastly different styles within Scotland itself. We'll get into a little history and geography lesson to explain all this in a moment. All the different types of music, though, share some characteristics—enough to get us started with a few different types of tunes in this book.

In the eighteenth and nineteenth centuries, Scottish music became marked by a series of celebrity fiddlers that are still revered to this day. These include Neil Gow, a fiddler who was hot in demand to provide the music for the most exclusive dance events. He was also a prolific composer who published many volumes of fiddle tunes.

Another personality was James Scott Skinner, who was known as "The Strathspey King." He studied and performed classical music as well as Scottish. He also wrote many tunes, but added some very technically challenging music to the repertoire. He toured Scotland, England, and even the United States and Canada, often dressed in a kilt and other "traditional" Scottish gear.

During this time, many collections of tunes, both traditional and original, were published in Scotland. The result is that there is a great amount of Scottish music available in printed form.

Traditional Scottish music is undergoing a massive revival in Scotland at the moment. At one point, traditional Scottish music almost died out. As a result, young people there who have rediscovered their tradition are not bound by convention. They are not afraid to mix their old music with the jazz and rock that they hear all around them, with some fun results.

History Makes Its Mark

Within Scotland itself, there are two main types of Scottish music: Highland, or West Coast Scottish music, and East Coast Scottish music. This division came about for reasons of history. If you've seen the movie *Braveheart*, you'll have some idea of what I'm talking about. Basically, hundreds of years ago, the eastern half of the country was much more assimilated into English politics, culture, and language. The big cities of Edinburgh and Glasgow also had their share of wealthy, "cultured" citizens. The western half was a mountainous, rural society with a long history of conflict with their Anglo rulers.

This division translated into the music as well. The result was that much of the music from the eastern part of Scotland is influenced by classical tradition and is more formal-sounding. Many of these tunes are heavy on technique and utilize a difficult, showy style.

The Highlands, on the other hand, retained their *Gaelic* language and culture in their more wild, mountainous country. The music from this area is more closely related to the music of the bagpipes. The fiddles often imitate the pipes through the use of droning open strings. In the Highlands, there weren't any fiddler concert events like in the cities. There, the music was mainly for dancing.

Fiddle Facts

The plaid kilt and many other aspects of Scottish kitsch never really existed. Rather, much of it was an invention of a Victorian Era hungry for cultural nostalgia.

def•i•ni•tion

Gaelic refers to the three Celtic languages of Scotland, Ireland, and the Isle of Man, as well as the people who spoke them and their culture. Very few people speak these languages at home nowadays.

Shetland and Orkney

The Shetland Islands are located to the northeast of Scotland and for many centuries were claimed by the Norwegians. As a result, their music is a great mix of Scandinavian and Scottish influences.

In Shetland, before the fiddle arrived in its present form, people played a two-stringed instrument called the *gue*, which was held more like a cello. The fiddle, as elsewhere, was quickly adopted as the new instrument of choice when it arrived.

As in Scotland, the fiddle was the main source of music in a strong dance culture. It was also a very important part of Shetland wedding ceremonies. There are many marches in the repertoire that derive from this aspect of Shetland's culture.

Fiddlers also were in demand on the many whaling ships that embarked from Shetland. Presumably, the sailors appreciated being reminded of home while out on the cold, dark northern waters.

The tunes themselves are of Scottish, and to a lesser extent, Scandinavian origin. They are mostly played with a droning open string under or over the melody, in a manner reminiscent of the Norwegian Hardanger fiddle's sympathetic strings. In the twentieth century, a fiddler named Tom Anderson was responsible for teaching hundreds of fiddlers on the islands until his death in 1991.

The Orkney Islands, just off the northeastern tip of Scotland, also have their own fiddle tradition that is a blend of Scottish and Scandinavian music.

Fiddle Facts
The fiddle was so popular in Shetland that a visitor at the turn of the nineteenth century named Sir Arthur Edmonstone noted that about 10 percent of Shetlanders could play the instrument.

Fiddle Facts
You often can find the same tunes repeated in Ireland, Scotland, Cape Breton, old-time, and even bluegrass music. These tunes started hundreds of years ago in the Old World, migrated, and evolved!

O Canada!

Much of the fiddle music in Canada is a result of Scottish history as well. In the 1700s, a large number of people in the Highlands of Scotland were thrown out of their homes by their landlords and other unsympathetic rich English types to make way for industries such as sheep farms. Poverty and oppression in the Highlands, as well as famines, also encouraged many people to leave their homeland.

Many of these people made their way to Nova Scotia. Their music was kept alive for centuries on the other side of the Atlantic. Cape Breton, the northern island of Nova Scotia, is heavily populated by fiddlers. The fiddle music there has its own particular jaunty style, which is usually accompanied by the piano. The music has thrived in Cape Breton since a revival began in the 1970s. Musicians like Natalie MacMaster and Ashley MacIsaac have achieved prominence in Canada, as well as the United States.

There is also a strong tradition of fiddle music from Prince Edward Island and the Ottawa Valley. All of these Canadian styles of fiddling have a strong Scottish heritage, but with an Irish influence.

Fiddle Facts
Though much of Canada has a strong connection to Scottish culture, the French-speaking province of Quebec boasts a vibrant tradition of fiddling that is a blend of French and Irish traditions.

Ornaments

So what are these *ornaments*, anyway? You might be saying to yourself, "I thought you only needed ornaments for the holiday decorations!" Ornaments in Scottish or Irish music are ways of embellishing the tune. This can be accomplished either through little additional notes from the left hand, or subtle and dramatic flourishes with the bow.

The ornaments are what give the tune character. Without them, the tune is simply a skeleton, and probably a boring one at that.

Actually, ornaments in fiddle music work in a similar way to that of the holiday tree. They add a little decoration and grace to a simple structure (a tree, or a folk melody). You shouldn't overdo it or it just might get gaudy. And the ornaments should be well made (or well played), otherwise, it will actually make your tree (or tune) seem worse off than if you'd just left it alone! But they are very important. You wouldn't play a tune without ornaments any more than you would put a naked tree up for the holidays. People would look at you funny.

Ornaments are the barometer of good taste and skill. However, good taste is always a little subjective, isn't it? How a fiddler chooses to ornament a tune is a hallmark of his or her individual style.

Grace Notes

Grace notes are the simplest form of ornament that is made with the left hand. Basically, they are little notes that don't stand on their own, but rather exist solely to decorate a note in the melody.

In Scottish music, grace notes sometimes are a definite, clear note, with an obvious pitch. Usually this type of grace note leads into another note. However, they also can work to break up the note, without really yielding a clear pitch of their own. These are reminiscent of the sound of the pipes. There are two characteristics to this type of grace note:

- The finger does not actually stay on the string, but rather glances off of it. The best way to do this is to move the finger in a hammering motion on and off the string.

- The grace note doesn't sound as much like a note as a little hint of musical static that interferes with a note. This is a result of the technique. Instead of shortening the string, the hammering action simply stops the vibrations for a second.

If you have ever heard bagpipe music, you might have noticed that every note has one or even two ornaments attached to it. Fiddlers aren't quite so dependent on constant grace notes, as they have more flexibility of sound from the bow. Still, grace notes are very important in all types of Celtic music. They add a lot of color to the tune, as plain notes become decorated and a simple melody becomes ornate.

Tune Up

Both the *type* of ornament and the *style* in which it is played make a melody identifiable as being Irish, Scottish, or some other fiddle style.

Grace notes look like this:

The grace notes can either lead into or break up the note.

In our "cheating" system, I'll put the fingerings for the grace notes in parentheses, so that you can distinguish them when looking at the numbers.

Triplets

Triplets are often used in Scottish music. They are especially common in tunes like the strathspey. Often, triplet after triplet is played in a long run of notes. This pattern is meant to show off a bit of virtuosity on the part of the fiddler.

Triplets are used in reels in lesser quantities. They simply add a little spice to the melody. You'll see the difference between these two types of triplets when you play some tunes.

Types of Tunes in Scottish Music

There is a wide variety of tunes in Scottish music, especially when traditions from Cape Breton and Shetlands are all bunched under the term "Scottish." Though most tunes were used for dancing, some types of tunes were used for other cultural purposes. Different tunes exude different personalities: staid, regal, driving, cheerful, beautiful, or haunting.

Finally, it must be said that while Scottish music does make use of these ornaments, the main component of Scottish music is the strong, rhythmic bowing style.

Marches

Marches are exactly what they sound like—that is, tunes to march to. They come in a variety of speeds and time signatures, but all feature a steady tempo. Here are a couple. If you have ever been at a parade, you will definitely recognize the second one. Just imagine the snare drums rolling and pounding along with you as you play these melodies, and you'll fall in step with the marching rhythm!

The Scottish march "Campbell's Farewell to Redcastle" also can be found in American music, under the name "Campbell's Farewell to Red Gap." It is a fairly straight-ahead tune in A Mixolydian. It doesn't have any ornaments and relies on scale patterns for the melody.

This tune introduces the combination of a dotted eighth and a sixteenth note. This pattern is found in much of Scottish music.

Key of D—A Mixolydian.

Campbell's Farewell to Redcastle.

The well-known march "Scotland the Brave" gives you a chance to start working on your grace notes. These first examples of grace notes will delay the actual note of the melody.

Instead of just playing the note straight, you will start the note a whole or half step below. Hang on the grace note just long enough to make your point, then move on to the "real" note.

Scotland the Brave.

Strathspeys

You know it's Scottish music when you hear a strathspey playing. These are actually a type of reel, but usually are played a bit more slowly and majestically, with great emphasis on the beat. Cape Breton players, however, play strathspeys faster, with a bit of wild energy.

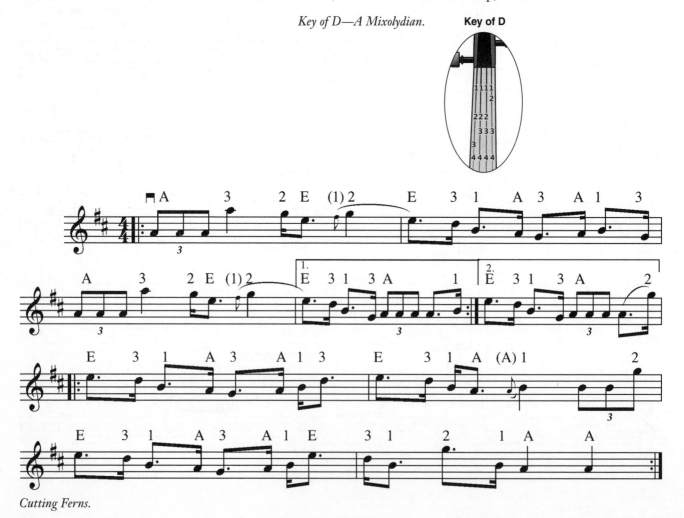

The major characteristic of a strathspey is the presence of the Scotch *snap*. A snap is written as a sixteenth note followed by a dotted eighth. In reality, it is played more abruptly than this, so that you literally "snap" out of one note into another. (Bagpipers refer to this by describing the tune as "pointed.")

You need a very small movement to get the snap; try to achieve this with a small flick of your wrist and fingers, rather than your elbow or arm. The goal is to get it sounding a little playful. One of the most challenging things about strathspeys is actually remembering which pairs of notes are snaps, which ones are dotted eighths and sixteenths, and which ones are the plain old evenly played pairs of eighth notes.

The tune "Cutting Ferns," from Cape Breton, can be found under the name "Cutting Bracken" in Scotland. You will play the same type of grace notes as in "Scotland the Brave," as well as the Scotch snap, in this tune.

Key of D—A Mixolydian.

Tune Up

Tap your feet to a strathspey every quarter note: "1-2-3-4."

Cutting Ferns.

The tune "Devil in the Kitchen" was written by William Ross, the piper to Queen Victoria from 1854 to 1891. It is a good introduction to strathspeys—there are a lot of open strings and simple patterns. However, there is a small bit of a "finger twister" phrase in the middle, so just take it nice and slow at first.

Key of D   *Key of D—A Mixolydian.*

Devil in the Kitchen.

Reels

Reels were invented in Scotland, and migrated to become a strong part of Irish tradition as well. They are ultimately played fairly briskly, with a driving rhythm that constantly moves forward.

"High Road to Linton" is a great starter reel. It is simple. When you listen to the tune, concentrate on the subtle but driving rhythm that you get with the bow. Then try to recreate it yourself.

Tune Up _____

This version of "High Road to Linton" is the original, traditional version. However, you'll hear most modern fiddlers play the tune with two extra parts that were composed by piano accordionist Bobby MacLeod about 50 years ago.

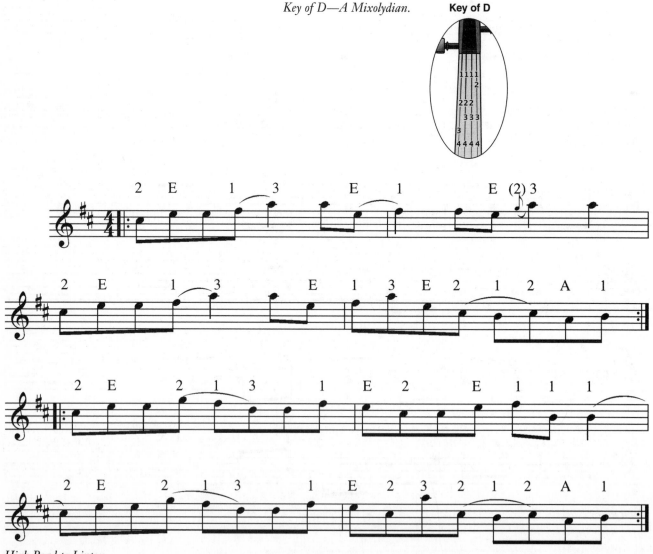

High Road to Linton.

"Sleep Soond Ida Morning" is a Shetland tune, and it should be played with great energy. In the A part, the second note of the slurs should be the one emphasized. Also, even though the key seems to be A minor, there are G♯ and F♯ notes. This is actually a typical sound for Shetland tunes.

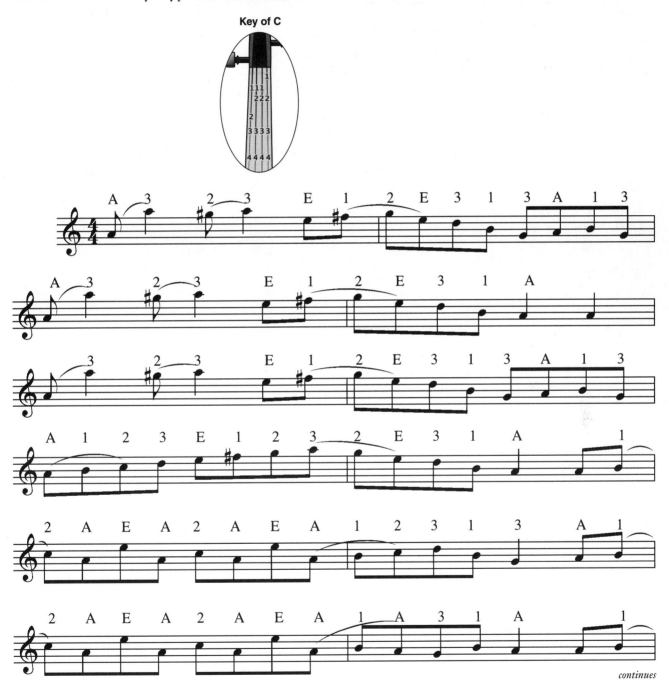

continues

Sleep Soond Ida Morning.

Triplets in reels are played a little grittier than the triplets in the strathspeys. Add a little pressure with your bow hand's index finger, just enough to add a little dirt to the sound. Try this in "Jenny Dang the Weaver."

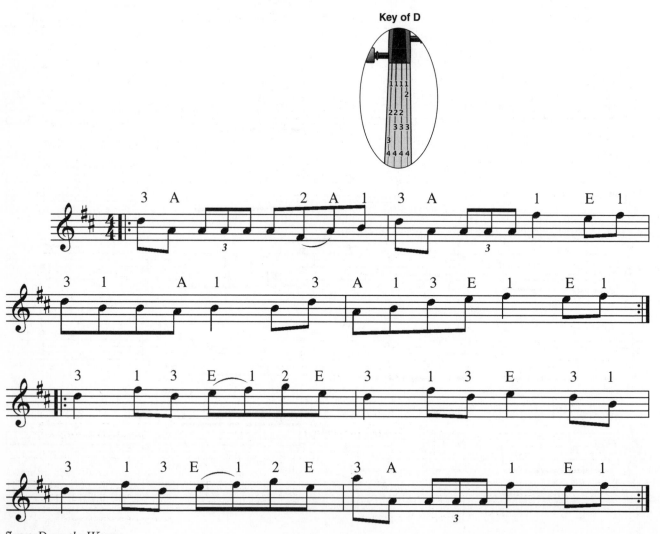

Jenny Dang the Weaver.

Fiddler Ashley MacIsaac hit the charts with the Cape Breton version of the reel "Sleepy Maggie." The tune can also be found as a three-part Irish tune called "Jenny's Chickens." Here is the version from Scotland.

In this tune, you'll try using a grace note to break up a note, instead of leading into it. Also, the triplet in this tune should be played lightly and delicately, with wrist and finger movements. The notes should dance up the little scale.

False Notes _____

Make sure that as you stretch the third finger out to reach a G♯ on the D string, your index finger doesn't slip up out of its anchor position.

Tune Up _____

The best way to practice grace notes that break up a note is to play a long note. As you do, execute your grace notes over and over, breaking your long note up.

The last thing I'd like to point out in this tune is in the final, descending phrase. In Chapter 7, I pointed out the advantages of leaving your finger down when you don't have to lift it. The reason for getting into this habit becomes clear: when you are playing a pattern like the one in the second to last measure of this tune, lifting your finger becomes a real hindrance.

With the two-part version of "The Mason's Apron" (there is also a four-part version out there), your third finger will be called to leave its familiar post, as its place on the D string will be raised to reach the G♯, courtesy of the key of A major!

In the B part, you'll get to try the crossing strings technique that you first

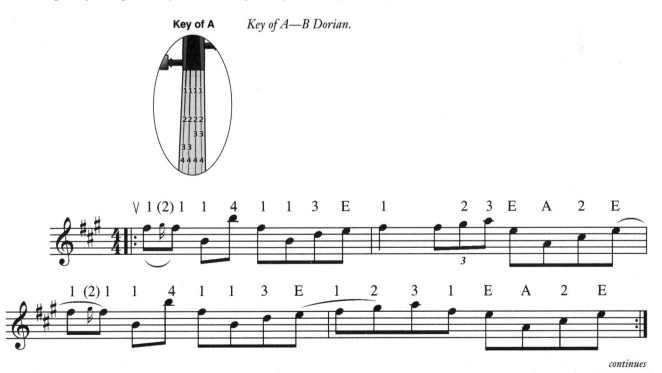

Key of A—B Dorian.

continues

learned in "Devil's Dream."

continued

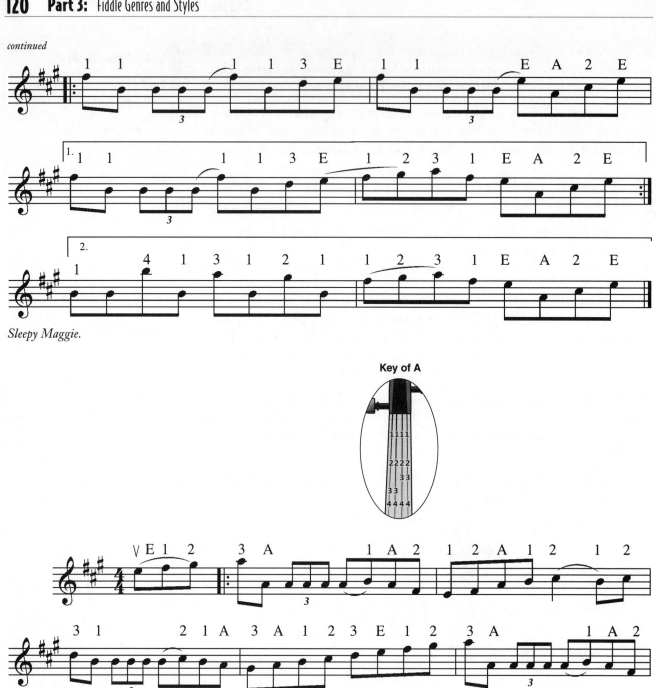

Sleepy Maggie.

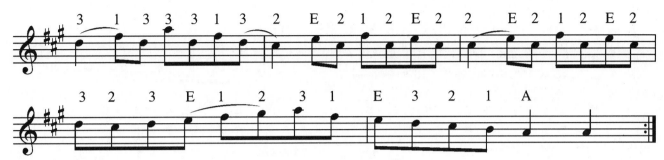

The Mason's Apron.

Jigs

Jigs, tunes in 6/8 time, are more common in Cape Breton music than in mainland Scottish music, perhaps because of the Irish influence.

The rhythm of jigs is important and more difficult than you might think at first. It is easy to play jigs in a very boring style: one note follows another, like a parade of ants, marching like drones.

To play a jig well, you want to emphasize the first note of the three. This should be done subtly, with pressure from the bow hand's index finger. A little increased speed of the bow on that note can come in useful as well. The notes should stay even; that is, none should be longer than another (you don't want to end up with the sound of dotted eighths).

A lot of this will come internally, after lots of listening and playing. But listening and playing consciously will help you reach the style.

There are a few grace notes in this "Jig of Slurs," composed by pipe major George Stewart McLennan.

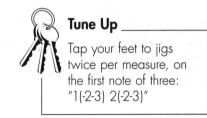

Tune Up

Tap your feet to jigs twice per measure, on the first note of three: "1(-2-3) 2(-2-3)"

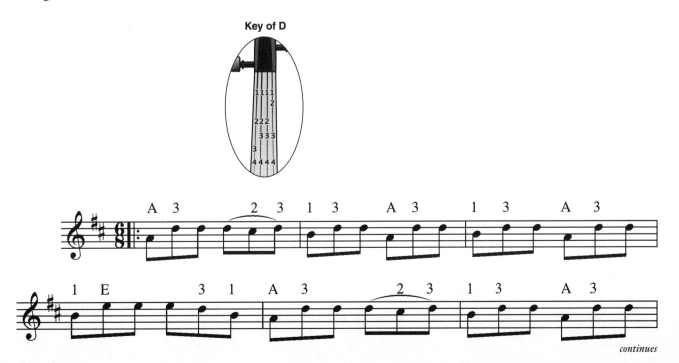

continues

continued

Jig of Slurs.

Slow Tunes

Many slow tunes in Scottish music come from the melodies of sad ballads. The song "Hector the Hero" was composed by James Scott Skinner in 1903, to lament the passing of his friend Sir Hector MacDonald, who committed suicide in the face of vicious public rumors.

This air uses both triplets and grace notes. These grace notes are fairly intricate, even when played slowly. These notes either tend to lead into the melody or to delay the start of a note. The trick to playing them well is to not labor them too much. Your fingers shouldn't linger on these notes. The action required to execute them is one of lightness and grace.

However, if you find all these grace notes difficult, just learn the basic melody (the big notes!) first and add the grace notes gradually. This tune has been recorded by many people over the years, so feel free to dig up some professional recordings and attempt to imitate various other interpretations as well.

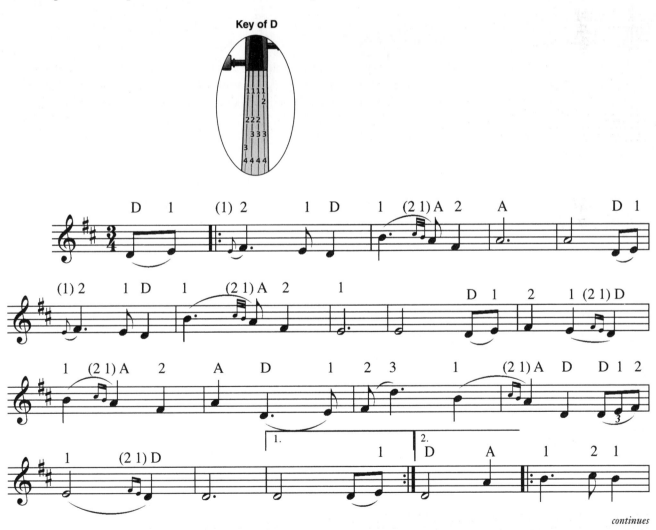

continues

continued

Hector the Hero.

None of the Above

The last tune for this chapter is not a common type of tune. It's a fun little tune that may have been from a type of song known as *mouth music*. It has a Gaelic title, but we'll use the English name, "The Twisted Bridge." To challenge yourself, as you play the final A of each phrase with your fourth finger, try to double the note with the A string.

def•i•ni•tion

Mouth music was vocal music sung with simple, or repetitive, lyrics. It was used to replace instruments like the fiddle and pipes when they were banned in historical times of excess religious or political extremism.

Key of D—A Mixolydian.

The Twisted Bridge.

The Least You Need to Know

- The umbrella term "Scottish" includes music from Scotland; the Shetland and Orkney Islands; and Cape Breton and the Ottawa Valley, Canada.

- Much Scottish music was collected or composed in written volumes of music starting in the eighteenth and nineteenth centuries.

- A major characteristic of Scottish music is strong, bold bowing style.

- Grace notes can be used to lead into a note, or to break it up into two.

- The Scotch snap, used in strathspeys, is an exaggerated sixteenth note followed by a dotted eighth.

Chapter 10

Irish Music

In This Chapter

- The history and culture of Irish music

- The different types of tunes from Ireland

- Ornamentation in Irish music

- A selection of tunes to learn

Irish music is definitely a success story of the twentieth century. This genre of traditional music hails from a little European island of only 3.5 million people. It has managed, in the last few decades, to become one of the most popular in the world. The Irish even have their own holiday in the United States—St. Patrick's Day. The festivities include a green-dyed river in Chicago and parades in almost every town where a citizen can claim a drop of Irish heritage.

But the mainstream image of Irish music is also a simplistic one, with songs like "Danny Boy" and "Irish Rover" dominant in people's minds. Traditional Irish fiddling, however, is actually an intricate craft. The left hand provides a constant stream of ornamentation, while the bow provides strong rhythm and variations in the sound. The result is distinctive—a style that can take years to master.

While it can be complex, Irish music is very accessible to beginners. The basic melodies are often quite simple. This chapter will take you through a little bit of Irish history and culture. Then, you'll learn a few different tunes and some basic ornamentation to add to them.

Traditional Irish Music

Ireland boasts a compelling instrumental music and song tradition. Like many other countries, it experienced many years of foreign conquest, which inevitably caused some hard times. Through years of turmoil, people kept their spirits up by holding fast to their unique cultural heritage. While the last century saw the popularity of the music ebb and flow even within Ireland, the music has survived and thrived.

Today, there is an astounding number of Irish musicians in Ireland. If you go into a local pub in the western part of the country, chances are good that you'll come across a *session*, or gathering, of musicians playing fiddles, pipes, concertinas, and flutes in the corner. However, you also can find people playing Irish sessions in the United States and countries like Sweden or Japan. The music of this small European nation really has traveled far to become a true "world music."

Fiddle Facts

Every July, over 10,000 students and fans of Irish music from all over the world attend Willy Clancy Week. This takes place in the tiny town of Miltown Malbay, County Clare (population: 1,042). Many people come to take classes from great Irish musicians, but the rest come to drink beer and soak up the omnipresent music.

From the Famine to ... Broadway?

Ireland probably couldn't have done it on its own, however. The country's history is one of strife, oppression, and emigration. Over a million immigrants left the country during the great potato famine of 1845 to 1851 alone. A great deal of them arrived in the United States, beginning a tradition of emigration from Ireland to the United States that lasted a century and a half. In fact, it is only in the last 10 or 15 years that Ireland's people stopped being the country's greatest export.

Fiddle Facts

According to United States census statistics, over 4.5 million Irish have come to the United States since the 1820s. The result is that 35.5 million Americans can claim Irish heritage! (Only the Germans can claim more.)

Homesick emigrants kept their music alive on this side of the Atlantic, and their ever-growing number of descendants proved a great market for Irish music and song. From crooners like Bing Crosby to the Clancy Brothers of the 1960s, Irish songs have enjoyed great popularity and have lasted in the public mind for decades. For decades, the best-selling band The Chieftans have collaborated with symphonies and mainstream artists like Emmylou Harris and Sting.

Most recently, a dancer/flute player from Chicago brought Irish music and culture to international audiences. Michael Flatley was an original member of a dance-based Broadway show called *Riverdance*. He then went on to start his own dance spectacular, *The Lord of the Dance*, which debuted in 1996. All of a sudden Irish dance and music were in everyone's mind, and another revival of Irish music was underway.

There are Irish music festivals all over the United States almost every weekend of the year, in obvious places like Chicago, but also in more surprising places like north Texas. Many public and free-format radio stations have a Celtic hour. All over the world, there are musicians who play Irish music just as authentically as those who grew up in Ireland. For many people, once they discover this music, they are driven to learn all about it. That's the reason Irish music is alive and well in our modern, global world.

The Regions

Unlike Scotland, Ireland was mostly a rural country, without big cities. As a result, musicians weren't exposed to as much classical music. Irish music remained firmly in the folk tradition. However, as in Scotland, the music of Ireland had different characteristics from region to region. Most of traditional music thrived in the more rural western half of the country. Here's a basic rundown of the various regional styles in Ireland:

◆ The southwest counties of Cork, Limerick, and Kerry boasted a dance tradition, with fiddles and accordions blasting out rhythmic tunes as people stomped and swung to set dances (a type of Irish square dance).

◆ County Clare was home to a slower, more intricate style. Its music made great use of complex ornaments and variations, and was largely played on the fiddle and *concertina*.

◆ Counties Sligo, Mayo, and Leitrim had quick tunes with showy ornaments that were made famous in their day by virtuoso fiddle and flute players who emigrated to America in the 1920s.

◆ County Donegal, in the isolated northwest corner, was influenced greatly by migrant workers to and from Scotland. The fiddle was king in Donegal. Fiddlers here had some unusual tune types in their repertoire, and used a driving, sparse style.

> **def•i•ni•tion**
>
> A **concertina** is a type of instrument similar to the accordion, but is small enough to hold on the knee with two hands and has a reedier, sharper sound.

In modern times, of course, people in these regions are no longer isolated from one another. As a result, these styles have merged and blended (some, with a more pessimistic view of life's changes, describe this as diluted and destroyed). Nevertheless, they are still important. There is much to learn from older players and recordings. Aspiring fiddlers often study the historical styles, in order to help develop their own contemporary, but rich and authentic, Irish fiddle sound.

Ornaments

Ornaments, as we explained in Chapter 9, are little flourishes with the left hand or the bow. They give the tune more character. After all, playing bare-boned note after note sounds a little ... bare! And frankly, I think hanging out bare is illegal in most states.

Ireland, being a cold and very Catholic country, demands that a lot of ornaments be draped on its bare tunes. No self-respecting fiddle player would be without them! Rhythm, of course, is still an intrinsic part of the music, but the bowing is more subtle. In general, the bow is not used nearly as vigorously as in Scottish music. This, along with the number of ornaments used, is the major difference between Scottish and Irish music.

> **Fiddle Facts**
>
> While most of Ireland's music was folk music, a harpist and composer named Turlough O'Carolan did compose many classically influenced pieces for Irish nobles in the 1600s. These are still played today.

How, when, and which ornaments are used in a tune are up to individual choice. No two musicians use the same ornaments in the same places. They might play the same type of ornament with different styles. Some use more ornaments, some fewer.

Irish tunes (like all traditional tunes) are never played just once. Each time the tune goes around, the musician will try to change his approach a little bit. He might change the pitch of notes; he might use more or fewer notes; he might switch, add, or remove ornaments, or add drones and chords to some notes. This practice is called *variation*. Great variations are one way to discern a good Irish fiddler from a great one.

Grace Notes

In Irish music, grace notes are small little hiccup notes that add a flourish to the note you are playing. They are similar to, but less obvious than, Scottish grace notes. A grace note should be here and gone before the listener can really register that you moved your finger. Timing-wise, it's easier to think of one as part of the note you're playing, rather than a separate note.

To make the grace note when you are playing a note with the first or second finger (an E or a B, for example), most Irish players use the *third* finger. In numbers, this is:

3-1 *or* 1-3-1

The key is to make that third finger barely register on the fiddle. To do this, don't put the finger that is making the grace note square down onto the string. Instead, the finger moves *across* the string, from left to right, in a sort of plucking motion. Put another way, the finger just flicks across the string—it says hi as it passes by.

Just like in Scottish music, grace notes can be used one of two ways in Irish music. They can *lead into* a note, or they can *break up* a note. However, either way, it pays to start out practicing them slowly.

Triplets

There are two types of triplets in Irish music. The first, which I'll call "noted" triplets, typically change two eighth notes into three, adding more notes to a tune. This can be one of two patterns:

Triplets can either jump up or down in pitch from a main note, or consist of three ascending or descending notes.

When played like this, the notes are clearly discerned (though they may fly by fairly quickly).

Irish "bowed" triplets change two eighth notes of the same pitch into three notes of the same pitch. When these are played, the notes are not heard so clearly. Rather, they are crunched slightly with the bow, producing a grittier sound. To achieve this effect, you need looseness and dexterity in your bow hand.

Triplets always start on the down-bow (there are a few fiddlers who ignore this rule, but not many). You often have to slur out of the last note in the triplet into another to continue that pattern. Try this exercise below.

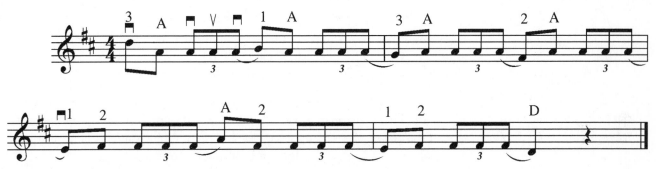

Slur the last note of the triplet with the next note.

Slides

Another way to ornament a note is to slide into it. To do this, you actually start out by purposefully playing the note a little flat. Next, you literally slide your finger on the fingerboard until the note reaches the correct pitch.

When you do slides in Irish music, they are much more subtle than the slide you are probably familiar with from country music. The slide happens quickly and is a more subtle change in pitch. The final effect is simply that— an effect on the note that might not be immediately easy to pinpoint.

> **Tune Up**
>
> If you find ornaments tricky, just play the tune as plainly as you want. Add ornaments later, when you feel confident using them.

Rolls

Ireland is the home of some great baked goods, including scones and brown bread. However, the rolls that we are talking about here are flourless fiddle ornaments. I go into more detail on these in Chapter 15, because they are actually difficult to pull off. Because they are a major feature in Irish music, though, I wanted to mention them in this chapter. They are a way of embellishing a note through a series of rising and falling pitches.

Types of Tunes in Irish Music

Jigs and reels are the most common types of tunes in Irish music. There are several other tune types in addition to these: the slip jig, the polka, the slide, the hornpipe, and the barn dance. Some of these were more common in a particular region. They all have a particular rhythm and all are fun to play.

Besides the list of tunes that I include in this section, there are also a variety of tunes from County Donegal, which picked up more unusual tunes in its connections to Scotland. These include the schottische, the strathspey, the mazurka, and the fling.

Jigs

Jigs are one of the most common tune types in Irish music. They are also probably the most recognizable type of Irish tune.

Jigs are written in 6/8 time, but it's important to avoid playing six notes that all sound the same. There is a small emphasis on the first of each set of three. To get this, just add a little more pressure using your bow hand's index finger.

The first tune, "Off She Goes," is an example of what is officially termed a single jig. This consists of a pattern of one quarter note followed by an eighth note. Don't labor this—aim instead for a cheerful, light sound. For this tune, let's skip any ornaments and let you concentrate on the rhythm.

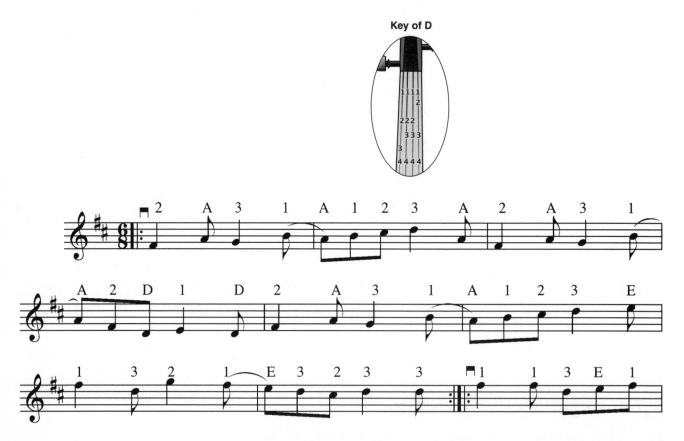

Off She Goes.

Slurring into the downbeat is one way of getting a subtle emphasis on the first note of three. Try this in "The Lilting Banshee." This one is a more standard jig, with the typical "1-2-3, 1-2-3" feel of most Irish jigs. There are also a few grace notes in this tune.

Key of G   *Key of G—A Dorian.*

The Lilting Banshee.

Another standard jig is "The Connaughtman's Rambles." You can definitely use this one to get people dancing next St. Paddy's Day.

There is a set of triplets in this tune. I've marked them to be played slurred, but you can change it up and play them separately and lightly for a different sound.

The Connaughtman's Rambles.

"The Irish Washerwoman" is more of an Irish tune in the popular imagination. While it's not played often by "real" Irish musicians, it is a fun tune and probably will be requested at holiday gatherings once your relatives find out you're learning the fiddle!

The second part is a bit tricky; you'll have to concentrate on your crossing strings technique here, as the notes descend on the A string. Instead of hopping, you'll have to slide your second finger over so that it reaches both the G and the C.

The Irish Washerwoman.

Polkas and Slides

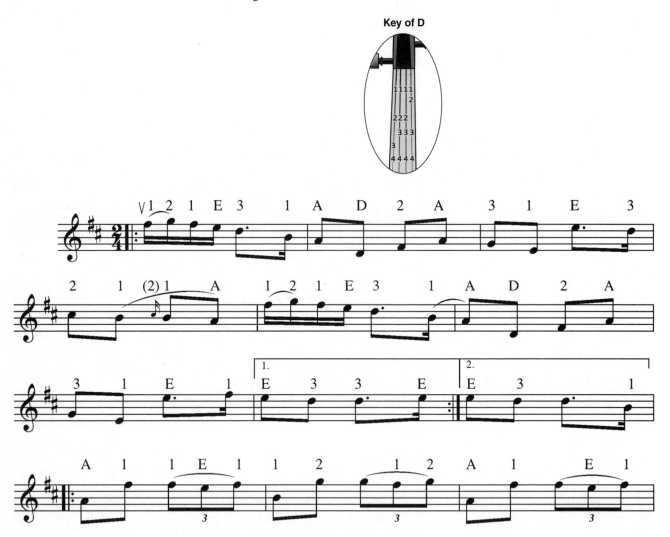

def•i•ni•tion

Sliabh Luachra is an area of Ireland that contains parts of counties Kerry, Cork, and Limerick.

Polkas are a tune type from County Kerry, or more accurately, the region called *Sliabh Luachra (Shleeve LOO-kra)*. You already played one polka back in Chapter 8.

Played authentically, polkas use an extremely subtle rhythm that is actually quite difficult to master (kind of like trying to imitate an Irish accent—it's harder than you think)! The goal is to accentuate the *offbeat*. However, for now, the melodies are quite accessible for the beginner fiddle player.

"Dennis Murphy's Polka" is a fairly simple melody, but watch out for the second-to-last measure of the tune. This will call for a bit of dexterity in your second finger.

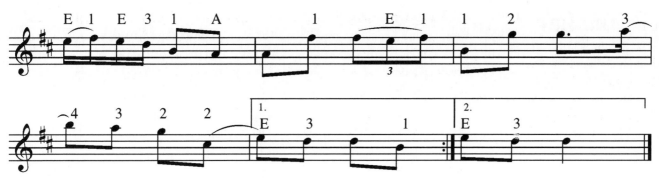

Dennis Murphy's Polka.

You should be able to get a cheerful sound from "Britches Full of Stitches."

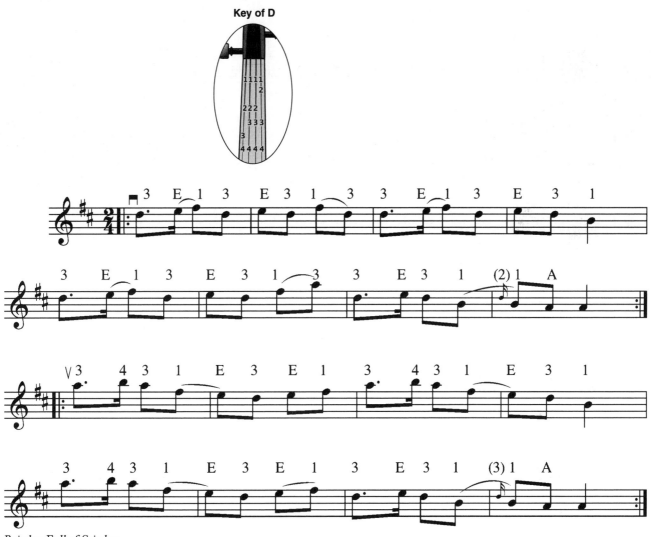

Britches Full of Stitches.

def•i•ni•tion

A **slide** is a type of tune from the region of Sliabh Luachra. It is in 12/8 time and is usually played fairly fast.

"The Road to Lisdoonvarna" is a *slide* from County Kerry. This type of tune should sound very light and cheerful. Try to put a lot of lift in your bow arm—that is, don't labor the strokes. This tune also makes great use of grace notes to break up notes.

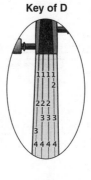

The Road to Lisdoonvarna.

Slip Jigs

Slip jigs are in 9/8 time, so there are three main beats that you tap your foot to.

Here is the "Dusty Millar," a slip jig that was recorded by the Irish band Altan on their groundbreaking album, "The Red Crow." In the manner of Donegal tunes, the melody is spare, without much ornamentation. The aim is to make the simple melody sound sweet and lyrical. Your bow arm should have a feeling of lift in it. As with "Off She Goes," don't labor the long note/short note pattern.

Fiddle Facts

Traditionally, only women dance to slip jigs. The style of stepping used is meant to show off delicate feminine grace.

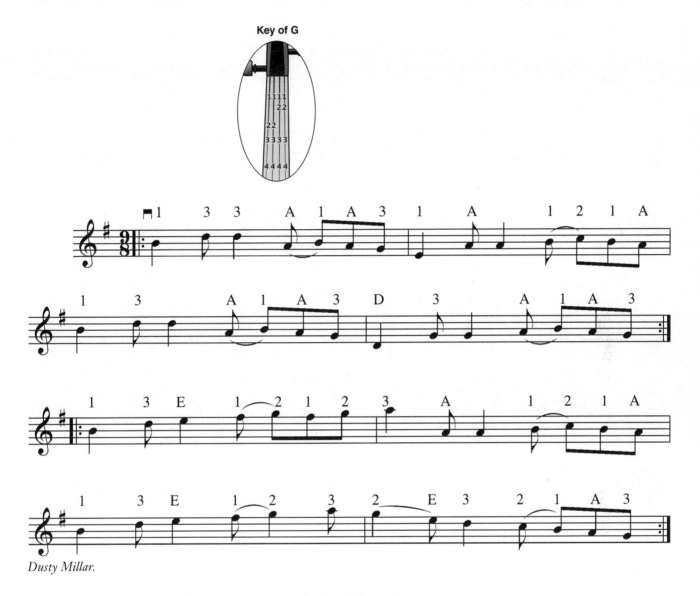

Dusty Millar.

"Drops of Brandy" can be played more vigorously than "Dusty."

Drops of Brandy.

Reels

Reels are the most common type of tune in Irish music. If you come across an Irish session in a local pub, there is a fair chance that you might hear nothing but reels all night.

"The Old Copperplate" is a fairly basic melody, but it can't be played without a few grace notes to liven things up.

Key of G—A Dorian.

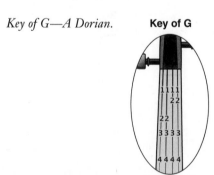

The Old Copperplate.

"Drowsy Maggie" is another tune that features crossing strings. This tune turns the pattern of "Devil's Dream" around, so you are starting with the first finger, not the third. There are also a few triplets in this one.

Key of D   *Key of D—A Dorian.*

Drowsy Maggie.

Hornpipes and Barn Dances

Hornpipes are usually written in 4/4, like reels, but are played more slowly, with a swingier feel. In the eighteenth century, men often danced the hornpipes because the dance steps called for stomping, showy moves.

In "The Harvest Home," there are several sets of consecutive slurs that help you achieve the swinging feel. The runs of triplets also slur into each other for the same reason.

Key of D

The Harvest Home.

There are a few tunes called barn dances in Irish traditional music as well. They originally made it into the music in the nineteenth century, an import from the dance music on the continent.

Here is a barn dance that was played by Lucy Farr, a fiddler from Ireland who lived in London for over 50 years. With this tune, you'll try some double stops—playing two strings at once. These enable you to play a little harmony with yourself.

Experiment with the angle of your bow so that you can hit two strings instead of one. Then you'll need a little extra pressure to play both strings at once. Be firm, but at the same time, keep aiming for a nice tone.

You can play several notes in a row like this. Or try to strike only the doubled open string once, and then let it ring out as you continue playing one string. I demonstrate both techniques on the accompanying CD.

Lucy Farr's Barndance.

Here is one more reel for you to learn. "The Earl's Chair" can make great use of double stops. I've put one in for you to try, but feel free to alternate and switch up using that double stop. The tied notes in the A part give the tune an unusual rhythm, as well.

The Earl's Chair.

The Least You Need to Know

♦ Irish music has become one of the most popular forms of traditional music in the world.

♦ While some of the tune types and ornaments are similar to Scottish music, the bowing style in Irish music is less vigorous, and the ornaments are more complex.

♦ Tunes in Irish music include the single, double, and slip jigs, reels, polkas, slides, hornpipes, and barn dances, as well as a few Scottish-derived ones found in Donegal.

♦ Good rhythm, well-executed ornaments, and interesting variations are extremely important in Irish music.

Chapter 11

Old-Time Music

In This Chapter

◆ The history and diversity of American old-time music

◆ Basic bowing styles in old-time music

◆ Droning and double stops

◆ Some old-time fiddle tunes

The last two chapters covered the music of Ireland and Scotland—the Old World. Now we're moving across the Atlantic to the New World, to introduce you to a bit of "old-time" music.

While old time is another niche traditional music pastime, it is music "made in the USA," which means that it can sometimes be a bit easier to find in the States than the more imported styles of Irish and Scottish music. The genre can seem mysterious to people who aren't familiar with it. In fact, a popular slogan on festival T-shirts and bumper stickers reads, "Old Time—Better Than It Sounds." It's a humorous acknowledgement of the fact that the fiddle tunes aren't often topping the Billboard charts. But the droning, pulsing, repetitive melodies of old-time music are *really* fun to play.

In this chapter, you are introduced to the most commonly played versions of some standards. First, though, you learn about some of the bowing styles, and how to really lay on the double stops and droning.

Scottish and Irish in America

It is hard to write old-time tunes down on paper. Their complex bowing patterns and syncopated rhythms aren't easily confined to a musical staff. If you decide that you want to dig deeper into the traditions of old time, you'll find that it's a music that is really only learned by ear. The sooner you find people to learn from and play with, the better!

The good thing about old-time *jams* is that, unlike at a majority of Irish sessions, each tune is played over and over many times. You'll always have many chances to pick up a tune by ear.

As you know already from Chapter 1, old-time music got its start when Scots and English (as well as some Irish) settlers immigrated to America hundreds of years ago. They brought their music with them. As these Europeans and their tunes encountered the people and music of Africa, they were changed to something completely American in several ways, including the following:

- The rhythm changed from emphasis on the *downbeat* (the first beat of the measure) to emphasis on the *offbeat*. This also is known as *syncopated* rhythm. In old-time music, you usually tap your foot to the second and fourth beat instead of the first and third.

- The strong melodies of Irish and Scottish music began to be played with more chords. Open strings often droned underneath or above the melody, for a ringing, full sound.

- A good, clear tone became less important to players, and good, strong rhythm and vigorous playing became even more important.

- The clawhammer banjo, an instrument of African descent, became a constant companion of the fiddle in much of the old-time repertoire. The clawhammer provides a percussive and chordal accompaniment to fiddle tunes.

- Fiddlers began making wider use of *alternate tunings*.

def•i•ni•tion

A **jam** is the old-time and bluegrass word used for what Irish and Scottish musicians call a session: an informal gathering of musicians who play tunes together.

Syncopated rhythm emphasizes a note that normally is not emphasized.

Alternate tunings means changing the tuning of the fiddle strings to an arrangement other than G, D, A, and E. This gives greater flexibility of fiddle sounds and results in some pretty cool chords, as well as some haunting and unusual sounds.

Dancing

As in Europe, the music of the fiddle in America was used for dancing. Here, European dance moves also evolved as they blended with different cultures. The more rigid, foot-based step dancing of Ireland and Scotland mixed with African dancing (which used the whole body) and became clogging. Irish set dancing and English and Scottish country dancing evolved into square, longways, and circular dancing in the South.

All this dancing was a huge part of the social fabric of rural America. As the dancing changed, so did the music. The rhythm of the music needed to match that of the dancing. Of course, this is a chicken-and-egg scenario (which came first, the change in the dancing or the music)? Most likely, they changed together, because one couldn't change without the other.

Fiddle Facts

Settlers may have been influenced by another continent as well: the hearty *stomp!* found in clogging is reminiscent of elements of Native American dance.

Singing

Singing was a huge part of the cultural fabric of the South as well. It was a constant source of entertainment that didn't require any instruments—or karaoke machines! During World War I, a British ethnomusicologist named Cecil Sharp toured the Appalachian Mountains seeking out songs. He "discovered" hundreds of songs that were descended directly from the old ballads of England and Scotland. Many of them still featured kings and queens in the plotline, despite the fact that the United States had been a democracy for over 150 years. (Who can blame them? Songs about "the vice president's daughter" falling into mischief just don't have the same ring to them.)

There was other singing in the South besides old, unaccompanied ballads. Singing is also done along with old-time fiddling. A fiddler could provide instrumental breaks between his or her verses, or even sing while playing.

You also might say that some singing was used to accompany the fiddling, too. Many old-time tunes are incomplete without a little associated verse—or several. The words are often humorous or a little nonsensical, and are usually belted out after a few times through the tune.

Fiddle Facts
The kind of research done by Cecil Sharp was portrayed in the 2000 "romantic ethnomusicology" motion picture, *Songcatcher*.

The Twentieth Century

From its beginnings, fiddling was a very central part of leisure time in much of the United States. This was certainly true in the rural South. Once the twentieth century began, though, many things changed. Transportation and revolutions in the agricultural economy meant that people now could, or were forced to, move away from their family homes. The recording industry meant that people didn't have to wait for "Fiddlin' Frank" to visit from down the holler with his fiddle. In the 1920s and 1930s, jazz and other forms of modern music became more popular. Fiddle music just wasn't the center of Southern life anymore.

But old-time fiddling has survived, despite several ebbs and flows of popularity. This would have been impossible, of course, without the stubbornness of older-generation musicians, who continued to fiddle in their rural homes for years, despite growing lack of interest in their craft. When urban folk musicians came calling looking for fiddle tunes in the 1960s, these older folks were more than happy to pass on to complete strangers what they had learned in their family homes.

Fiddle contests have also been a form of entertainment in the United States since Revolutionary days. In the 1920s, there was an old-time revival, spearheaded in part by automobile magnate Henry Ford. He asked his Ford dealerships across the country to host contests in the car showrooms. In Atlanta, Georgia, the Georgia Old Time Fiddler's Convention was a well-attended annual event from 1913 until 1935.

Fiddle Facts
Henry Ford was so passionate about old-time music and culture that he required his company executives to attend Friday night dances and classes.

The revival of the 1920s and 1930s eventually waned, but the 1960s brought a renewed interest in folk and traditional music. People began seeking out the last of the "old timers" in their rural homes and learning tunes and techniques from them.

Ironically, old-time music started to thrive in urban places like New York City. The larger population of cities meant that enough people interested in the same music lived in the same place. The music wasn't kept alive through tradition anymore—instead, people were part of "scenes"—where newcomers were welcomed and taught the ropes.

So these days, the kitchen has been replaced with festivals. People gather at these events from all over the country to jam, learn, and just hang out around other old-time musicians. Nowadays, the best old-time musicians are just as likely to be from New York or Seattle as from a tiny town in Virginia. In more recent years, younger "revivalists" have brought old-time music to mainstream audiences again—in Hollywood films like *Cold Mountain,* or in authentic but polished bands that appeal to the modern audience.

> **Fiddle Facts**
>
> Where did you come from, where will you go? Where did you come from, Cotton Eyed Joe?
>
> —Refrain to "Cotton Eyed Joe"

The Regions

The term "old-time music" is actually a product of the recording industry. No one had a name for it back in the day. It was just the music that people played at home and in the community. They lived, partied, married, and died where their families had lived for decades or centuries. Sometimes, several generations of families rarely met anyone who lived farther than 30 miles away.

However, at the start of the twentieth century, fiddlers traveled from the rural places where they lived and went into the recording studios. The record labels' marketing executives decided that they needed a name. What to call string band music, music that had been a part of American history for centuries? The labels first tried out less flattering titles such as "hillbilly," but "old time" seemed to fit the bill, and stuck.

But old time covers a lot of ground. In geographic terms, Ireland and Scotland together encompass about 60,000 square miles. The United States? Over 3.5 *million* square miles. Well over half of that area boasts some form of music that is considered old time. You can spread a lot of jams over all that land! Different regions of the United States, of course, created different styles of music from place to place:

- ◆ Appalachia is probably the most well-known region for old-time music. People associate the sound of twanging fiddle and banjo with the mountains, and they're not wrong. The states of Kentucky, Tennessee, West Virginia, and Virginia all have very strong traditions of old-time music. The music survived for centuries, as generations were isolated in the hills and mountains. These pockets created by the hills and hollers also meant that, even within each state, there are many distinct and different styles of music.

◆ The South isn't all mountains, though. The eastern half of North Carolina, known as the Piedmont, is a great area for old-time music, as are the states of the non-Appalachian South, like Alabama, Mississippi, and Georgia.

◆ There is also a strong fiddle tradition in the Midwest, mostly to be found in the Ozarks of Missouri and Arkansas.

◆ In the Southwest, Texas and Oklahoma's version of old time often featured a more "long-bow" style of playing that later evolved into Western swing music.

Bowing

If you find the ornaments of Irish and Scottish fiddling just twists your fingers into a tizzy, then old time might be for you. Aside from the occasional grace note, old-time music doesn't depend on ornamentation to give tunes personality. Complexity and individual style are largely found in the bowing. The bowing alone renders the powerful syncopation, accents, and phrases that characterize old-time fiddling.

If you continue to learn old time, you'll discover a whole range of more complicated bowing patterns that vary by region and style. In this book, we stick to the simplest versions of these:

◆ The saw is what it sounds like. It means, basically, no slurring. You simply move the bow back and forth, using one bow stroke for one note. The music that uses this type of bowing, which is most of old time, is called "short bow" music, as opposed to "long bow," which is a main feature of modern bluegrass. A good saw bow stroke gives a tune a simple yet powerful drive, and a real straight-ahead feel.

◆ The shuffle is a combination of sawing and slurring. The Nashville shuffle is the most basic version. This is a two-beat note (or a two-note slur) followed by two separately bowed notes. The sound is probably familiar to you, as the pattern is often used to kick off country tunes. There are other, more complex shuffles as well.

As they use these different bow strokes, old-time musicians make use of changing pressure from their bow hand to create effects on the notes they are playing. In the middle of a long note, the fiddler can throw some pressure onto the bow to create an accent. This adds rhythm to a note that otherwise would be long and unadorned.

Droning

Irish and Scottish music can make use of drones to emphasize certain notes. Old time, however, takes this to the next level. Being on one string at a time is more of an exception than a rule. Old-time fiddlers are constantly letting an open string ring out over or below their melodic line.

Tune Up

One way to get an instant old-time sound is by droning an open string with a fourth finger of matching pitch. For example, try playing your open A and at the same time, a fourth-fingered A on the D string.

Droning can be almost constant throughout the tune. Other times, a musician might lay off the drones and then stick them back in order to bring out a passage, or emphasize some syncopation. Some fiddlers prefer more droning than others, and some regional styles feature more droning than others, as well. Here are two things to think about when learning the basic technique behind droning:

- Droning is achieved by playing two strings at once. To drone well, you need to get your bow hair at the precise point where it draws across both strings with a good, strong, steady tone.

- When you play on only one string, you actually have a fairly large angle to work with. To see what I mean, play an open string. As you bow back and forth, play with little movements of your arm angle. You will find that when playing one string, you have more room to work with than you thought. So when you are playing music that uses drones, try to let your bow hang out as *close* to a double stop as possible. Then, when you want to produce a double stop, a little movement from your bow arm or a little added pressure from your index finger will do the trick.

Double Stops

Droning is one form of chording—while you play the main note, an open string provides some harmony. Sometimes you want a little more variety than just an open string while you fiddle, though. Double stops can give a clearer sound than droning. They also can vary up the chord you have been playing.

If you play two strings that are both fingered, it is a double stop. This is a little trickier than droning, because it means that you have to pay attention to the intonation of two notes, not just one. If either note is sharp or flat, then the chord won't sound good.

Tunes

While many of the tunes in the old-time repertoire are directly descended from the music of Scotland and Ireland, the tune types are not as diverse. The majority of dance tunes fall into what would probably be considered a reel in the Old World. Tunes like jigs and polkas are not really found in old-time music, though waltzes, and to a lesser extent, hornpipes can be found.

 Tune Up

With so much droning in old-time fiddling, I'm not going to write it into the tunes. Just listen for it in the audio DVD, and as you try the melody, at the same time, play an open string below or above it.

To start you off with that old-time sound, here's a really simple old-time tune, "Black-Eyed Susie." Leave that third finger down on the A string when you are leading into it for a smooth sound.

Black-Eyed Susie.

"Sally Ann" is one of the best-known tunes in the repertoire, and you should be able to work on your fourth finger droning.

Sally Ann.

Tune Up

Find some old recordings of "Cluck Old Hen," and at some point you'll hear the fiddle being plucked with the left hand to imitate the chicken.

The tune "Cluck Old Hen" is another simple tune, but it makes great use of a syncopated rhythm, so that each part actually starts before the downbeat. This one is almost entirely made up of fourth finger and open-string droning. Try to toggle the bow to be stronger on one or the other in order to create some pulses in the melody.

Key of D—A Mixolydian.

Key of D

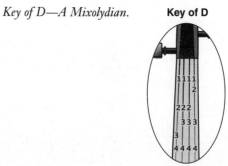

Cluck Old Hen.

"Turkey in the Straw" is a tune that is familiar to most Americans, since it has been used in popular culture for over two centuries.

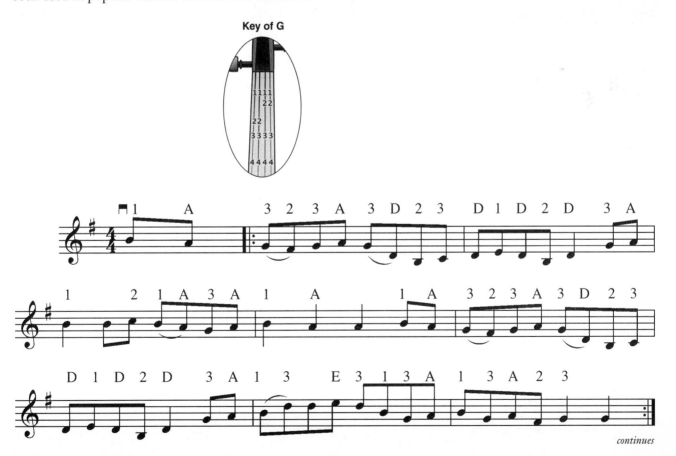

continues

Turkey in the Straw.

"Hop Light Ladies" is a tune that shows the connections between Scotland, Ireland, and old time, because it is the American cousin of the commonly played Irish tune "Miss MacLeod's Reel." This and "Arkansas Traveler" are based on the playing of fiddler Gordon Tanner. His father, Gid Tanner, led a popular band of the 1920s, The Skillet Lickers.

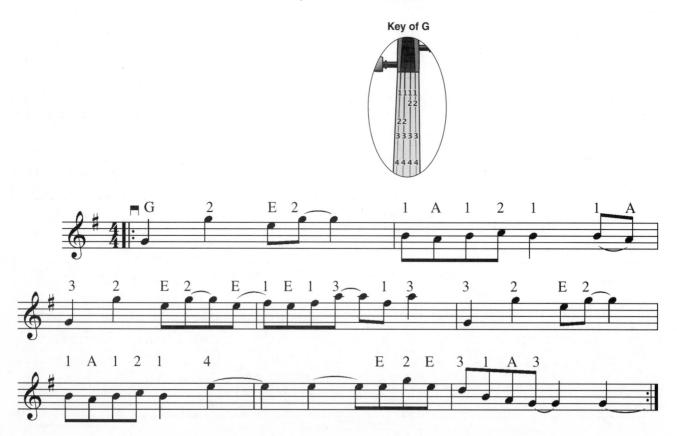

Hop Light Ladies.

continues

continued

Arkansas Traveler.

Key of D—A Mixolydian.

Key of D

Old Joe Clark is another common old-time tune.

"Cotton Eyed Joe" is a simple melody with many variations. But fair warning—
it is a much trickier tune to play than it looks. It is a good one for changing up
the notes each time you play it. You should be pretty much constantly droning
either the A or the E strings.

Cotton Eyed Joe.

Here is the "Fisher's Hornpipe," just for something fun to finish the chapter up with.

Fisher's Hornpipe.

The Least You Need to Know

♦ The offbeat nature and complex bowing style of old time makes listening to the music especially important.

♦ The term "old time" encompasses a wide range of regional styles of music.

♦ Old time depends greatly on a strong rhythm, and utilizes a great deal of droning and chording to achieve a full sound.

Chapter 12

Bluegrass Music

In This Chapter

- ◆ How Bill Monroe invented a musical genre
- ◆ Why you never hear solo bluegrass fiddle
- ◆ How a bluegrass band works
- ◆ Bluegrass bowing and style
- ◆ Some traditional bluegrass breakdowns

Bluegrass music is truly an all-American style of music. It is a descendant of old time, but also has some influences from blues and jazz. Unlike old time and other traditional music, it is music for the stage. Bands put together arrangements and harmonies that are pleasing to a modern audience's ear. The music is marked by tricky double stops, haunting melodies, and improvisational solo breaks.

Traditional fiddle styles depend on crafting a specific feel and rhythm within a "simpler" tune. But the best bluegrass fiddlers today exhibit technical skills that easily rival the most virtuoso classical musicians.

This chapter is a little start in that direction for you. You get to try a few of the standard tunes, many of which were pulled out of the old-time tradition to become bluegrass standards as well. You learn about double stops and chords, and also try out a few "tags"—little phrases that mark the end of a tune.

Bill Monroe and the Blue Grass Boys

Bluegrass is definitely an all-American form of music, born and raised here. The most interesting thing about it, though, is that it is also pretty much the creation of one man, Bill Monroe. He was born into a farming family in Rosine, Kentucky, in 1911. His mother played several instruments and loved to sing and dance. After his older brothers took up the fiddle and the guitar, he took up the mandolin. Eventually, he would revolutionize the way the instrument and his native music was played.

In the 1930s he and his brother Charlie left their jobs at an oil refinery near Chicago to try their hands at a music career. They began performing on the radio as a duo called The Monroe Brothers, and were very successful. The act lasted until the two headstrong and competitive men needed to part ways.

Monroe's next step was to form a band, which he eventually called Bill Monroe and his Blue Grass Boys. He took his new act and auditioned for the Grand Ole Opry. He was asked to start that Saturday. He toured with the Boys from 1938 until his death in 1996 and was the only member to be in the band from beginning to end.

Monroe took the music from his rural Kentucky home and rendered it into something new. He played his music fast, with strong percussive rhythm from the mandolin, guitar, and banjo. He sang in a high voice, often falsetto, and worked out concise and haunting harmony lines to old gospel songs and new compositions he penned. Monroe liked to try out harmonies with fiddles, too, and sometimes used up to three fiddles at once.

Some believe that his greatest score was the addition of Earl Scruggs to the band's lineup. Earl's three-finger-roll banjo style became an indispensable part of the band's sound, and of the genre itself.

Many bluegrass fiddle players got their start by spending some time as a Blue Grass Boy. Monroe demanded a very high level of musicianship of anyone in his band. When a musician left the band after a stint of touring with Monroe, it's almost certain that they left able to play better than when they had started.

Modern-Day Sounds

While Bill Monroe may have invented bluegrass single-handedly, there is no doubt that the music has grown within and beyond his creation. There are hundreds of bluegrass bands that work within the framework and sound that he pioneered. But there are countless others that are experimenting with the sound, blending it with other forms of music.

Many bluegrass musicians and fans consider the definition of "bluegrass" to mean the sound and repertoire of Bill Monroe—period. Anything else is an imposter. In this way, bluegrass has joined Irish, Scottish, and old-time music. In all of these genres, people are constantly arguing, sometimes passionately, about what constitutes "real" music, and what does not—and perhaps, what is an affront to the very notion of music itself. These people often are called purists. They consider themselves defenders of authenticity.

Purists are valuable to any musical tradition. They keep the essential elements of the music alive. As a result, aspiring musicians can continue to learn from them. Many musicians believe that to become great at any style of music, you've got to start with the music or musicians who began it. By learning the "pure" form of the music well, you make sure that you understand the spirit of the music. This is what is referred to as putting the music in context.

Fiddle Facts

Over Bill Monroe's performing career, he hired almost 400 different musicians to play in the Blue Grass Boys.

Fiddle Facts

Bluegrass is nothing but a hillbilly version of jazz.
—Kenny Baker

From there, if you choose to branch out with the music, expanding its horizons, you can. You know that the roots are there holding you down no matter how far you wander. In the end, only the audiences can decide whether or not the music is worth listening to.

In recent decades, younger, more experimental musicians began to use jazzy chords that expanded what was possible with the bluegrass harmonies. Particularly modern-sounding bluegrass is often referred to as "newgrass." Mandolinist David Grisman pioneered a jazz/bluegrass hybrid he called "Dawg." His collaboration with Grateful Dead guitarist Jerry Garcia probably helped vastly expand the fan base of bluegrass music.

In recent years, fiddler and singer Alison Krauss has imbued bluegrass with a more modern Nashville singer/songwriter sound. This has been very successful with audiences and critics alike: Krauss has won 20 Grammys. Dan Tyminski, a member of her band Union Station, was featured on the soundtrack to *O Brother, Where Art Thou?* It became the best-selling bluegrass album of all time. Young bands like Nickel Creek and stalwarts like the Del McCoury Band continue to tour successfully around the United States. Interest in bluegrass continues to expand to include not only audiences in America, but abroad in places like Europe and Japan.

Fiddle Facts
It seems like bluegrass people have more great stories to tell than other musicians.
—Dan Fogelberg

Chops, Anyone?

Bluegrass is different from the other genres of music you've learned so far. For one thing, the Irish, Scottish, and old-time traditions have a long history of solo musical performances. At a country dance event, a solitary musician would provide the music as people got down to the mean sound of ringing metal strings. Even today, you can go and hear a concert of solo fiddle music, and it wouldn't be too strange. Traditional fiddle music is meant to be self-contained.

But there is no such thing as solo bluegrass fiddle, because bluegrass is band music. It is almost never performed with less than four, or (even better) five people. Most likely, a band's instrumentation includes guitar, mandolin, bass, five-string banjo, and of course, the fiddle. A *dobro* often is thrown into the mix, too.

So you're not going to hear any solo fiddles sawing away in bluegrass music. But the four or five members of the band aren't just up there playing randomly, either. Bluegrass has a definite format. Here's how the musical arrangement of one song might flow:

def•i•ni•tion

A **dobro** is a guitar with a metal resonator built into the instrument instead of a sound hole.

A **breakdown** is the bluegrass word for a fast fiddle or banjo tune.

1. The fiddle (or the banjo) starts off the *breakdown*, or kicks off a vocal number with an instrumental theme. The bowed melody rings out, intertwined with the rhythmic strums of a guitar and the three-fingered rolls of the five-string banjo.

2. The fiddle fades out as the vocalist begins the song. Most bluegrass music is centered around the vocals.

3. During verses or other instrumental solos, the fiddler gives up the role as the big-cheese melody instrument, and becomes part of the rhythm and chords of the song. The bow is used percussively, as short, steady chops against the string produce a crunchy-sounding chord. The fiddler might play a counterpoint to the vocal melody as well.

4. In between verses, the fiddler throws in a short little phrase or two, to fill the vacuum left by the singer. This phrase will lead into the next verse.

5. At some point in the song, the singer takes a break. (Or if it is an instrumental number, the fiddler finishes playing through the breakdown.) It's time for solos. This is where bluegrass resembles jazz more than any older fiddle tradition. Each instrument—guitar, banjo, dobro, fiddle, bass—can take a turn improvising. The banjo will throw out a solo full of three-finger rolls. The guitarist shows off his flatpicking skills. The bass player might roll out her percussive slaps and double time plucks. And the fiddler will blaze a path of lightning-fast scales and arpeggios, chords, and double stops. All these hint at the original breakdown, or perhaps the melody of the song. But this is also each musician's moment to emerge from the rolling texture of the band's sound; the audience will see all members show off their chops—that is, just how darn good they are on their individual instruments.

Fiddle Facts

One of Elvis Presley's first hits, "Blue Moon of Kentucky," was a Monroe cover song.

In bluegrass, fiddlers have become very technically proficient. From the start, Bill Monroe usually chose "fiddle-unfriendly" keys to suit his singing voice. This meant keys with lots of sharps and flats, so fingering was rarely simple. Fiddlers quickly had to learn to play in odd keys. This immediately raised their playing technique to the next level.

Many of these keys meant that open-string droning didn't work as well anymore, so fiddlers learned to pull off some complex double stops. They learned to change smoothly from one double stop to another.

Bowing also became complex. Bluegrass fiddlers use several different types of shuffles. They mostly use a long-bow style of playing, with lots of notes crammed into one bow stroke. During all of this, the fiddlers must achieve a great tone.

Bluegrass fiddling also involves a lot of "playing up the neck." Most traditional fiddlers keep their hand in the *first position* on the neck (with the exception of a few tunes). In first position, the first finger is placed one whole step above the open string. This is what you have used so far.

However, bluegrass fiddlers are constantly called upon to *shift positions*. They regularly pull up the anchor and move their hand up and down the neck. This is done when the fiddler wants to reach higher notes, such as the ones above the high B on the E string. Another reason to shift is that many double stops are difficult to play in first position. By shifting, some chord configurations are easier.

Modern country and bluegrass has demanded even more technically proficient players than in the past. Today's studio fiddlers need a flawless tone, impeccable intonation, and great chords. They also need the ability to go in and "nail" a solo or two on a song.

All of this means that if you learn how to play bluegrass fiddle, you probably will have gained enough technique to play in any other type of modern band as well.

Bowing Patterns

The bowing in bluegrass, like all fiddling, is largely up to the player's individual style. However, there is a lot more slurring of notes in bluegrass than there is in any of the traditional music we've learned so far. This is called long bow (as opposed to the short bow of old time, which involves a lot of sawing back and forth).

The most basic form of bowing in bluegrass is the Nashville shuffle. This is, in 4/4 time, two quarter notes slurred followed by two sawed notes.

In most of the tunes in this chapter, I keep the bowing fairly basic—a few Nashville shuffles here, a couple longer bows there. As you speed up the tunes, bowing that worked when it was being played more slowly might feel strange when played faster. Change it up if you like some other way better. Just make sure it works with that strong bluegrass backbeat!

Slides

Bluegrass music makes great use of slides. You definitely are familiar with this if you've heard any form of country music. Popular country singers often slide into their notes, and their fiddlers do, too.

The country fiddle slide is much less subtle than the one used in Irish music. It definitely conjures up that "yee-haw!" feeling. The ultimate tune for sliding—back and forth, even—is the famous tune "The Orange Blossom Special." That degree of sliding isn't out of place in any bluegrass song. (Okay, maybe I exaggerate just a little.) Just start with your finger almost a whole step below the note you are aiming for, and then slide it up into place as you bow. Of course, this should work within the tempo of the tune you're playing—but you want to add some nice twang into your playing, and you're not ashamed to, either!!!

Double Stops

Old time uses a few double stops, but it mostly makes use of droning open strings. However, bluegrass makes great use of double stops, some simple and some tricky. This is out of both necessity and growing virtuosity, because many bluegrass songs are in keys that just don't work with a droning open string.

Fiddlers can double stop out of one chord into another. This involves changing one finger while the other one holds down a solid note. Or it can mean changing both fingers. Either way, it has to be done smoothly.

> **Tune Up**
>
> One way to ensure good-sounding double stops is to make sure that the bow and both fingers are pressing firmly on the strings.

Try this combo of the Nashville shuffle with some double stops, and you've got the intro to many a bluegrass song—at least the ones in the key of D! If you are feeling really crazy, try sliding into the double stop to start it off, too.

A simple double-stopped shuffle kicks off a tune.

Tags

A bluegrass song is almost never complete without a tag ending. This is a short little phrase that ends the tune. There are a few basic ones, and then hundreds of variations on them. No matter what form it takes, the tag should always make it clear that the song is ending, leaving you in that country state of mind.

Here is one of the most generic of tag endings. The second half is all droned, so play both the D and G string. There are many versions of this ending, with the first half almost intact and the second half improvised to the fiddler's personal taste.

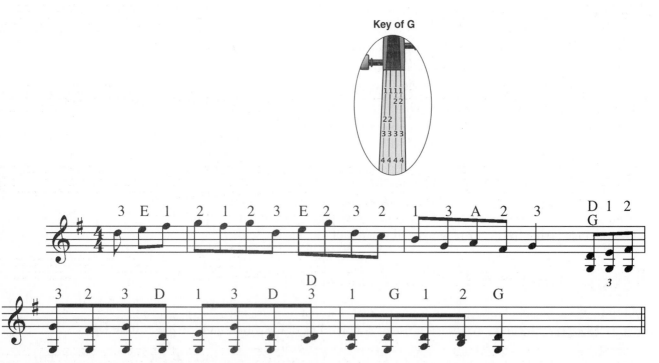

After the last time through a melody, end it something like this.

The Breakdowns

Let's start off with "St. Ann's Reel," a bluegrass tune that comes from old time and is common in French Canadian repertoire as well. Try out some simple double stops in this one.

continues

St. Ann's Reel.

The classic "Red Wing" has lots of long notes in its most basic form. The better you get at improvising, of course, the sooner you can turn those long notes into a frenzy of runs. In the meantime, try a few double stops, especially the fourth finger/open-string droning.

Red Wing.

False Notes

The improvisation in bluegrass means that a written version of the tune is used as a *jumping-off point,* rather than a "skeleton." Once the tune is played through for the first time, you might not hear it in that form again until the end. Only the chords stay the same. What each instrumentalist does with it is up to them. This means that in this book, I've written out my own interpretations of the basic versions of the tunes—but it is only one version of hundreds.

So don't depend too long on the written music in this chapter—eventually, you'll need to listen to a lot of different versions, and learn how to come up with your own version, and then improvise the heck out of it!

"Whiskey Before Breakfast" is a tune that is constructed mainly of scales, and once you get going, it should flow right under your fingers. Aim for super-smooth bowing on this one.

Key of G

Whiskey Before Breakfast.

"Forked Deer" is a fun one with a fairly straight-ahead A part in D major. The more syncopated second part switches to A Mixolydian. The second part can be made even more dense by adding drones over the melody. Experiment with it.

Forked Deer.

"Temperance Reel" is another one that can really flow smoothly under your fingers once you get it. "Bill Cheatham" is an enjoyable one, too. "Katy Hill" brings in an abrupt, early ending of the phrases.

Temperance Reel.

continues

continued

Bill Cheatham.

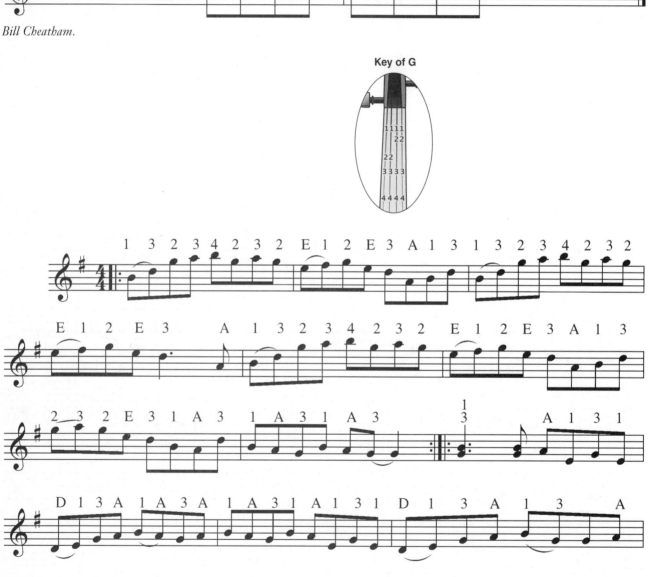

Katy Hill.

Try changing from double stop to double stop in the tune "Dixie Hoedown."
This is a simple change, but it could be tricky if you've never done it before.

continues

continued

Dixie Hoedown.

Tune Up

A great tune to listen to for double stop changes is the tune "Lonesome Moonlight Waltz" on the recording *Kenny Baker Plays Bill Monroe.*

The Least You Need to Know

◆ Bluegrass was invented by mandolin player Bill Monroe, who toured with his band the Blue Grass Boys for nearly 60 years.

◆ Unlike other traditional music, bluegrass tunes aren't played over and over; rather, they are improvised on—much like in jazz.

◆ Bluegrass can demand technical proficiency, because fiddlers often play in higher positions at rapid tempos.

◆ Use lots of double stops, drones, slides, shuffles, and slurring to obtain a good bluegrass sound.

Part 4

Movin' on Up

At this point, you've played around with some of the different types of melodies from various fiddling genres, all while improving your basic technique. This part takes you to the next level—you continue learning a mix of styles, but as you do, you'll be mastering some of the more difficult skills of fiddle playing. There is a chapter of tunes to just have fun with once you've gotten through all the tutorials in this book, too.

And that's not all—at the end of the book is a chapter on ways to hear more music, and how to successfully get out of the house and play with other people.

"My next piece is called Turkey in the Straw.
Feel free to loosen your bow ties and take off your tiaras."

Chapter 13

Changing It Up

In This Chapter

◆ Using different tunings for the fiddle

◆ How fiddle vibrato can sweeten a long note

◆ Crooked tunes

◆ Variations, improvisation, and backing up singers

So far, you've had a great introduction to the fiddle itself as well as to four genres that often are played on it. Take the time now to go back and play all the songs you've learned. Make sure you've really got that bow under the control you want, and that you can make the left hand do what it is supposed to. Make sure you've got a good bow-arm flow—fingers and wrist first, and elbow and shoulder next. Make sure that your bow arm has the proper mix of balance and strength. Get good and comfortable with the tunes you've learned.

Once you've done that, you're ready for the next few chapters. This chapter lets you try some new and fun things with the fiddle, like alternate tunings and vibrato. You also get an idea of the things you should think about if you want to accompany songs, or vary up tunes.

Alternate Tunings

Hopefully, by this stage you've gotten the hang of tuning up your fiddle in the arrangement known as standard tuning—that is, G, D, A, and E. However, in the past, fiddlers weren't always satisfied with this arrangement. Perhaps they were trying to achieve some different sounds, and they found that tuning the fiddle in the standard way was limiting them—so they started using *alternate tunings.* That is, they decided to change the tuning of their strings so that it wasn't the usual setup. This is especially common in old-time music, where droning is such an important part of the sound.

Some of the ways musicians arrange the strings include tuning the strings an octave apart or a third apart rather than a fifth apart. Obviously, these alternate tunings allow for different harmonic possibilities. In fact, it can change the sound of your fiddle enough that you feel you are playing a completely different instrument altogether!

False Notes

Playing in alternate tunings means that your pegs should be at their optimal "mobility vs. snugness" factor. The pegs should be easy to move, but also easy to secure in place. Otherwise you'll end up spending much more time tuning (and cursing!) your fiddle than actually having fun with alternate tunings.

Here are some of the alternate tunings you'll find in old-time music:

- ADAE: the G string is tuned up one whole step
- GDGD: the A and E strings are tuned down one whole step
- DDAD: the G string is tuned down to a D that is one octave below the normal D string, and the E is tuned down a whole step

Tune Up

With alternate tunings, our "cheating" system will need a little tinkering. I indicate the open string with a letter—if we are in ADAE tuning, then watch out for the "A" that is the G string.

Another method of alternate tuning is to tune the bottom and top strings to the same notes, only an octave apart. This is a trick that was used by Scottish and Irish fiddlers in the past (though players don't use it very often today). When the fiddle is tuned in this arrangement, the two or three strings that are not being played often act as sympathetic strings, ringing along with the music. This gives your fiddle an especially vibrant sound. There are at least three ways of doing this:

- AEAE: the bottom two strings are tuned up one whole step
- GDGD: the top two strings are tuned down one whole step
- ADAD: the G string is tuned up a whole step, and the E string is tuned down one whole step

Tune Up

Playing the fiddle in alternate tunings calls for a whole extra step of memory. Not only do you have to remember how the tune goes and what the name of it is, but you have to remember how to tune the strings before you play it.

The biggest challenge to using different tunings is that your fingers will lose their automatic pitches. For example, in AEAE tuning, instead of a G, the third finger on the D string makes an A. This makes droning along with the A string quite easy. However, it is also easy to forget that you have tuned the strings differently, and hit some truly wrong notes!

The more you change tunings, obviously, the easier it will get, both to tune and retune the fiddle before playing each melody. And once you learn the tune, it's not hard to remember how your fingers go. And then you'll find that playing in different tunings is a great deal of fun. It really is amazing how much changing one or two strings can change the whole sound of your fiddle.

The common old-time tune "Angeline the Baker" is in ADAE tuning. Simply take your low G string and tune it up one whole step to an A.

Angeline the Baker.

The tune "Cumberland Gap" is in ADAD tuning.

Key of D—ADAD tuning.

Cumberland Gap.

Fiddle Facts

The Cumberland Gap was a natural path through the Appalachian Mountains, located on the Kentucky/Virginia border. Originally carved out by a river, it was widened for settlers' wagons in 1796. It was also of great strategic importance in the Civil War.

Here is the tune "Cripple Creek," in AEAE tuning. With this tuning you can take the whole A part and play it down an octave, on the lower two strings, using the same fingering. You'll just have to hop back up an octave for the last few notes at the end, when the melody goes below the A string.

Key of A—AEAE tuning.

Cripple Creek.

Vibrato

Among fiddle players, *vibrato* usually is associated with the lyrical and sweet sound of classical violin, not the rhythmic, dirtier sound of fiddle music. However, fiddle players often use vibrato. The difference is in the style of the vibrato used.

A classical violinist's vibrato is very visible (some awe-inspiring alliteration there, eh?) to a listener at a live performance. When the violinist hits a longer note, she begins to move her left hand back and forth. This causes a strong wiggling of the finger that is pressed against the fingerboard. Often the whole arm is engaged in this movement. This changes the note from a steady one to one that wavers—the pitch goes up and down quickly. The basic note, however, stays the same. It just has a lot of frill on it. The vibrato used by classical violinists is part of the reason that the music has such a formal sound.

Let's say that the vibrato used by a classical player offers the same effect as the decorations you might see in a wealthy person's room a hundred years ago. Lots of lace, gold trim around the edges of the walls, intricate silver teapots on a fancy wooden table.

The vibrato on a fiddle, however, is more like folk art decorating a cabin wall. The tablecloth is a checkered gingham, and the teapot is a brown-clay vessel. Simple and sparse, it all still manages to add a little flair to its surroundings! This is what you are looking for in fiddle vibrato.

Now, there is no one style of fiddle vibrato. Different fiddlers definitely have different approaches. Bluegrass players these days actually can have fairly powerful vibrato that is closer to classical music than the type other fiddlers use. But old time and Irish players, with their more spare, rustic sounds, would definitely stick to vibrato that is on the simpler side.

Vibrato is used on longer notes. It's not necessary on faster notes. It would get in the way, and bow-hand rhythm and left-hand ornaments will ensure that the note is interesting enough. But when a note is drawn out, or a slow waltz or air is on the menu, vibrato is not out of place.

Here's the most basic technique for fiddle vibrato: vibrate or shake your hand—almost imperceptibly, but very quickly—as you hold down a note (not an open string, of course). The result should sound like the note is slightly shivering, as opposed to the strong wavering sound of a classical violinist. However, the back-and-forth motion should be in a fairly steady rhythm. Otherwise, it will just sound like your hand is spazzing out! The hand actually needs a bit of tension to achieve the sound—a tension that should be released once the note is over, of course! The result is a note that has a little more color to it. Voilà!

Obviously it is difficult to demonstrate vibrato in the pages of a book. So listen, observe, and learn—then try it out for yourself. Eventually you will find a sound that makes you happy.

Fiddle Facts
Before the advent of the recording industry, even classical violinists didn't use the strident vibrato so common today. But when recorded using the rudimentary technology of the early twentieth century, violinists found they could cut through the static when they added a good ole' warble.

Off the Beat-en Tunes

Up to now, you've played tunes in 4/4, 6/8, 2/4, and so on. When you got a time signature at the start of a tune, you expected it to dictate the entire tune. Also, at this stage you have probably gotten used to tunes that consist of A, B, and maybe C or D parts that are made up of four or eight bars.

However, in old-time and bluegrass fiddle, you'll often encounter tunes that are "crooked." This means that there are extra bars or half bars, when extra notes are added. A fiddler back in the day decided that a note just had to be held longer, or started earlier, to sound the best. There can be bars left out, as well. Crooked sometimes simply means that phrases don't go as expected.

"Clinch Mountain Backstep" is a tune made famous by the Stanley Brothers, on their very first recording. It goes crooked in the B part with an extra half bar. Learn it, then go find a five-string banjo player to jam with!

Key of G   *Key of G—A Dorian.*

continues

continued

Clinch Mountain Backstep.

Irish and Scottish tunes generally follow a straight AB, AABB, or AABBCC pattern (and so on). Old-time music, however, is more loose with this concept. There are tunes that don't follow a strict AB pattern. Parts are likely to jump around. Try out the tune "Jenny on the Railroad," which goes AABBCCB.

Key of D—A Mixolydian.

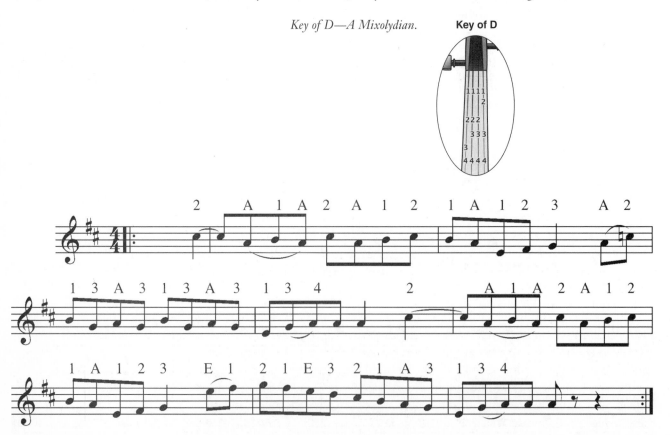

Jenny on the Railroad.

Playing with Songs

If you are content to only play tunes, whether in your own kitchen, at jams, or onstage, then you never have to worry about this particular topic. Playing with songs can be a challenge for someone who has only played fiddle tunes. That's because the fiddler is always the melody instrument in traditional music. As a result, many fiddlers are content to play the melody and let someone else (usually the guitarist) worry about trifles like the key of the song. After all, the fiddler just has to play the notes and a tune is born!

Playing with songs, however, takes a completely different way of thinking about the music. When a fiddler is playing with a singer, they have to think as an accompanist, not just a melody maker. A fiddler has to be aware of things like *chord progression*, the order of chords in the song. Thinking about chords means you have to think about the notes that surround the central note. For instance, if you are playing a D, is it a D major, a G major, or a B minor chord? Each of these three chords means that you'll need different notes to play harmony.

The other thing to remember when playing along with songs is that *not playing* sometimes becomes even more important than playing. In a song, the singer is the star, not the fiddler! So everything you play has to complement what the singer is doing, not compete with or ruin it. This often means not playing at all.

If playing underneath the verse, the fiddler has to match the chords and also provide a nice harmony to layer under the singer's voice.

Between verses, you can simply play a fiddle rendition of the verses. Or you can come up with some clever passage that hints at the melody, while achieving its own identity. Or you can come up with a riff that just makes the song sound cooler, but doesn't really sound anything like what the singer is doing.

The best way to learn how to play along with songs is, as always, to listen to how other fiddlers do it. Nashville country fiddle players are the masters of this craft, as the best ones have played on hundreds, if not thousands, of songs. Listening to bands can provide some insight as well. Then find a singer near you who is willing to let you have a go as she belts out her favorites.

Variations

Like lightning, a version of a fiddle tune should never strike the same performance twice. In traditional music, as I've said, the tune written down on paper is a "skeleton" of that tune. Each individual player will have their own version, and also make changes—variations—to the melody as they repeat it.

In general, Scottish music doesn't make much use of variations. Irish music makes huge use of it, and so does old time. No self-respecting fiddler would play a tune the same way twice in either of these traditions! Variations can be accomplished in a number of different ways:

- **Change the pitch of certain notes.** Finding which notes to change is the tricky part. You want to maintain the melody, but add a few surprises—instead of going up a note, you could go down. Instead of a G, you could play an A, B, or D, depending on what kind of effect you're going for.

- **Change the length of notes.** A note could be held longer (substituting for notes before or after it) or a pair of notes could be changed to a triplet, and vice versa.

- **Make good use of chords and drones.** If you want to accentuate a note, add a drone or a chord to it. If you have used drones on a passage once, try it without it next time. Use a different chord than you did last time.

- **Stop!** That is, put a pause in at an opportune moment. Silence is golden, and it will add a bit of drama to the tune. This technique should be used sparingly, as it's definitely heavy-handed. It can really be effective if you pull it out of the hat at the right time, though!

- **Change up the ornaments you are using.** If a note was ornamented last time, you can use a different ornament, or you can you leave it out altogether. Or vice versa.

- **Change the *dynamics*.** This is a more modern idea—in the old days, you just played as loud as you could, so as to be heard over the dancers. In a session or jam, this kind of variation is a bit pointless unless it is felt by the whole group (which happens, and it's kind of cool when it does). However, when performing, going quieter or louder to emphasize a certain passage can be a very effective tool.

def•i•ni•tion

Dynamics means how loudly or softly a musician plays a note or series of notes.

Improvising

Improvising is definitely a bluegrass schtick. It is a form of variation, but taken to the next level. Instead of playing the basic melody, you change it up or leave it behind altogether. Teaching improvising is a little like teaching a baby how to talk. You can show and tell, but it's up to the learner to listen and figure it out, and finally, to come up with his own ideas about what to say.

Most people learn how to improvise by—big surprise here—listening. The more you hear, the more certain tricks and runs will get into your head, and then your fingers.

Improvising can call for some plain old-fashioned technical practicing. As I've mentioned, bluegrass makes use of some keys that are on the more difficult side for the fiddle. Make sure you are familiar with your scales, arpeggios, and keys. You don't necessarily have to practice these things endlessly, but it can only help your playing to do a bit of it.

When you practice improvising on a song, start out by making a note of the key. Play a scale based on the key. Then play a few modes. If you are in E flat major, then play an E flat major scale, up and down a few times. Then try the F Dorian mode, or the A flat Mixolydian mode. Play these scales. Some runs based on these will sound great in your solos. Also, knowing your scale means you can try to pull off some of the blistering runs that are a staple of bluegrass.

Tune Up

Here's the best way to learn improvisation: pick your favorite bluegrass (or jazz, or Western swing) fiddler. Pick a song that he or she has recorded, and learn the solos note by note. After a few songs of this, you might find that coming up with your own solos gets easier and easier.

The Least You Need to Know

- Old-time musicians often play tunes for which the fiddle is tuned in an arrangement other than G, D, A, and E.
- Vibrato should be used sparingly and subtly, but can add great color to the right notes.
- A fiddler should aim to be unobtrusive and complementary when playing with a singer.
- In Irish, old-time, and bluegrass music, no fiddle tune should ever be played the same way twice.
- Practicing scales and arpeggios can be good preparation for improvising, but learning actual solos note for note is the best way to go about kindling your creative impulse.

Chapter 14

Playing "Up the Neck"

In This Chapter

◆ Shifting your left hand on the fiddle neck

◆ Avoiding a "fear of heights"

◆ Trying out different positions

Fiddlers, in general, remain down in first position on the neck. This is where your left hand has been in all the tunes you've played thus far. In fact, many fiddlers *never* leave first position. If you want to stay there, that's fine with me. But you may find that you want more of a challenge. Or you might find yourself most interested in bluegrass fiddling. If this is the case, you'll have to leave your comfy spot near the peg nut, and venture further up the heights of the neck. Because part of being a hot bluegrass fiddler is playing some high notes!

This chapter goes over some of the rudiments of shifting positions. There are a few different resting spots once you leave first position. I give you some pointers on the best way to find your way around up there in the fiddle neck stratosphere!

Shifting

So you've decided that you're ready for the next step. You are feeling restless where you are—that is, in first position. You're feeling cramped. Stuck. Kind of … low. You want, in short, to play tunes with higher notes. And you're wondering how to get there.

Don't call Dr. Phil! You just need a little coaching on technique and you'll be good to go. Your left hand is the key. Now is a good time to check and make sure it is in a good state. Even in first position, it should be relaxed, loose, and gently circling the neck. This becomes even more important if you want to shift up the neck.

False Notes

When you shift up, don't leave your thumb behind—take it with you so it doesn't interfere with good intonation.

Being relaxed is necessary once you start moving around. You don't want to find that you are stuck because your thumb has a death grip on your instrument! At the same time, you want your hand to feel sure where it is, not blindly groping around for notes. The key is to lose tension, but at the same time, to be very sure of where each finger needs to go. This is what will produce a solid, clear, in-tune note no matter how high up you go.

Before we try playing any actual notes in other positions, just experiment with the feeling of moving your hand up and down the neck. Don't worry so much about whether the distance is correct, just make a note of how far your hand has to move when your first finger goes from a B to a C natural on the A string. For now, just introduce yourself to finding first position again correctly once you have left it:

1. Move your hand up a half-step distance, and go back to first position. Test with your bow to see if you've gotten back to the right spot.

2. Move up a whole step, go back to first.

3. Shift three whole steps up, and then return to first.

4. Shift up so that the fingers are reaching for the part of the fingerboard that hangs over the belly of the fiddle itself. Try playing a few screechy notes up there. See if you feel loose, then shift back down to first position and play a few notes. Get yourself used to the feeling of pulling up anchor and letting your hand be mobile on the fiddle neck.

Avoiding Vertigo

Playing in different positions can be a bit daunting at first. For one thing, you've probably gotten mighty comfortable in your first position comfort zone. When all of a sudden, a tricky melody demands that you move from first and go up the neck, it can be a bit disconcerting! Here's why:

Once you begin shifting positions, you have to lose the association of numbers, notes, and fingers we've used so far. The A on your E string, for example, no longer belongs to the third finger. It might be played by your second or third finger, or you might be sitting above it, which means you'll have to play it with the A string.

Tune Up

Shifting is a major reason to stop depending on numbers for fingering. Instead, associate a pitch with a note on the staff, and learn to instinctively feel how far apart the notes are on the fingerboard.

Here's another thing: you thought no frets was bad before? Well, the small, persnickety increments on the neck of a fiddle get even smaller as you move up. Each time you move up to a higher position, you'll have a smaller space for squeezing in your scales and your fingers. If you found it difficult to stay in tune in first position, you're in for a real treat now. (In fact, if you still have real trouble finding your notes in first position, do us all a favor and keep practicing there for a while.)

On top of all these developments is some more added pressure: a note that is out of tune in the upper registers, in this case on your E string, sounds more grating than one that is out of tune in the lower registers. (This is a universal truth. Remember all those screechers on *American Idol?*) Also important is your tone: if you still don't have good tone, the higher registers will really shine the high beams on that defect in your playing.

All in all, if you're not confident or solid on the fiddle, once you reach those upper registers, you will gain the powerful and awesome ability to send people fleeing from the room with their hands to their ears. I suppose this is one way to get rid of your pesky in-laws during the holidays. Really, though, this is a power for evil, not for good. So if you don't want to find yourself wondering if everyone in the room is eating lemons (except those sometimes lucky souls who can't identify an out-of-tune note to save their life. This comes in handy in these situations!), then keep working on your intonation!

You can, however, learn to shift positions with confidence. You'll start exploring the different positions in the next section. As you do so, try to identify the finger in each one that, for you, feels the easiest to find. This might be the finger that feels the best to you, or sounds the best to you. Make that finger your anchor. Then play notes. Get used to how the intervals between that finger and the other notes need much less distance between them.

> **Tune Up**
>
> One good note to anchor from in second and third position is the slot where your third finger was (A on the E string, for example). When you go even higher, anchor from the note that matches the string above (E on the A string).

Positions

So the root position for your left hand is first position. While fiddlers often don't mention the names, there are also the second position, third position, and so on. These are the places you will go as you move up the neck.

Let's use the key of G to introduce you to shifting, because this is a scale that starts right at the lowest open string of your fiddle. It's also a key you should be very familiar with by now after all those fiddle tunes.

> **Fiddle Facts**
>
> The notes that are one octave above your open string are also a *harmonic*. With your left hand, gently touch the string, instead of pressing down, while bowing. If your finger's in the right spot, it will produce a clear, though airy version of the note, and you're in tune. This is another good spot to anchor from.

Take a moment to play a couple scales in the key of G. Go all the way from the open G string to the E string. Get the intervals of this scale firmly in your head before you go up into the stratosphere.

Now, here's a little sketch of the fiddle neck that you are used to, but with the higher notes of the E string included.

Notes of the fiddle, including the higher registers.

Second position means that your first finger shifts up a half or whole step, so that it now sits where your second finger did in first position. Try this scale.

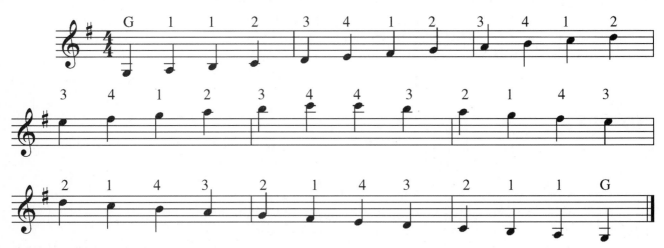

On the G string, you'll shift your first finger up to a B after playing the A.

You'll probably find that one of the trickiest things in second position is keeping your first finger in tune. So far, this finger has always been in the same spot. In a G scale second position, the first finger needs to alternate between the higher position of an F♯ and the lower position of a C♮.

Third position calls for your first finger to shift up to the spot usually filled by your third finger. Try this scale.

Tune Up

Don't flog scales like a dead horse. They are good to practice, but once you've got going on them, try to practice the higher positions by playing real tunes that utilize them. This will keep you more interested.

You'll play the B on the G with your second finger, and then shift up to use your first finger to produce the C.

Fourth position means your first finger is now where your fourth finger would have been—for example, the B on the E string. In this position, you play the same scales as you do in first position, except for the space for your fingers is smaller.

The fourth finger in fourth position is also one full octave above your open string.

For some real-life practice in fourth position, look for the introductory passage to "Monroe's Hornpipe" on the album *Kenny Baker Plays Bill Monroe*. It starts in fourth position, and then shifts down to first at the end.

After playing the C on the G string, you'll shift up to use your first finger to play the D.

Now try to figure out a few more scales, on your own. Play a C major scale, a D major scale, and an A major scale. Try the scales in the second position, third position, and so on.

Try to Fly

Most bluegrass tunes that utilize positions are more modern. Look for the fun and universally known tunes written by Bill Monroe that send you up the fiddle neck. "Jerusalem Ridge" and "Road to Columbus" are two examples.

For now, try the traditional number "Salt Creek." It will take you up into second position. Take a look at the fifth to last measure. You should shift up to second position a note before you actually have to be there, so shift your first finger onto the G. That works a little more smoothly than shifting with your second finger onto the A. I've marked these passages below the notes to give you a further hint.

Salt Creek.

"The Contradiction" is a fairly well-known show tune in the Irish and Scottish traditions. It has been found in different versions in Scotland, Ireland, and Cape Breton. The C part is the one designed to show off your shifting know-how.

In this section, you will first shift up to third position. Next, you will shift up to fourth position in order to reach the high E with your fourth finger without stretching.

3rd Position.......................................

continues

continued

The Contradiction.

Tune Up

Some fiddlers play the entire C part of "The Contradiction" in third position, simply stretching farther to reach the high E. Try it both ways, and do what works for you.

The Least You Need to Know

◆ To reach higher notes on the E string, you'll need to shift up the neck of your fiddle.

◆ Playing in higher positions is a necessary skill if you want to master bluegrass fiddling.

◆ As you shift up the neck, the distance between notes will become shorter—you'll need to adjust your fingerings accordingly.

◆ The key to shifting well is to be relaxed, find a finger to anchor from, and be sure of your fingerings.

Chapter 15

Like NASCAR ... on the Fiddle

In This Chapter

◆ Using your bow arm efficiently for rapid notes

◆ When playing fast is appropriate

◆ Irish rolls

What fiddle player doesn't want to play fast, at least once in a while? After all, it's the ultimate way to impress people. However, it's only impressive if you can pull it off! Otherwise, the only impression you'll leave is a musical scene evocative of a train wreck.

In this chapter, we go over a few basic techniques for exceeding the fiddling speed limit, without going off the rails! Then we'll give you the controls—that is, the fiddle bow—and let you fly on a few tunes.

What Your Bow Arm Needs to Do

So you want to integrate some speed-racing ability into your fiddle playing. First off, you've got to ask yourself if you are ready.

Playing fast is another situation for which you really need to have your rudiments down. If you don't have your technique in order when you are playing slowly, then you are going to sound worse when you start playing at the speed of light.

This chapter gives some pointers on how to speed up your playing, but remember: it is essential that you pay attention to what you are capable of (not just what you *wish* you were capable of)!

Playing quickly requires clean playing. The cleaner, the better. By clean, I mean mixing some good pressure and tone with great coordination. There are three basic ways of squeezing in notes when you play really fast:

False Notes

Some fiddlers can get the false impression that playing something faster makes it sound better. Actually, whizzing by your technical problems can make you feel better, but you are fooling no one!

Tune Up

When really sawing through fast notes, find the point at which the bow is balanced, and try to bounce the notes on and off the string. This clearly separates the notes and yields a percussive effect.

def•i•ni•tion

Musicality does mean good technical ability, but more importantly, it is the ability to infuse music with emotion and moods that affect a listener.

♦ You can put lots of notes in one long bow, resulting in a stream of music.

When you do this, the most important thing is to keep a great tone on the bow while moving a short distance. The goal is to squeeze as many notes in as short of a distance as possible. That way you can concentrate on the notes, instead of worrying about running out of room on the bow.

♦ Play lots of notes separately, using your bow-hand fingers to make tiny movements of the bow.

With this technique, you need to have mastered using only your finger and wrist to move the bow. You may have tried this when playing Irish music triplets; you will need it for every single note when you speed up. Trying to play fast notes with a stiff bow arm is like trying to speed-paint a room: it's only going to look sloppy, there will be spills and missed spots everywhere, and everyone is going to know it, too.

♦ Play with a mix of slurs and sawed notes.

There are certain notes that are more conducive to being played with slurs, and others that do better when played individually. When changing strings quickly, it's often easier to use separate bow strokes. When playing a run on one string, it is easier to use slurs. The rest is feel and timing, and it's up to you to figure out what works best through trial and error, as well as discerning what is going to be your own style.

If you start speeding up and notice you are sloppy, then slow it back down. Only play as quickly as you can match the bow arm to the left-hand fingers.

Good Taste?

You may be familiar with the saying, "More money than sense." Well, the musical equivalent is "more technical ability than sense!"

This is the other issue you'll find with fast playing—that is, the matter of taste. Playing fast is a party trick—a fun and valuable one, for sure—but it is a technical accomplishment more than a musical one. Holding a note a hair longer than expected, then moving on to a note that is out of the ordinary but effective, can really show off musicianship far more than playing fast. So can the simple act of not playing (leaving a little space in the music) if you are in an ensemble or band situation.

This is the question of *musicality*. If you can play fast without difficulty, great! Then you should start to pay attention to whether or not you are spitting out notes that sound interesting to an audience.

Music is, after all, a bit of being human. So do your best to make your music *sound* human, too! And always ask yourself the question: Just because you can play fast, should you?

In some respects, the answer depends on the genre you are in. Lightning-fast runs are a hallmark of bluegrass fiddlers. If you are hoping to play Monroe tunes like a champ, then there is no doubt that blistering solos are definitely something you should be striving to pull off well.

But even in bluegrass, the true artistry comes down to some of the slower riffs. Just as practicing slowly forces you to pay attention to the more difficult parts of fiddle playing, performing a slow tune gives you a chance to show off the fact that you really have polished over your bumps.

So basically, all I'm saying is to make sure that the tempo you've picked out is going to do justice to the music. It can be fun to play fast—but the true test of a musical genius is knowing *when* to put the pedal to the metal, and when a tune is just going to sound better a little slower.

Tunes That May Be Saturated with FAST

So with your technical accomplishments (or limitations!) in mind, here are a few tunes to try out with a higher amount of horsepower—that is, bow-horse-hair power!

"The Laird of Drumblair" is a Scottish tune—a strathspey, but it can also be made straighter (take out the dotted rhythms) and played as a reel. The late fiddler Johnny Cunningham was famous for taking this tune to a speed that made the triplets into a streaming blur of notes. You can find a recording of this feat on the original *Celtic Fiddle Festival* CD. Have fun.

> ### Fiddle Facts
> We consider that the man who can fiddle all through one of those Virginia Reels without losing his grip, may be depended upon in any kind of musical emergency.
>
> —Mark Twain

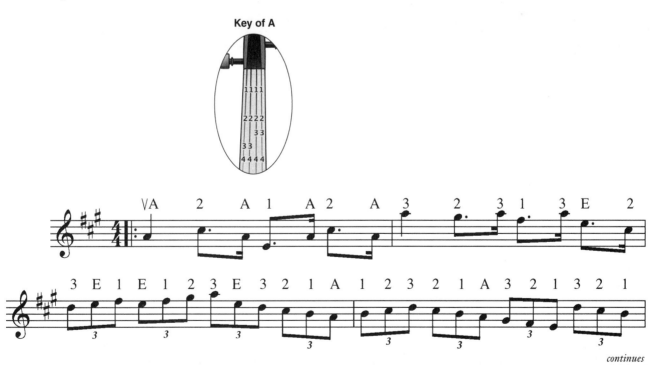

continues

continued

The Laird of Drumblair.

In the bluegrass world, pretty much every tune you've learned can be played blisteringly fast—the tune "Soldier's Joy" included. Try to put your own bowings on this—shuffles, saws, whatever works.

Tune Up _____

I've also thrown in a special bluegrass-style double stop in "Soldier's Joy"— playing a fifth above, instead of the more natural fourth. You'll know it when you hear it. Fiddlers sometimes play runs of quick notes in fifth-interval double stops like this for a really weird effect.

Soldier's Joy.

Irish Rolls

Fast fingers aren't needed for just for those lighting bluegrass runs and solos. In Irish music, the tunes themselves aren't always so fast. In fact, Irish music is often better when it is played a little more slowly. Great artistry comes in Irish music with a rock-solid sense of rhythm and well-executed ornaments. In Irish music, it's the ornaments that often call for quicker fingers.

In Chapter 10, you learned about triplets, grace notes, and slides. I also mentioned rolls, but didn't go into them then. This is because for most people, rolls are the most difficult ornament to master in Irish music.

Part of this is that you need some quickness of fingers to pull off a roll. Rolls can come in several different speeds, but even the more leisurely variety call for some real dexterity of fingers. On top of that, a successful roll demands some real attention to subtlety. Even if you are hitting the fingers just right, the proper feel of a roll is hard to master.

A roll is an elaborate little decoration that definitively brands a piece of music as being Irish. It is basically a way of adding a trill to a note.

Rockin' the Rolls

When you play a roll on a note, first you play the note itself. This identifies which note you are actually on, which is important because it will quickly get decorated beyond recognition! After playing the note, you play a note above, go back to the note, play a note below, and then end on the note.

When you are ornamenting a note played with the first or second finger, you use the *third* finger to play the upper note of the roll. If this is all sounding confusing, here is how it works using our number system:

> 1-3-1-A-1 or 2-3-2-1-2

When you are rolling a third-finger note, you use the fourth finger to play the upper note. Written in numbers, this is:

> 3-4-3-2-3

This is how it is written out in music:

Practicing rolls up and down the scale is also a great way to get them in your fingers.

Start out practicing rolls very slowly. Don't think of them as an ornament at first. Just get your fingers used to the patterns that I outlined in numbers above. Once you feel like you're in a groove, start ramping up the speed a little at a time. The effect you are looking for in rolls is related to that of grace notes. The roll notes should flicker by, and not be heavy-handed. Once you feel like you've got the mechanics of the roll in order, then try playing some in an actual tune.

The timing of rolls is also important. The first note of the roll is emphasized the most. When you play a roll, especially a more leisurely one, this is where you should linger. The rest of the notes will tumble out more quickly. Again, this is subtle and tricky to master, so listen to other fiddle players if you want to master this technique. Everyone has their own style of playing rolls. Shoot for the sound that appeals to you the most.

How Rolls Are Written

I'm going to take a little shortcut, by the way. I'm not going to write out every note of a roll in every tune. (Looking at all those grace notes on a page can make a fiddler's head spin!) Instead, it's up to you to learn what a roll on a note is and put it in yourself.

For example, a roll (left) will be symbolized with the swirl above the note (right)

Jig Roll and Reel Roll

Rolls in jigs and rolls in reels end up working slightly differently. As you can see in the illustration above, a roll is usually actually replacing a three-note set.

In a jig, this is a whole beat (or actually, one tap of the foot, which in jigs is two per measure, or three beats). In a reel, it's usually three-quarters of a tap of the foot. In both cases, the roll needs to fall evenly across the space. This way, it's not rushed. This, in turn, leaves enough space for the next note.

A roll shouldn't be too long or late, either. That will end up throwing off the rhythm of the tune. It's like arriving to a party—if you're a little early or really late, it's a little awkward. Keep things smooth!

Try the following jig first, "Ward's Favorite." The tune is named after an Irish tenor banjo player named Jim Ward, who was an early member of a historical band from Clare called the Kilfenora Ceili Band.

The melody is fairly simple, so you can concentrate on the rolls. As you listen to the recording, note how the roll falls across the beat.

Key of G

Ward's Favorite.

Another easy jig to try out rolls in is "Willie Coleman's."

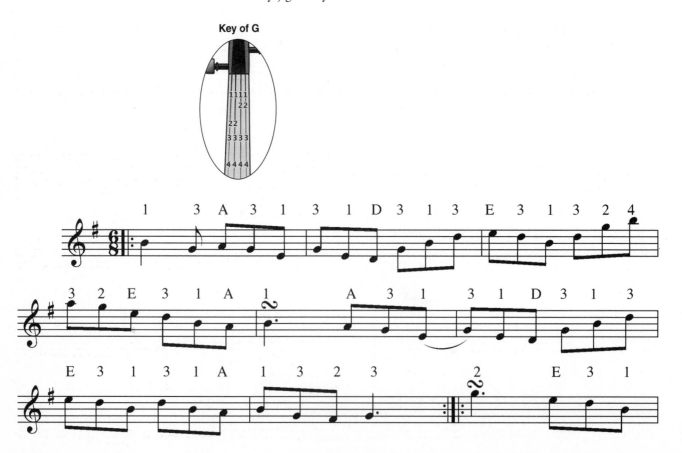

Willie Coleman's.

Compare this to the reel "Ships Are Sailing." The rolls need to move at a little less leisurely pace than in the jigs.

Ships Are Sailing.

The "Boys of Malin" is a reel that displays great rhythm and drive in the first half, and then brings in some rolls for some easygoing grace.

Boys of Malin.

Tune Up

If you continue with Irish music, you will encounter short rolls in reels that replace two notes instead of three (that last one beat, instead of a beat and a half). This demands even faster fingers.

The Least You Need to Know

◆ Make sure your technique issues have been addressed before playing at speedy tempos.

◆ If you are ready to speed up, you are ready to pay attention to good musicality as well.

◆ Rolls are an integral part of Irish music, but they do demand both speedy fingers and a good sense of timing.

Chapter 16

Let's Play "One for the Road"

In This Chapter

◆ Why learning the fiddle never ends

◆ Discovering your individual musical style

◆ A few more tunes to play

At the end of a great session, musicians end the night by playing one for the road. This one often turns into quite a few more! This chapter has some tunes from all styles that will allow you to try out all you've learned, or to just have some fun.

Finding Your Own Style

With the music in this chapter, we're at the end of our musical adventure together. You've learned a lot about playing the fiddle, and learned a lot about what you still have to learn. And if you haven't figured it out yet for yourself, here's the biggest rule of fiddle playing of them all:

> There's always more to learn!

No fiddle player is ever satisfied with his playing. In fact, no musician should be. (If she is, then she's fooling herself.) No matter how good you've gotten, there is always something you can do better, or something new to learn. This is why music never gets old.

Also, there always will be times when you feel like you are not improving, or that you are frustrated with your playing. This is what we call being in a rut. It's important to keep playing anyway—one day, you'll find your musical subconscious has been hard at work fixing the problem and will let your fingers or bow arm know. It's a great feeling—and part of what makes all the practicing worthwhile.

Fiddle Facts

Now, mister, they ain't nobody mastered the fiddle. There's notes in that fiddle ain't nobody found.

—Tommy Jarrell, old-time fiddler of Toast, North Carolina

(Alden, Ray. Liner notes to *Tommy & Fred: The Best Fiddle & Banjo Duets*. County Records, 1993.)

Tune Up _____

One thing to remember is if you feel frustrated by your instrument, not your playing, then it might be time to upgrade to a better-quality "axe."

If you really are frustrated, sometimes taking a break for a few days helps. You might find that some technique finally falls into place when you pick your fiddle back up.

Listen to or go see people who are accomplished on the instrument. Don't obsess too much about their technique—enjoy the music and just let it soak in. It is possible to learn only through listening and absorbing someone else's musicality.

Listening to your favorite players and even learning their music note for note, inflection for inflection, is an invaluable way to learn. The ultimate goal in doing this, though, is to find *your* voice. This is the voice of musical expression that you make through the fiddle, and what marks a great musician.

When you learn through other people's playing, you encounter many different styles, tricks, and techniques. It is up to you to take what you like and leave the rest! And one day, you'll find that you are making the music that you would want to hear yourself.

And a Few for the Road

So, here we are at the end of the music lessons. But we certainly can't leave it at that ... so here's a few more tunes to play. A couple are a little trickier, so I left them for the end. And others are just some that I thought would be fun to play. Sometimes, you don't want to work too hard—you just want to play music!

You might say the first tune here is not a "fowl" melody at all. "Duck River" is a common tune in the old-time tradition.

Fiddle Facts

The actual Duck River is the longest river contained within the Tennessee state line. It was named a State Scenic River by the governor in 2001.

Key of D

Duck River.

"The Butterfly" is an Irish slip jig that is very well known in the tradition. It is a good exercise in keeping things lovely, because the tune can be grating if not played well. Keep your bow arm nice and light, and try to get some emotion through your playing.

Key of G   *Key of G—E minor.*

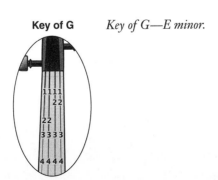

The Butterfly.

"My Love Is in America" is another common Irish reel.

Key of D

My Love Is in America.

"S'Beag S'Mhor" is a waltz written by the Irish harper Turlough O'Carolan in the 1600s. It's a nice piece of music, and well known.

Key of D

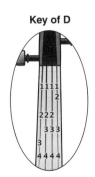

S'Beag S'Mhor.

"Blackberry Blossom" was not named after the personal digital assistant device. It's another common bluegrass tune, with a tricky B part. Just improvise your way out of it if you don't like the way it goes, because everyone else does!

Blackberry Blossom.

Here is another commonly played Irish jig, "Tobin's Favorite."

Tobin's Favorite.

The tune "Red-Haired Boy" is the bluegrass version of an Irish tune called "The Little Beggarman." Hopefully by now you've figured out how different Irish and bluegrass music can be. The tune is almost the same melodically in both traditions … but they are treated very differently. The rhythm, bowing, and ornamentation really change the sound. And, in the bluegrass of course, you will improvise on the melody.

So here is the bluegrass "Red-Haired Boy."

Key of D—A Mixolydian.

Red-Haired Boy.

False Notes

You've been able to try out several different styles in this book. While dabbling is always encouraged, it's best to pick one genre to concentrate on for a while if you want to get really good at one—otherwise, you will most likely end up a jack of all trades, master of none.

Here is the Irish "Little Beggarman." It's actually a hornpipe, so give it a nice swingy feel.

Little Beggarman.

The Least You Need to Know

◆ The fiddle is a lifelong occupation—there is always more to learn, and more to practice.

◆ There will be times when you feel like you are not progressing, but practice through it or even take a short break, and you'll break out of your rut.

◆ Listening to other fiddlers can provide inspiration and ideas for your own playing.

Chapter 17

Get Out and Hear the Music

In This Chapter

- ◆ Ways to find a private teacher
- ◆ How to find more fiddle music to listen to
- ◆ Where to find other people to play with

While this book is an excellent introduction to the world of playing the fiddle, there's no denying that it's impossible to learn everything you need or want to know from one book. You may want to continue exploring all types of music, or you may be steering toward getting really good at one particular style.

There are many ways to improve as a musician. You can enlist the help of a local private fiddle teacher. Going out or staying in and listening to the music you love is essential. There are also many books, websites, and recordings that can further your technique and introduce you to even more tunes. We cover all the ways you can find these resources.

Playing by yourself all the time is no fun, either. Here are some tips on getting out and playing with other people and making sure that you are welcome back in the future, too. All in all, this chapter will help ensure you're fiddling happily for years to come.

Finding a Good Teacher

It's never too late or too early to find yourself a good private teacher. Learning out of a book, of course, is an inexpensive and relaxed way to learn. A book, for one, doesn't get annoyed when you don't practice, and it only costs money once. You can learn the fiddle on your own time without pressure, and without someone listening to you struggle through your beginning techniques. As you're reading this, you obviously already have figured out all those benefits, of course!

That said, it can't be denied that a good teacher can be a great way to enhance your learning. He will point out things about your playing that need improvement immediately. He can answer your nagging questions. He can demonstrate something to you if you don't understand it. He also can provide a bit of motivation—knowing you are spending good money can make you practice harder. So does knowing that you have a lesson coming up, and you will be taking up an hour of someone's time. After all, you want to sound like you're actually learning something.

Fiddlers who teach, however, often aren't in the phone book. Here're a few places you could check out:

◆ Inquire at the local music store. They might have lessons there. Often, musicians seeking students will advertise through flyers or cards. Check the bulletin boards. If you don't have luck there, ask the store if they have lessons in-house, or if they know of someone who will teach the fiddle style you are seeking.

◆ Seek out local music organizations and venues. Many styles of music have local practitioners who sponsor occasional workshops or ongoing music classes. These classes are a great way to get lessons while meeting other people who also are learning. The teachers of workshops and classes often will be willing to take on private students as well.

◆ Ask local performers. They might be taking students on themselves, or they might know someone they can recommend.

◆ Craigslist and other Internet sites often are used by teachers seeking students.

Tune Up

Keep in mind, the best players aren't always the best teachers. People who are very gifted often can't explain to others what they are doing, because it comes so naturally to them.

False Notes

Many teachers will charge you for a lesson anyway if you don't show up, or cancel less than 24 hours beforehand. Dem's the rules ... after all, they may have refused good paying work to make time for you!

It's always good to keep in mind that some people are better teachers than others. A good teacher should be willing to answer your questions, demonstrate techniques, and play for (or along with) you once in a while. They should be patient when you are struggling and push you when they can see that you are capable of more.

You also have a part to play. Be a good student! Practicing hard between lessons means your teacher won't feel like she is wasting her time (of course, she will still gladly accept your money!). And of course, you've spent valuable time and money to be there, too. You'll get more bang for your buck if you practice, improve, and can learn something else at your next lesson—instead of just rehashing what you did last week.

Be respectful of the fact that someone has set aside valuable time for you. Don't cancel at the last minute or just "skip" your lesson without giving at least 24 hours' notice, or as much as you can, unless it's really an emergency. The same goes for your teacher as well, of course—if she constantly flakes out on you, find someone else to teach you.

Be patient with yourself at the lesson. Remember that your teacher once struggled through the fiddle at the beginning, too. He knows what it's like, even if he is not at the pinnacle of his talent. Don't apologize for not getting something right away at the lesson. Teachers are there to help you learn, not judge how quickly you pick something up. Also, believe it or not, you will not be the only student they've ever had that sounded less than stellar when learning the fiddle.

Take it slow and remember that a new technique will usually take a while to master. Give it all your best shot and enjoy yourself! Laugh when your attempt at something comes out in a mere squawk. Your teacher will appreciate it, and you'll get more enjoyment out of your hobby that way. Life is too short to let something you do for fun stress you out.

Tune Up

What is "practicing hard"? To some extent it depends upon your own goals for your playing. But picking up your fiddle for at least 20 to 30 minutes a day, with a solid hour or more here and there, will definitely mean some improvement.

Where to Hear the Music You Love

A great way to improve your playing is to listen to it. You certainly don't want to only listen to yourself when you are aiming to improve your style! You can't know what you want to sound like without exposing yourself to the different sounds and styles of various players.

There is no "right" way to play the fiddle. Even within a certain style, different players will have a different approach. The more you listen to great players as you continue your own practicing, the more you will start to hear little details and techniques that you hadn't noticed before—techniques that you can aim for with your own playing.

Live music is still alive and, well, despite all the competition from iPods, Xboxes, and Internet chat rooms, you just have to look a little harder for it these days. Concerts and festivals are around, showcasing the current crop of talent. And the Internet has allowed people to market their music worldwide, so that even a genre of music that people play thousands of miles away is accessible to you with the click of a mouse.

Local Venues

The most obvious place to look for music is at the local venues in your area. If you live in a place with a thriving music scene, then it could be easy to find music venues. Local bars, coffee shops, universities, music clubs, and performing arts centers are all possibilities.

Sometimes the music is free, but usually you'll have to pay. The cost of music usually is commensurate with how talented or popular the band is, so if it's high, it's usually worth it. Once you start going to fiddle music concerts, you'll find that the price of a ticket rarely reaches the heights of today's more popular artists. Also, by going out to concerts you are supporting the music you love and ensuring that it can continue to be performed.

Tune Up

When you are feeling "stuck" in your practice, going out and listening to a great musician live can provide just the inspiration you need to get out of your rut.

House Concerts

As things like DVD players and cable TV made it more tempting for people to just sit at home, many music venues closed their doors. This especially goes for the type of venues that might have showcased much of the fiddle music that you have been learning in this book. As a result, some avid music fans around the country began opening their homes and producing small concerts for their favorite musicians.

While these can be hard to find at first, once you go to one there will often be a mailing list to join. The owner of the house will e-mail you if there are future events. Usually you can find one of these events by watching the itinerary of a musician you would like to see. If she is playing a house concert, her concert listing will say as much and usually contain an e-mail address or phone number for further information.

Festivals

A weekend of music in the summer can be an inspiration when you are feeling stuck or frustrated at your instrument. Look around for bluegrass festivals, Celtic festivals, or other folk and eclectic festivals that might feature the fiddle music you are looking for. You can find a few of the bigger ones in Appendix B.

Check the schedule of the bands or musicians you love in the summer months—they are sure to be playing at festivals at that time of the year. Check the listings in the paper for local events. Along with hearing the bands you love at a festival, you are also sure to discover some new musicians that you haven't heard of before. It's also a great way to spend a lovely summer day outside after a week inside an office.

Fiddle Facts

Music is always a sign of feasting and merriment.

—Sancho, in *Don Quixote*

Recordings

When your favorite musician isn't available live, there are always recordings to listen to. A compilation CD from a particular genre is always a good way to start out if you have no idea who to listen to. The people who put these things together know who the stars of the genre are. Of course, some compilations are better than others. Generally, the more information about the artists on a compilation CD, the better it is. This indicates that someone passionate about the music wanted to put a CD together for people like you, who want to know more about a particular genre. Ones with less information are sometimes thrown together as a cheap way for a record label to make a few more bucks and can be so-so representations of the music.

Most fiddle music isn't available at your local chain music store. However, there are fewer chain music stores available these days anyhow. This is partly because people aren't dependent on them to find the music they want to hear. Now, it's easier and easier to find it. There are great websites and stores that ship world-wide. There are many genre-specific retailers of fiddle music as well. You might have to poke around to find them, but once you do, you will discover more recordings of this type of music than you ever thought existed. To get you started, I've listed a few online and specialty retailers of fiddle music in Appendix B.

Radio

Be sure to check out your local radio stations for music. The lower and upper parts of the dial often contain the more *freeform*, small-scale, and local stations that tend to carry more diverse music than the "Hot 97X" and other type mainstream stations. Local colleges in your area might have a radio station that is freeform. One hour it might be some loud and violent heavy metal, but the next could be the sweet strings of bluegrass. Just check out their websites to find the show schedule.

These smaller stations also are willing to stage live interviews and performances from artists right in their studios. These appearances often coincide with a concert tour appearance near your area that night, so radio is another way to find out who is playing in your area. They often happen early in the day, so it's a good way of hearing what your favorite musician is like before they've had their first cup of coffee for the day. It can get interesting sometimes!

The Internet

The Internet has exponentially expanded the opportunities for learning about—and playing—fiddle music. In the past, people were confined to what music was around them, or what their local record store would carry. Nowadays, any music from around the world is available at the click of a button. You can sample music on people's website. Purchasing music by download means that you don't have to buy a whole album at a time, so you can pick and choose. There are also great online-only radio stations that exist to promote specific genres of music. And of course you can discover a wealth of books and DVDs for sale online to keep learning more about the fiddle.

The Internet is also a great place to learn new tunes and get answers to your pesky fiddle questions. There are forums and information sites dedicated to the fiddle that are chock-full of information. Searching under your topic, from "buzzing sound fiddle" to "bluegrass music," can bring up a wealth of information. (Of course, it always pays to double-check on accuracy when getting your facts from the anonymous web.)

Many websites exist where people have catalogued tunes in various formats. Sometimes people even put little midi files or old recordings up to listen to for free. In a way, I suppose the Internet has replaced brainpower and community memory in our society. Now, if I can't remember how a tune goes, I can usually find it somewhere on the Internet to remind me.

Your favorite artists' websites are always a good place to start when looking for information and resources. Their links page will often lead you to the sites of *their* favorite musicians, music stores, and other troves of information.

def•i•ni•tion

Freeform radio means that the DJ—not the station or some corporate outfit—decides what music to broadcast.

Tune Up

Many people use a format called ABC to put tunes online. It uses the names of the notes written out in certain ways instead of traditional written music, and can be played with little computer programs. Since this format personally makes my head spin, I think I'll just let you know it's out there, to check out for yourself.

Of course, there's always a caveat when it comes to these new technologies. They are great to have around in a pinch. But remember that sitting at your desk chatting with people online is no substitute for practicing or getting out and playing! So resist the addiction of online surfing (I, unfortunately, can speak from experience here), as it can be too easy to end up clicking your mouse for hours.

Music Organizations

Fiddle music is a more niche pastime than some other things (like being a baseball fan, for example). People often have gotten together to form an organization to support and promote a type of music in the area. These organizations can take up various functions. They can sponsor concerts. These might happen sporadically, or on a more regular basis. Some will put together workshops when a fiddler comes through town to perform. These organizations also might be the driving force behind a festival in town as well.

Others will have regular meetings, sessions, or classes that aspiring fiddlers can join to hear and learn more, or just get together to play. This can be a valuable resource when you are sick of sitting at home practicing alone.

Playing in Sessions

So, we've established that an aspiring fiddler should get out and hear music, and practice hard at home, too. Eventually, you may want to get out, meet others with similar interests, and *play* some music, too. In fiddle music, a gathering of musicians playing together for fun is often called a jam, or a session.

Sessions or jams are held at various types of venues. Local bars often have them. Your local Irish pub might have an Irish music session. A local cafe might have a Sunday afternoon bluegrass jam. A local music organization might sponsor a session at another venue.

Many people assume a session is an open-door event and that anyone can come in, sit down, and try to play. This is sometimes true, but the format varies depending on the type of music and who is running the show. Some sessions are more open than others. Sometimes just anyone can show up and play, no matter what your level. These sessions are sometimes referred to as "open." Other times, the session is a free format, but made up of a more cherry-picked group that is aiming for a higher level of performance. In this case, the musicians might not be seeking or welcoming people who want to just show up and play. Or they might be willing to have people sit in, but prefer to keep control of the music that is played. It's up to you to figure out what kind of session it is, because musicians often aren't so good at coming right out and explaining it. One slight rule of thumb is that the more open a session is, the more friendly people are. The other thing is that if you follow the rules doled out in the next section, you are more likely to be able to weasel your way into hanging out with the musicians who like to keep their session more controlled.

Session Etiquette

You've just learned about the various types of sessions out there. While these are a treasure trove of people and music just ready to be learned from, it's important to remember one important point before heading out the door. This is what I'll call the musicians' Golden Rule:

Don't be "*That* Guy" (or Gal!)

I am referring to what is actually known among musicians as "session etiquette." Sorry to say, this is not included in the topics found on the Emily Post website, so I will do my best to outline the requirements below. (Thank you very much!)

It's really not very hard to get yourself welcomed back to a session once you have poked your head in. The usual rules of politeness and friendliness (for questions on these, do consult Emily Post), of course, always apply. You can pretty much take these rules, turn them into music, and you've got the rules for playing at a session. If you are a nice and reasonable person, why wouldn't people be happy to see you? Unfortunately, sometimes there is "*That* Guy" running around a session that tends to drive the more accomplished musicians (or everyone) a little bonkers. So here're the tips that can help you avoid being … "*That* Guy."

Tune Up _____

When walking into a session for the first time, it's always a good idea to ask, "Is it alright if I join in?"

♦ Don't forget to tune your instrument before you start playing. And check it periodically after that. Asking for an A from your neighbor is a sure sign that you are attuned to your own sound and are there to make some good music. On the other hand, nonstop tuning can be annoying, and trying to tune while people are playing is a general no-no.

♦ Pay attention to what's going on around you. When you first walk in the door, take the time to find out what kind of session it is and what the format is. If one person seems to be in charge of leading the session, everyone will appreciate it if you don't try to come in and take the bull by the horns. On the other hand, if the session seems to be more of a free-for-all, try to take only your fair share of time. No matter how excited you are about the 15 new songs you learned last week, it is a fact that no one else is as excited about it as you are. Launching from one of your songs straight into 14 more while everyone begins staring blankly into space is going to earn you few friends. Everyone is there to play, too, not just listen to you!

♦ Be realistic about your level compared to the group's. If you are still pretty scratchy and out of tune, and your sense of rhythm or control of the bow still needs work, then make the session a learning experience for you.

♦ Try to *listen* to what the other musicians are doing. If you don't know a tune, don't play. Observing, as opposed to playing as loudly as you can, will only endear you to the musicians there. You probably will also learn a few things as well. This is especially important when there is a lead instrument, or even a singer, trying to belt out the melody. If you can't hear them over your own fiddle, chances are your neighbor can't, either.

- Notice whether or not there is a social component to the session. Some groups like to stop in between tunes and chat a bit. If you take the first moment of silence to start playing, let's face it—you are musically interrupting people. *Timing* is important both within your tunes and in between them, too!

- When playing, concentrate not just on your own sound, but listen to see how your playing fits in with the group sound. After all, being able to listen and react to other musicians is part of what makes an excellent musician.

Again, most of these points are just common sense and manners. If you start out going to sessions with the tips we've gone over here, you are probably well on your way to becoming a great fiddler.

So good luck, practice hard, and happy fiddling!

The Least You Need to Know

- A good private teacher can provide added motivation and help you improve.

- Look for a private teacher through your local music store, local fiddlers, music organizations, and Internet sites.

- Local radio, festivals, house concerts, local venues, and recordings are all great ways to hear the music you are learning to play.

- The Internet is a great resource for purchasing, hearing, and looking up music that you can't find in your community.

- Sessions and jams are great ways to get out and play and meet new people—just make sure you use good session etiquette to make playing fun for everyone there.

Glossary

A string   The second highest string on the fiddle. It's the one second from the right.

action   This refers to how hard it is to press down on the string with the left hand. "Low" action means the strings are very close to the fingerboard. "High" action is the opposite.

air   A slow melody, sometimes played without a steady tempo.

alternate tuning   Tuning the strings of the fiddle in an arrangement other than the standard tuning of G, D, A, and E. Often used in old-time fiddle music, but can be found in Scottish and Irish music as well.

Amati   A family of fiddle-makers from Cremona, Italy, that made some of the best fiddles in the world in the seventeenth century.

backbeat   The second and fourth beats in a phrase of music; instead of counting ONE-two-three-four, one would count one-TWO-three-FOUR.

bagpipes   A reed instrument that produces music by forcing air from an inflated bag, rather than blowing air directly through the reeds. Various types of bagpipes are found throughout Europe. The most common bagpipes are the voluminous Highland pipes of Scotland.

bar line   A vertical line that divides the musical staff into measures, or bars.

bass bar   A length of wood, usually spruce, that is fixed in position inside the body of the fiddle, on the underside of the belly. The bass bar acts as a structural support. It also helps transmit vibrations throughout the body, helping it to resonate and produce sound.

belly   The front of the fiddle, which has two f-holes cut into it.

breakdown   A bluegrass term referring to a fast banjo or fiddle instrumental tune.

bridge   The carved wooden arch that holds up the fiddle strings. It also transmits the vibration of the strings to the rest of the instrument.

camber   The curve of the stick of the bow.

carpal tunnel syndrome   A compression of the arm's median nerve that can cause symptoms including pain, tingling, numbness, and decreased ability to grip well.

chin rest   A small oval concave piece of wood that attaches to the bottom left, on the fiddle's belly. This is where the chin is placed when the fiddle is played.

chops   Slang; "has some chops" means that an instrumentalist knows what he or she is doing.

chord   Three or more notes played at the same time.

chord progression   The order of chords in a song or piece of music.

chromatic scale   A scale that consists of only half steps.

clawhammer banjo   A style of playing the five-string banjo common in old-time music. Also refers to the instrument itself.

concertina   A "free reed" instrument (related to the accordion), held on the lap between two hands, that is used in Irish music.

Cremona   The town in Italy where fiddle making reached its peak in the seventeenth and eighteenth centuries.

crooked   Describes a tune or phrase that takes an unexpected turn. This includes melodies that have an extra bar or half bar; are short a bar or so; or contain an unexpected turn in the melody.

crossing strings   Moving from one string to the next while playing.

crwth   (Rhymes with "tooth.") The crwth is an early European form of a bowed stringed instrument. It continued to be used in Wales long after it died out in the rest of Europe.

D string   The second lowest string on the fiddle, or the second from the left.

dobro   A type of guitar with a metal resonator built into the body where the sound hole normally would be. There are two types of dobro; in bluegrass music, a square-neck version is used and it is played sitting flat on the player's lap.

Dorian   A musical mode. The Dorian scale starts and ends on the second note of a major scale.

double stop   Playing two strings at the same time with one bow stroke.

down-bow   A bow stroke in which the player pulls the frog of the bow away from the fiddle, or to the right.

downbeat   The first beat of a measure.

droning   A type of *double stop* in which a player plays the melody on one string while simultaneously sounding an open string above or below.

dynamics   How loudly or softly a musician plays a note or series of notes.

E string   The highest string on the fiddle, or the farthest to the right.

ebony   A black wood, used to make fingerboards on the fiddle.

eighth note   A note that is one-half the length of a quarter note. It is indicated by a black dot with a stem and one flag.

end button   A black button, centered in the bottom rib of the fiddle. A length of *tail gut* wraps around the end button, securing the tailpiece to the instrument.

f-holes   The two holes carved into the belly of the fiddle, shaped like the lower-case letter f—one of them is reversed. These allow the sound to exit the interior of the fiddle.

fiddle   The same instrument as a violin. This term is used when played by musicians from nonclassical musical genres, including Celtic, American old time, and bluegrass.

fiddle contest   An event in which fiddlers perform a tune in front of judges, who then gauge the best performers.

fifth   A musical interval of two notes that are five degrees apart.

fine-tuner   A small knob that tightens or loosens a fiddle string in small increments. It is part of, or located in, the *tailpiece*.

fingerboard   The strip of wood, usually made of ebony, that starts at the top of the neck and extends down the belly of the fiddle. It sits under the strings. By using a finger to press down a string onto the fingerboard, the string is shortened, and therefore makes a higher pitch when it vibrates.

flag   A small mark that indicates a note is shorter than a quarter note in length.

flat   1) A symbol that indicates a note is a half step below its natural form. 2) A state of being out of tune because the pitch is lower than it should be.

frequency   The number of vibrations in a sound wave per given length of time.

fret   Frets are thin metal bars embedded across the fingerboard of a stringed instrument, like a guitar. They divide the fingerboard into sections, each representing a musical pitch.

frog   The handle of the bow. This is also where the hair is fixed into place at one end of the stick, and tightened or loosened as needed.

G string   The G string is the one farthest to the left, and is the lowest string of the fiddle.

grace note   A small, quick note that embellishes another note in the melody. In fiddle music, a grace note can either lead into a note or break a note up in the middle.

half note   A note consisting of two quarter notes, or one-half of a whole note. It is symbolized as a hollow note with a stem.

half step   A tonal step that is equivalent to one key (black or white) up or down on a piano keyboard.

Hardanger fiddle   A Norwegian fiddle that is shaped like a fiddle, but has four or five sympathetic strings.

harmonic   A spot on a string that when lightly touched, allows both sides of the string to vibrate, and emits another note.

hornpipe   A form of dance music. In Irish music, this is usually played in a "swingy" 4/4 time. There are also English hornpipes in other time signatures.

improvisation   Playing a free-form interpretation of a tune or melody that follows the chord progression the song is based on.

intonation   The degree to which a player is in tune. "Good" intonation means one is in tune, and "bad" intonation means one is out of tune.

jam   A gathering of old-time or bluegrass musicians who intend to play music. Can occur in public or private, at festivals or in homes.

jig   A type of tune in Scottish and Irish music, almost always played in 6/8 time.

key signature   The collection of sharps and flats (or complete absence of any) at the left of the musical staff, which indicate what notes are sharp or flat in a given piece of music.

learning by ear   The ability to learn a piece of music by hearing it, as opposed to learning it from musical notation.

ledger lines   The small lines that extend the musical staff when a note needs to be written above or below the five main lines.

long bow   A bow stroke that uses most or all of the length of the bow.

luthier   One who makes and/or repairs stringed instruments. Comes from the word *lute*.

major scale   A scale that ascends according to the following whole (W) and half (H) step pattern: WW H WWW H.

march   A slower, methodical tune that was traditionally used to march people in a parade or procession of some sort.

measure   The spaces on a musical staff indicated by two bar lines; the music within each measure contains a specific number of beats.

metronome   A device, whether electronic or mechanical, that clicks or beeps a steady beat in perfect time.

microtone   A note that falls somewhere between the half and whole steps of the modern Western scale.

minor scale   A scale that starts and ends on the sixth note of a major scale, and ascends in the following whole (W) and half (H) step pattern: W H WW H WW.

Mixolydian   A musical mode. The Mixolydian scale starts and ends on the fifth note of the major scale.

mode   A mode is a scale that starts and ends on a different note than the note that starts the major scale, thereby changing the sound and mood achieved by the music. For example, a scale based on G major but starting on the note A is in a different mode—in this case, A Dorian.

musicality   The condition of being both technically accomplished at a musical instrument, as well as the more elusive ability to infuse the music with emotion and mood that affect the listener.

mute   A small device that dampens the natural vibrations of the bridge, lowering the volume of the fiddle.

Nashville shuffle   A two-beat note or slur, followed by two separately bowed one-beat notes.

natural   The version of a note that is neither sharp nor flat.

octave   Two notes that are eight notes apart on a musical scale; the high note vibrates at exactly double the frequency of the lower one, and the two notes also have the same note name.

old time   A general term that refers to the diverse types of music played by American string bands in the early part of the twentieth century and before. It is descended either directly or indirectly from the music of Scottish, English, and Irish immigrants and was heavily influenced by the music of Africa. The title "old time" includes the music of Appalachia, east of Appalachia, the South, Texas and Oklahoma, and the Ozarks.

open string   A string that is played without any fingers pressing down on it.

ornament   An embellishment of a note made with the left hand or the bow. Ornaments include grace notes, rolls, triplets, and slides.

peg box   The rectangular hollow above the fingerboard. Four holes, two on either side, hold the four *pegs* into place on the peg box.

peg nut   The small block of wood, embedded in the top of the fingerboard, which slightly elevates the strings as they exit the *peg box* to span the fingerboard. The peg nut also separates the strings into even lengths apart, through four small notches that hold the strings in place.

pickup   A device that converts the vibrations of a string into an electrical signal, which then can be sent to an amplifier, audio loud speaker, or recording device.

piezo crystals   The devices in a violin pickup that sense the vibrations of the bridge.

polka   In Irish music, this is a dance tune that is in 2/4 time, usually from the *Sliabh Luachra* region of Ireland.

purfling   The thin black line on the belly of the fiddle that outlines its shape. In all but the most inexpensive violins, this is made by carving out a thin groove that is then filled with a different kind of wood from the belly.

quarter note   A note that is one-quarter length of a whole note, and is represented by a black dot with a stem.

reel   A tune that originated in Scotland, it is played in Irish and Scottish music. It is in 4/4 time.

rehair   Replacement of the horsehair on the bow.

response   How fast a string begins making sound after it is played upon with the bow.

rest   A moment of silence in music. Different symbols represent different lengths of rests, which correspond to lengths of notes.

ribs   The sides of a violin.

roll   An ornamentation of a note in Irish music. In quick succession, the central note is played, then a pitch above it, then the central note, then a pitch below, then the central note again. For example, the note C is ornamented in the following pattern: C-D-C-B-C.

rosin   Pine sap, or resin, that has been collected, processed, and turned into a cake or block. This is rubbed on the horsehair of the bow in order to obtain friction needed for playing.

run   A scale or series of notes, usually played rapidly.

saw   A style of bowing in old-time music, in which there are no slurs; the bow simply moves up and down with each note.

scale   An ascending or descending series of notes.

scroll   The decorative knob at the top of the fiddle. It serves no purpose for the sound, but is traditionally carved into a spiral shape.

session   A gathering of Irish and Scottish musicians who intend to play music. A session can be formal or informal and can happen in public or private. Sometimes a session is open to all, and other times it consists of a select group of musicians.

session etiquette   Refers to the fact that a new musician should be courteous, be in tune, and be aware of his level of playing and volume as compared to the other musicians.

set up   Refers to the process of ensuring that all the parts of an instrument are put together well—the strings' height, bridge position, sound post position, etc. If an instrument has been set up correctly, playing it will be less frustrating.

sharp   1) A symbol that means a note is a half step above its natural pitch. 2) The state of being out of tune because the pitch is higher than it should be.

shift position   To move the left hand up and down the fiddle neck, in order to reach higher or lower notes.

short bow   A bow stroke that uses only a small length of the bow.

shoulder rest   An accessory that attaches to the back of a fiddle, allowing the fiddler more space between the chin and shoulder.

shuffle   A combination of saw and slurring bow strokes.

sixteenth note   A note that is one-half the length of an eighth note. It is indicated by a black dot with a stem and two flags.

Sliabh Luachra   The region of Ireland consisting of sections of counties Cork, Limerick, and Kerry. Musically, it is known for its slides and polkas.

slide   1) An ornament in which the finger is placed a microtone or even half step below the targeted note. The finger then slides up the fingerboard until the proper pitch is reached. Very common in country fiddling, it also is used more subtly in Irish and Scottish fiddling. 2) A dance tune, usually from the *Sliabh Luachra* region of Ireland, that resembles a fast jig in 12/8 time.

slip jig   A type of jig that is played in 9/8 time. Traditionally danced by women due to its graceful dance steps.

slur   When two or more notes are played with one bow stroke.

snap   A style of playing two notes in Scottish music, in which the first note is very short and the second very long. Usually written as a sixteenth note, then a dotted eighth note.

sound post   A moveable wooden dowel that is inside the fiddle. It is wedged between the belly and the back, underneath the treble side of the bridge. Its placement is important—it supports the thin plate of wood that makes up the belly, and allows the bridge to transmit its vibrations to the rest of the instrument.

staff   The five lines and four spaces that are used to indicate the pitch of a note in written music.

standing wave   A wave that oscillates between two fixed points; that is, the back-and-forth movement of a vibrating string.

steel strings   Strings that are made of 100 percent metal.

stick   The technical term for the wood of a bow.

Stradivari   The most famous maker of violins, he arguably perfected the form of the modern violin. He lived from 1644 to 1737, and worked in Cremona, Italy.

strathspey   A Scottish tune in 4/4. It is characterized by sharp dotted rhythms known as Scotch snaps. Bagpipers refer to these tunes as being "pointed."

sympathetic strings   These are not played on directly, but rather are placed below the main set of strings. They enhance the instrument's sound by responding to the vibrations of the main strings.

syncopation   When a beat that is emphasized becomes deemphasized, and another beat is emphasized instead. You will hear terms like "offbeat" and "back beat" associated with songs that are syncopated.

synthetic core strings Strings that are made with an imitation gut core, wrapped completely with a thin metal wire.

tail gut The thick, strong cord that attaches the *tailpiece* to the *end button.*

tailpiece The black, wedge-shaped piece that holds the strings of the fiddle in place. It sits at the bottom center of the belly. The other end attaches to the *tail gut*, which connects to the *end button*, which is fixed in the fiddle.

tie Two notes of the same pitch played continuously, resulting in a longer note. On the staff, this is marked by a curved line that joins the two notes.

time signature Two stacked numbers that are placed at the beginning of the musical staff. The bottom number indicates the length of note that equals one beat, and the top note indicates how many beats are in a measure.

tip The pointed end of the bow.

tone Refers to the sound quality of the fiddle. While every fiddle has an inherent tone quality, the tone also can be changed through bow pressure and speed, as well as left-hand fingering.

treble clef The symbol on the left of the staff that indicates a piece of music is in the upper registers of the scale.

triplets Three notes played in the span of one beat.

tuner A device that provides a correctly tuned pitch, or tests a pitch that needs to be in tune.

tuning peg The wooden piece that holds the string in place inside the *peg box.* By turning it, a player can either tighten or loosen, and therefore tune, the string.

up-bow A bow stroke that is made by moving the bow hand to the left, or the frog toward the instrument.

variation An alteration of notes or bowing made by a player, in order to change a melody from the way it was played the last time.

varnish The shiny coating of a violin. It gives the violin its color and protects the wood.

vibrato A form of ornamentation, it is produced with a back-and-forth movement of the left-hand finger that is holding down a note. This causes a slight wavering in pitch.

viol de gamba A European stringed instrument that is the precursor of the fiddle.

violin An unfretted, bowed instrument that has four strings.

whole note A note that is made up of four quarter notes; represented by a hollow circle.

whole step A one-tone distance in the Western musical scale. This is represented on a piano keyboard by the musical distance between two white keys that also are separated by a black key.

B

"More Fiddle? Yes, Please!"

Magazines

Fiddler Magazine (www.fiddle.com) A magazine devoted to all things fiddling. Each issue spotlights a different style of fiddling and includes tunes to learn. It also covers a variety of other topics related to fiddling and fiddles.

Strings Magazine (www.stringsmagazine.com) Originally focused primarily on classical players, this magazine expanded its coverage to include all genres of music. Look for their annual buyer's guide for some advice on purchasing an instrument.

Dirty Linen (www.dirtylinen.com) This bimonthly magazine covers folk and world music, and is good for album reviews and concert dates of your favorite artists.

Bluegrass Unlimited and *Bluegrass Now* (www.bluegrassmusic.com and www.bluegrassnow.com) Two magazines chronicling the bluegrass scene.

Old Time Herald (www.oldtimeherald.org) A magazine dedicated to the music of the southeastern United States and all its kin.

Irish Music Magazine (www.irishmusicmagazine.com) Contains touring schedules and CD release information for bigger-name Irish music acts.

Fiddle Books

There are many fiddle books out there these days. Some are straight tune collections, others are specific to teaching one style of music. There are more books for Irish and Scottish music, as old-time music is very hard to write down, and bluegrass music is so dependent on band and improvisational formats.

No matter what format, though, one should never be completely dependent on books for learning fiddle music. That said, they can be handy for reference, new material, and some added advice!

Mel Bay Publications (www.melbay.com) publishes how-to and tune books, CDs, and DVDs for various fiddle styles (as well as for many other instruments). These can often be found at your local music store:

Fiddler's Fakebook A popular, pan-traditional tune book, compiled by David Brody.

O'Neill's Music of Ireland Police Chief Francis O'Neill lived in Chicago in the late nineteenth century and collected thousands of tunes from his fellow Irish musicians. The original version, now published by Mel Bay, is complete; Miles Krassen's version of this book for fiddlers, from Oak Publications, contains ornaments written into the tunes.

Ceol Rince na hÉireann A series of printed collections of Irish tunes compiled by Breandán Breathnach.

Scottish Collections

The MacKintosh Collection Robert MacKintosh of Tulliemet, Perthshire, published four collections of music from 1783 to 1803, which are now found in one volume.

The Skye Collection A collection of over four hundred tunes, published by Keith Norman MacDonald in 1887.

The Caledonian Companion Written and compiled by Alastair J. Hardie, this modern collection has many tunes, as well as instruction on bowing and technique.

Fiddle Info Online

www.theviolinsite.com While designed for the classical musician, this thorough site contains information on violins, brands of strings, and other accessories; lists violin makers; and has some teaching tools.

www.violinonline.com/interactivefingerboard.htm This page, from a website full of basic violin instruction, has an interactive fingerboard that shows you the fingering for many different notes. There is also a page with a violin tuner for all four strings on this site.

www.comhaltas.ie Comhaltas Ceoltóirí Éireann (pronounced "COLE-tus Kee-ol-tori Erin") is an organization dedicated to preserving traditional Irish music and culture started in Ireland, but has branches all over the world. The site has many audio and video samples of music, and can help you find the closest branch to you.

www.irishfiddle.com A site with a decently comprehensive list of respected Irish fiddlers past and present, articles and information on Irish fiddling, and links to videos.

www.abdn.ac.uk/scottskinner/index.shtml The University of Aberdeen has put together a nice website showcasing James Scott Skinner; you can read about him and the history of Scottish music and dance, look at old manuscripts and tune collections, and hear some old recordings.

www.oldtimemusic.com   Information on old-time music, with featured fiddlers and lots of links to record labels, bands, and more.

www.fieldrecorder.com   A site dedicated to releasing rural American music that currently is only in private collections to the public.

www.bluegrassworks.com   A site with info on bluegrass, festivals, musicians, and CD reviews.

www.ibluegrass.com   Another informative site, including an index of local bluegrass bands by region of the United States.

www.bluegrassmessengers.com/fiddle.html   A great site that has documented a number of recordings and versions of many old-time and bluegrass tunes.

www.youtube.com   Check out YouTube for fiddle lessons, performances, and concert clips. You can find lovely performances, and some fairly awful ones, too. If nothing else, all these will help you distinguish the great from the mediocre (and the massacring). The real gems, though, can be found when people post old clips of those musicians long deceased, but still revered. It's the next best thing to going back in time and seeing them play live.

Tunes to Learn

www.cranfordpub.com   Lighthouse keeper and fiddler Paul Cranford, of Cape Breton Island, maintains this vast resource of fiddlers from Cape Breton, Scotland, and Ireland, and their tunes. There is a treasure trove of great info, as well as tune books and CDs for sale.

www.thesession.org   An interactive site containing thousands of searchable Irish tunes in sheet music format, as well as discussions, comments, and events posted by users.

www.madfortrad.com   Online lessons from well-respected masters of Irish traditional music.

www.bbc.co.uk/radio2/r2music/folk/sessions   Play some Irish and Scottish tunes along with some well-respected musicians on the BBC's "Virtual Session."

Listen to or Purchase Tunes

www.homespuntapes.com   Get more in-depth instruction for many specific styles on DVD, including old time, bluegrass, jazz, Irish, Cajun, and Cape Breton.

www.smithsonianglobalsound.org   The Smithsonian's digital music store, with a good collection of music from all around the world. Recordings span the century of recording, including old bluegrass, old-time, Irish, and Scottish music.

www.tradtunes.com   A download site specifically for Celtic, traditional, and roots music.

www.sugarinthegourd.com   Old-time music online radio station.

www.1001tunes.com   Information, downloads, and photographs of old-time music, with vintage recordings available to purchase.

www.cdbaby.com   An independent music retailer that sells CDs from musicians not on a record label (many fiddle musicians today fall in this category). Any musician in their catalog also can opt to be sold on digital music outlets such as iTunes and Rhapsody.

Music Retailers

These retailers will be well informed about the music and carry a great selection of recordings and method and tune books.

Rampant Lion Celtic Traders
47 S. Villa Ave.
Villa Park, IL 60181
630-834-8108

You can often find Celtic music retailer Rampant Lion at Midwestern Irish festivals; they have a retail store in the Chicago area and will ship.

Ossian USA
118 Beck Rd.
Loudon, NH 03307
603-783-4383
www.ossianusa.com

Ossian USA has a small store in New Hampshire, and will ship. They sell Irish music, books, and videos.

Celtic Grooves
www.celticgrooves.com

A website dedicated to sales of very traditional Irish music.

County Sales
Floyd, VA
540-745-2001
www.countysales.com

The largest retailer in the country for books and recordings of old time, bluegrass, and related genres.

Fiddle Camps, Festivals, and B&Bs

There are a great variety of "fiddle camps" out there—some actually do involve camping, others in more "civ'lized" quarters. They are a good way to meet and play with other people. You'll get a vacation and get a good dose of fiddle instruction from some of the musicians listed in Appendix C, as well as others that are equally talented. I have listed a few of the big ones here; there are many more that might be in your local area. Many of these might be advertised or even run through local music festivals.

Instruction

Rocky Mountain Fiddle Camp (www.rmfiddle.com) Several different styles of fiddle playing are taught, in Colorado.

Swannanoah Gathering (www.swangathering.org) A series of weeklong workshops in North Carolina, including "Celtic Week" and "Old Time Week."

Augusta Heritage Festival (www.augustaheritage.com) In West Virginia, another series of weeklong workshops, including swing, Cajun/Creole, Irish/Cape Breton, bluegrass, and old-time weeks.

Mark O'Connor's Fiddle Camps (www.markoconnor.com.moses.com/fiddle. camp) Learn swing, Texas, bluegrass, Celtic, and Klezmer styles at camps in California and Tennessee.

Valley of the Moon (www.valleyofthemoon.org) Two camps in California where you can learn Scottish, Shetland, Norwegian, and other related fiddle styles.

Catskills Irish Week (www.east-durham.org/irishartsweek) All Irish music in a historically Irish-American resort town north of New York City.

Ashokan Fiddle and Dance Week (www.ashokan.org) Choose from a Northern week, a Southern week, or a Western and swing week.

Fiddler's Retreat (www.fiddlersretreat.com) The Irish B&B meets fiddle (or tin whistle) class with Theresa Bourke, who is a breakfast cook, fiddle instructor, and County Tipperary concierge, all in one.

Listening

Hear some music at the biggest festivals in each genre. There are hundreds of festivals all over the country, so I'm just going to list a few of the biggest and most well known. Many of them also have workshops during the festivities.

If you can't make the festivals, go to their websites, see who's playing—and then go to the artists' sites, and see when they are playing near you.

Grey Fox (www.greyfoxbluegrass.com) One of the biggest bluegrass festivals in the country.

Appalachian String Band Music Festival (http://www.wvculture.org/stringband) Five days of old-time fiddle contests, concerts, and classes in Clifftop, West Virginia.

Milwaukee Irish Fest (www.irishfest.com) The biggest Irish music festival in the United States.

Celtic Colours (www.celtic-colours.com)   A long series of performances, at a variety of locations, held every fall in beautiful Cape Breton Island.

Celtic Connections (www.celticconnections.com)   A winter festival in Glasgow, Scotland, set up like Celtic Colours.

Online Violin Shops

The two retailers that follow will carry most fiddle accessories, as well as cheaper-model fiddles and bows. They always have good deals on strings.

- Southwest Strings: www.southweststrings.com
  1-800-528-3430

- Shar Music: www.shar.com
  1-800-248-SHAR
  Check out their "outlet" for discounted, cosmetically blemished, or used instruments.

Folk Instrument Shops

Both of these shops will have an extensive collection of how-to and tune books, DVDs, and CDs. They also sell various instruments of the folk traditions.

Elderly Instruments
1100 N. Washington
Lansing, MI 48906
1-888-473-5810
www.elderly.com

House of Musical Traditions
7040 Carroll Ave.
Takoma Park, MD 20912
301-270-9090
www.hmtrad.com

A Sampler of Players

You can't learn music in a vacuum, or course. One of the best ways to improve your playing is just to listen to some good fiddlers. The more you listen, the more an authentic sound will seep into your practice. And, of course, listening to music is a universal pastime while you're doing dishes, setting mice traps around the house, or whatever your chore is this weekend.

Picking out some recommendations is subjective and difficult to narrow down. I've tried to get a good mix of older, traditional "roots" players and some more modern players that may or may not be willing to "mix it up" a bit. Of course there will be lots of people who deserve to be on this list, but aren't. We've got to save trees somehow, and I guess it's those fiddlers who will have to make that sacrifice for us!

Scottish Fiddlers

Here's a small sampler of Scottish and Shetland fiddlers to check out.

Alasdair Fraser

Alasdair Fraser was born in Scotland and currently lives in California. He has done a great deal to revive Scottish fiddle playing in Scotland and in the United States. Along with his prolific touring, recording, and composing career, he has run his Valley of the Moon summer camps for almost 20 years.

www.alasdairfraser.com

Johnny Cunningham (1957–2003)

The fiddling world will miss Johnny Cunningham, a well-respected producer as well as very gifted fiddler—with a sense of humor that always had audiences laughing between sets. A native of Scotland, he spent much of his life in the United States. He played with his brother Phil in the band Silly Wizard in the

1970s. Starting in 1997, he began touring with the very successful show "The Celtic Fiddle Festival," which showcased three different styles of playing (originally Irish, Scottish, and French).

www.johnnycunningham.com

Aly Bain

Shetland fiddler Aly Bain was a founding member of band Boys of the Lough, and has performed for almost 20 years with accordion player Phil Cunningham. He has done a great amount of solo work as well. His strong style brought both Scottish and Shetland music to audiences around the world.

www.philandaly.com

John McCusker

A Scottish fiddler from the younger generation, John McCusker played with the Battlefield Band for over 10 years. He is also well known as a producer for other artists from Scotland and the United Kingdom, especially singer Kate Rusby. He is worth checking out in either capacity.

Catriona MacDonald

Catriona MacDonald learned fiddling from a respected Shetland fiddler named Tom Anderson. Her playing is a great representation of the strong Shetland style, but she is not afraid to experiment with modern musical influences. She is also the only female member of the band Blazin' Fiddles, an ensemble of six or more fiddlers that hail from all the different musical regions of Scotland and play some rockin' sets of Scottish fiddle tunes.

www.peerieangel.demon.co.uk

Hanneke Cassel

Hanneke Cassel is another example of America's now-authentic claim as a birthplace of great Celtic fiddlers. Originally a Texas contest fiddler from Oregon, she discovered Scottish music and then spent her summers at Fraser's Valley of the Moon fiddle camp. She graduated from Berklee College of Music and has been touring nationally for several years, as a member of trio Halali, and more recently with her own band.

www.hannekecassel.com

Cape Breton Fiddlers

Over 100 years after the great emigration from Scotland to Nova Scotia, here are a few fiddlers that demonstrate even the darkest hours of history can have a silver lining (or some golden fiddlers …).

Buddy MacMaster

Buddy MacMaster was actually born in Ontario in 1927, but luckily, his parents soon returned to Judique, in the tiny but musical island of Cape Breton. He is an icon in the fiddling world and has been an inspiration for the flock of young fiddlers that have since taken the music from this tiny musical island in Canada to the world stage. He still plays weekly at the packed local square dances.

Natalie MacMaster

Buddy MacMaster's niece, Natalie MacMaster, has been a major force in bringing Cape Breton fiddling to an international stage. Her fiddling is high energy and lyrical, as is her stage show, which she is on the road with for most of the year.

www.nataliemacmaster.com

Jerry Holland

Although he has lived in Cape Breton since 1975, Jerry Holland was born in Boston. Thanks to his father, who was one of many emigrants from Cape Breton living there, he grew up surrounded by fiddle music. He was exposed to Cape Breton fiddling as well as Irish and Scottish music, and all three elements can be heard in his great playing. He is also a well-respected composer of many popular tunes.

www.jerryholland.com

... And the List Goes On

A few more fiddlers from the Scottish, Shetland, and Cape Breton traditions to get you going might include Laura Risk, Brenda Stubbert, Wendy MacIsaac, Duncan Chisolm, and Elidh Shaw.

Irish Fiddlers

The sheer number of musicians playing traditional Irish music today is astounding. I could name a hundred players off the top of my head who are worth listening to. But I've managed to whittle it down a bit.

Michael Coleman (1891–1945)

Coleman emigrated to the United States from County Sligo, Ireland, and landed in New York City in 1914. Starting in the 1920s, he recorded numerous 78s of his native fiddle music. When these recordings made it back home to Ireland, it spurred a renaissance in traditional music, as people were awed at his virtuoso style. It's still great to listen to Michael Coleman's fiddle playing, full of great runs and rolls. Just be warned that the piano and guitar accompanists were studio players who knew nothing about Irish music, and it shows. (A lot.)

Bobby Casey (1926–2000)

Bobby Casey was a fiddler from Clare who lived most of his life in London. His music is a great example of West Clare fiddling, and his ornaments and variations are elaborate. For the modern ear used to studio precision, it can be a jolt to hear the microtone pitches that he uses to great effect. But it is well worth listening to Bobby if you want to hear some truly authentic Irish fiddling.

Andy McGann (1928–2004)

Andy McGann was born in New York City of Irish parents. He was one of the original Americans who proved you could be born on the western side of The Pond and still play authentic Irish-style fiddling. He often played with Michael Coleman in his younger days, and his style is derived from that Sligo playing. His recording with Longford fiddler Paddy Reynolds, *Andy McGann and Paddy Reynolds*, is a great album of fiddle duets.

Tommy Peoples

Tommy Peoples is a fiddler originally from Donegal who lived for many years in Dublin and then County Clare, and was the original fiddler for the 1970s band The Bothy Band. His style is an original mix of counties and personal flair. His unique ornaments, variations, and original tunes are well worth a listen, and can be heard on his album *A Quiet Glen*, among others.

Frankie Gavin

Frankie Gavin, originally from County Galway, played with bouzouki player Alec Finn for many years in the band De Danaan. He is a fantastic player, who plays with great energy and technique and isn't content to stay completely within a traditional framework.

Liz Carroll

Chicago native Liz Carroll is the star of the American-born fiddlers working today. Her style is completely authentic and yet firmly American, with hints of a twang in her strong playing. Her skillful variations are something to listen for. She is a prolific composer as well, and many of her tunes are firmly ensconced in the repertoire from here to Ireland.

www.lizcarroll.com

Martin Hayes

Martin Hayes sparked a flurry of interest in Clare fiddling when he released his first recording in 1993. He draws on the slow and lyrical nature of his home county while infusing it with a modern sensibility. He largely performs as a duo with guitarist Dennis Cahill, who supplies thoughtful and original chords. Their beautiful music is very accessible to a large audience.

www.martinhayes.com

Irish Bands

The 1970s sparked a revival in Irish music, and many bands became well known in the scene. While arranging Irish music in a group setting wasn't traditional, it has become a solid part of the tradition. The band setting for the music is often the most accessible way to listen when you are first starting out. Here are a few to check out:

◆ The Bothy Band—one of the original bands of the 1970s, there are still great tunes and fun arrangements here, along with some of the best players. It's also got a great vintage '70s flavor to it.

◆ Altan—Donegal fiddling was the oft-spurned black sheep of the Irish music family for a long time. Then Altan released their debut album, *The Red Crow*, in 1990. Their driving fiddle duos, along with flute and bouzouki, sent everyone scurrying to learn these "new" Donegal tunes. After the death of flute player (and husband of main fiddler and singer Mairead Ni Mhaonaigh) Frankie Kennedy in 1994, the band was determined to forge on, and continues to play around the world to this day.

www.altan.ie

◆ Younger bands like Dervish and Danu are very accessible and fun to listen to. They carry on the tradition of playing Irish music in bands that became so popular in the '70s.

www.dervish.ie and www.danu.net

... And the List Goes On

These are just a few musicians worth hearing if you want to explore the possibilities in Irish music. A more comprehensive list might include fiddlers John Carty, Paddy Glackin, Kevin Burke, Liz and Yvonne Kane, Brian Rooney, Dennis Murphy and Julia Clifford, Matt Crannitch, Seamus Creagh, Cathal Hayden, James Kelly, Tommy Potts, Randal Bays, and probably a hundred other fiddlers as well.

Old-Time Fiddlers

There is a huge list of old-time fiddlers, as the definition of the music spans such a huge geographic and stylistic area. But here are a few!

Tommy Jarrell (1901–1985)

Tommy Jarrell was a hugely influential fiddler from the Round Peak region of North Carolina. He received a National Heritage Fellowship from the National

Endowment for the Arts in 1982, and performed in many places around the United States. He welcomed many aspiring old-time musicians into his home, and they would often visit for days, learning old-style fiddle music.

Eck Robertson (1886–1975)

Texas-style contest fiddling owes much to Eck Robertson. A consummate entertainer and performer in his day, he became the first commercial country recording artist when he recorded in New York City in 1922. His fiddling was traditional, but he wasn't afraid to try new things and was technically very accomplished.

Joe Thompson

Old time and bluegrass music wouldn't exist without the African American influence on the music of Ireland and Scotland in the United States, and in fact, old-time string band music was played by black musicians all over the South at one time. Joe Thompson is one of the last living musicians from this side of musical history.

Bruce Molsky

Bruce Molsky was born in the Yankee stronghold of New York City, but after discovering old-time music, he went and studied with, among others, Tommy Jarrell. He is one of the premier performers of old-time music today, and often tours and collaborates with a wide range of performers as well.

www.brucemolsky.com

Dirk Powell

Dirk Powell learned the music from his grandfather in Kentucky, and has gone on to a very successful career in music. Among his impressive roster of recordings, film, and television work, he was one of the musical consultants for the film *Cold Mountain*, as well as many other films.

www.dirkpowell.com

Rayna Gellert

The daughter of an old-time musician from Indiana, Rayna Gellert played classical music until college, when she felt compelled to start learning old-time music herself. She released her solo album *Ways of the World* in 2000, and tours with old-time band Uncle Earl.

www.rayna.utopiandesign.com

... And the List Goes On

Check out the Carolina Chocolate Drops for a young group that is continuing the legacy of fiddlers like Joe Thompson. Other old-time fiddlers include the Carter Brothers, the Stripling Brothers, Doc Roberts, John Salyer, Marcus Martin, Hiram Stamper, Gid Tanner and his Skillet Lickers, Clyde Davenport, Bob Holt, Mike Bryant, Brad Leftwich, and Chirps Smith.

Bluegrass Fiddlers

Bluegrass fiddling has been technically difficult from the beginning, and the more modern players have continued to stretch what is possible on the instrument. Take a listen to some of these cats!

Kenny Baker

Kenny Baker grew up in Kentucky and, after joining Bill Monroe's Blue Grass Boys, would remain in the band longer than any other member (aside from Monroe himself, of course). His style has been a model for generations of aspiring bluegrass players. Many standard bluegrass tunes can be found on the recording *Kenny Baker Plays Bill Monroe*.

Chubby Wise (1915–1996)

Florida native Chubby Wise joined Bill Monroe's Blue Grass Boys in 1942, and continued touring and performing for over 40 years. He is considered one of the best early bluegrass and country music artists.

Aubrey Haynie

Aubrey Haynie, originally from Tampa, is one of the most respected and hard-working session musicians in Nashville, for good reason. His fiddling is both extremely tasteful and technically amazing. You can find his fiddling on many great country artists' recordings, but look for his solo work to hear some fantastic renditions of old classics and new compositions alike.

www.aubreyhaynie.com

Stuart Duncan

Stuart Duncan, originally from Southern California, is another prolific Nashville session musician. He was named Fiddle Player of the Year seven times in a row by the International Bluegrass Music Association. His fiddling can be found on albums by Lyle Lovett, Dolly Parton, and many, many others. He performs and records as a member of the Nashville Bluegrass Band.

... And the List Goes On

For more great fiddling, check out the bands Alison Krauss and Union Station, Blue Highway, Mountain Heart, Old School Freight Train, and the Del McCoury Band. Ron Stewart and Andrea Zahn are two more great studio fiddlers.

And More Fiddle Styles

I've covered four basic styles in this book, but the truth is there is an amazing spectrum of fiddle styles and genres out there. Here are a few great fiddlers who can't be put in one specific genre, or at least the genres we've worked on!

Vassar Clements (1928–2005)

Vassar Clements was a Blue Grass Boy starting in 1949, but his career led him to record with a wide range of artists from various genres, including pop and rock. He grew up listening to swing and big band, and incorporated many of those sounds in his playing. He pioneered a style he called "hillbilly jazz."

www.vassarclements.com

Bob Wills (1905–1975)

Not many fiddlers have been inducted into both the Country Music and the Rock 'n' Roll Hall of Fame, but "Texas Playboy" Western swing fiddler Bob Wills achieved both honors. He also was given a Grammy Lifetime Achievement Award in 2007. His band performed for decades, using horns in the big days of swing and moving to electric guitars as rock 'n' roll became king.

Elana James

Elana James is a Western swing and jazz-influenced fiddler originally from Kansas City but now living in Austin, Texas. She performed for many years in the Hot Club of Cowtown trio (under the name Elana Fremerman) and then, after spending a hiatus working with Bob Dylan and Willie Nelson, recorded her solo debut in 2007.

www.elanajames.com

Mark O'Connor

Mark O'Connor made his mark at a young age when he wowed everyone at Texas fiddling contests. He went to Nashville for a while, but has moved on to explore many genres including classical, jazz, and folk music, and has worked with musicians like cellist Yo-Yo Ma, "newgrass" banjo player Bela Fleck, and jazz trumpeter Wynton Marsalis. He has composed music for television and orchestras as well.

www.markoconnor.com

Darol Anger

Californian Darol Anger started life as a bluegrass fiddler, but has become well known as someone with great technical chops, exploring bluegrass and jazz (he was a founding member of the Turtle Island String Quartet). He is a strong collaborator with fiddlers from all different genres, including Celtic, jazz, bluegrass, and old time—meaning that you never know what you will hear next.

www.darolanger.com

Jazz Violinists

Darol Anger once said in *Fiddler Magazine*, "Fiddling is an incredibly valuable skill to bring to playing jazz violin." While we didn't cover jazz in this book, I think it's worth it to listen to jazz—even if you don't intend to play it; the chords and technique are always good for ideas and inspiration.

Stuff Smith was a great swing player from the 1920s to the 1940s, who learned much of what he did from trumpeters rather than fiddle players. Stephane Grapelli was a European fiddler who played with famed guitarist Django Reinhart, most famously in the band The Hot Club of Paris.

Modern-day jazz violinist Regina Carter is a virtuoso musician with amazing technique, though I would stick to later recordings by her, as the early ones tend to be heavy on synthesizers.

What's on the DVD

The DVD included with this book contains an approximately 30-minute-long video. This video is made up of a series of short fiddle lessons.

The last hour of the DVD consists of audio recordings of all the tunes that are taught in the book. Each tune is a separate track on the disc, and is easily located using the DVD menu.

The video lessons highlight techniques I thought would be especially useful for you to see, not just read, about. It isn't a straight half-hour lesson, like one you'd get if you came to my house. (After all, the whole *Idiot's Guide* is worth well over a year—or more—of lessons!)

I recommend that you don't go straight through the video from the very beginning. Rather, use it to clarify and practice new techniques along with me as you learn them in Chapters 7 through 12. There are also a few full-speed versions of tunes that are meant to inspire you.

Here are the lessons on the DVD (video):

Preparing to Play (see Chapter 7)

Shoulder-rest position; rosining the bow, and the tuning of the four fiddle strings.

Fiddle & Bow Technique (see Chapter 7)

How to hold the fiddle and the bow, how to move your bow arm, and how to place your left-hand fingers on the fingerboard. Demonstration of the D Scale.

Simple Tune (see Chapter 7)

The tune "Shortnin' Bread," played very slowly.

Slurring Notes (see Chapter 8)

How to slur, demonstrated with the tune "Red River Valley," from the beginning of Chapter 8.

Using One Finger on Two Strings (see Chapter 8)

Learn how to use your finger on two strings for certain fiddle passages, using "Devil's Dream." Ends with a full-speed performance of the tune.

Grace Note #1 (see Chapter 9)

Using the tune "High Road to Linton," demonstrates a grace note that leads into another note, as found in Chapter 9. Ends with a full-speed version of "High Road to Linton."

Grace Note #2 (see Chapter 10)

Demonstrates a grace note that breaks up a note, as found in Chapter 10, using the tune "Connaughtman's Rambles." Ends with a full-speed version of "The Connaughtman's Rambles."

Droning (see Chapter 11)

Demonstrates the technique of droning—playing an open string as well as a string with the melody—using the tune "Sally Ann." Ends with a full-speed version of "Sally Ann."

Same Tune, Different Styles (see Chapter 16)

My guitarist friend Flynn Cohen and I demonstrate the Irish and Bluegrass versions of "Red-Haired Boy."

List of Tunes (Audio Only):

1.	D Scale	16.	Ryan's Polka
2.	A Scale	17.	Danny Boy
3.	G Scale	18.	The Girl I Left Behind Me
4.	Mary Had a Little Lamb	19.	Devil's Dream
5.	Two-Octave G Scale	20.	Campbell's Farewell to Redcastle
6.	Twinkle, Twinkle Little Star	21.	Scotland the Brave
7.	Shortnin' Bread	22.	Cutting Ferns
8.	Row, Row, Row Your Boat	23.	Devil in the Kitchen
9.	I'll Tell Me Ma	24.	High Road to Linton
10.	Amazing Grace	25.	Sleep Soond Ida Morning
11.	Red River Valley	26.	Jenny Dang the Weaver
12.	Home on the Range	27.	Sleepy Maggie
13.	The Parting Glass	28.	The Mason's Apron
14.	Auld Lange Syne	29.	Jig of Slurs
15.	The Ash Grove	30.	Hector the Hero

31. The Twisted Bridge
32. Off She Goes
33. The Lilting Banshee
34. The Connaughtman's Rambles
35. The Irish Washerwoman
36. Dennis Murphy's Polka
37. Britches Full of Stitches
38. Road to Lisdoonvarna
39. Dusty Millar
40. Drops of Brandy
41. The Old Copperplate
42. Drowsy Maggie
43. The Harvest Home
44. Lucy Farr's Barndance
45. The Earl's Chair
46. Black-Eyed Susie
47. Sally Ann
48. Cluck Old Hen
49. Turkey in the Straw
50. Hop Light Ladies
51. Arkansas Traveler
52. Old Joe Clark
53. Cotton Eyed Joe
54. Fisher's Hornpipe
55. Bluegrass Intro
56. Bluegrass Tag Ending Example
57. St. Ann's Reel
58. Red Wing
59. Whiskey Before Breakfast
60. Forked Deer

61. Temperance Reel
62. Bill Cheatham
63. Katy Hill
64. Dixie Hoedown
65. Angeline the Baker
66. Cumberland Gap
67. Cripple Creek
68. Clinch Mountain Backstep
69. Jenny on the Railroad
70. Salt Creek
71. The Contradiction
72. The Laird of Drumblair
73. Soldier's Joy
74. Ward's Favorite
75. Willie Coleman's
76. Ships Are Sailing
77. The Boys of Malin
78. Duck River
79. The Butterfly
80. My Love Is in America
81. S'Beag S'Mhor
82. Blackberry Blossom
83. Tobin's Favorite
84. Little Beggarman (also known as Red-Haired Boy, Irish version)
85. Red-Haired Boy

Index

Q-R

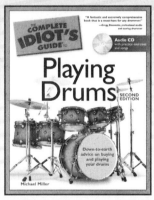

WARRANTY LIMITS

READ THE ENCLOSED AGREEMENT AND THIS LABEL BEFORE OPENING AUDIO PACKAGE.

BY OPENING THIS SEALED VIDEO PACKAGE, YOU ACCEPT AND AGREE TO THE TERMS AND CONDITIONS PRINTED BELOW. IF YOU DO NOT AGREE, **DO NOT OPEN THE PACKAGE.** SIMPLY RETURN THE SEALED PACKAGE.

This DVD is distributed on an "AS IS" basis, without warranty. Neither the author, the publisher, and/or Penguin Group (USA) Inc./Alpha Books make any representation or warranty, either express or implied, with respect to the DVD, its quality, accuracy, or fitness for a specific purpose. Therefore, neither the author, the publisher, and/or Penguin Group (USA) Inc./Alpha Books shall have any liability to you or any other person or entity with respect to any liability, loss, or damage caused directly or indirectly by the content contained on the DVD or by the DVD itself. If the DVD is defective, you may return it for replacement.